First Generation

HINCKLEY TRIUMPH (T300) MOTORCYCLES

MAINTENANCE, RESTORATION AND MODIFICATION

TRIUMPH

First Generation

HINCKLEY TRIUMPH (T300) MOTORCYCLES

MAINTENANCE, RESTORATION AND MODIFICATION

David Clarke

THE CROWOOD PRESS

First published in 2021 by
The Crowood Press Ltd
Ramsbury, Marlborough
Wiltshire SN8 2HR

enquiries@crowood.com

www.crowood.com

British Library Cataloguing-in-Publication Data
A catalogue record for this book is available from the British Library.

ISBN 978 1 78500 943 3

Disclaimer
Safety is of the utmost importance in every aspect of an automotive workshop. The practical procedures and the tools and equipment used in automotive workshops are potentially dangerous. Tools should be used in strict accordance with the manufacturer's recommended procedures and current health and safety regulations. The author and publisher cannot accept responsibility for any accident or injury caused by following the advice given in this book.

Triumph Motorcycles do not endorse or support the switching of parts between bikes they were not originally intended for, or the modifying of bikes beyond their original purpose, so any maintenance or changes you make as a result of reading this book are not the responsibility of Triumph Motorcycles, the author or the publisher.

Typeset by Jean Cussons Typesetting, Diss, Norfolk
Cover design by Maggie Mellett
Printed and bound in India by Parksons Graphics Pvt Ltd

contents

acknowledgements

This book would have been impossible without the help and support of a number of T300 riders and friends. Postings on the various Facebook Triumph groups (T300, Mk 1 Speed Triple, Modified Hinckley Triumphs, Daytona and so on) have also been enlightening. Friends who have contributed include Gordon Smith (who also took some photographs used in the book), Ivan from National Triumph (whose knowledge of T300 parts is unparalleled), Mark Gaylard (again supplying many photographs and some text), Paul Messenger, Sean Symonds, Trevor Smith of Sprint Manufacturing, Cavan Holden, Christian Forward, Bob Cornforth, Denis Fitch, Chris Foxley, Paul Humphreys, Paul Barnett and Phil Ogden. I also thank my wife, Glenis, for proofreading and supporting me in my passion for T300 motorcycles.

I make no apology for using text in various sections in the book supplied by Mark Gaylard, Gordon Smith and Paul Barnett as they know what they are doing! I would have liked to use official Triumph material but that was not possible.

Lastly, if you plan to do any major work on the engine and carburettors, then go on one of the two-day courses run by T300 guru Clive Wood in Lincolnshire. These are normally run over a weekend in the winter months and cover the major jobs on an engine, particularly stripping an engine down for a sprag clutch change. The course will give you an insight into how it's done and the confidence to go ahead. Clive has been servicing, building, modifying and racing T300s since 1991 and is extremely knowledgeable. This course is a must have if you want to learn more about the T300 engine. Clive can also service and repair your bike.

introduction

I have been a first generation Hinckley Triumph owner since 1997, when I bought my first new bike, a Triumph Sprint Sports; this has been followed by three different Mk 1 Speed Triples (one Black, one Racing Yellow and one an ex-Speed Triple Challenge race bike), a Daytona Super 3 and a Daytona 900, which I turned into a café racer using the excellent kit from CRK (Café Racer Kits). I still have the first Speed Triple in the rare Racing Yellow, which I bought back in 2010 and am keeping it in original condition while doing a rolling restoration on it. I also have the Café Racer along with a more modern 2008 Triumph Thruxton, which has been heavily customized.

I had carried out basic maintenance such as oil/filter changes, but when I acquired a 1994 ex-Speed Triple Challenge bike that was in a very poor condition (despite only having 3,200km/2,000 miles on the clock) as it had been stored for many years, I was faced with moving to a new level of restoration and maintenance. The bike was complete with all the original racing parts, so, after taking a deep breath, I commenced of a full rebuild. I stripped it down to the frame and either refurbished or replaced parts as required. In the course of the restoration, I replaced the swing arm, had the engine rebuilt (by Triumph guru Chris Foxley) and refurbished/overhauled lots of parts – brake calipers, carburettors, forks, rear shock absorber (it was fitted with a Proflex as authorized by the race series and rebuildable) – including re-powder coating many of them. Consumables like the chain and sprockets, air filter and spark plugs were replaced while servicing the bike.

This was the first time I had stripped a bike down completely but it was with the assistance of friends who were also Triumph enthusiasts and who gave me plenty of help and advice. What was very helpful was using a small digital camera to photograph everything at every stage as I dismantled each part before putting the bits into a bag marked up with a description. This saved the day more than once, as there was often a long time gap between taking things apart and reassembling them.

Researching the Speed Triple Challenge and the Mk 1 Speed Triple became a bit of an obsession with me after working on these early Triumphs, though I don't consider myself a mechanic and this book is **not** intended to replace the Triumph factory workshop manual. With the right tools, and the tips and hints in this book, however, you should be able to maintain better your T300 and know your way round the main components and which parts will fit from one model into another. I have also included a number of bikes that have been modified to illustrate the potential of the interchangeable parts, as well as given details of parts suppliers and individuals who can help where you are not confident your own skills (or tools) can do what you require. All the suppliers I mention are ones I have used over the years or are known to be purveyors of the right parts and services.

Before starting any job, have a look at the official Triumph workshop manual (supplemented by the excellent Haynes manual #2162, now revised) and check that you have the correct tools and have ordered any parts required. Read the relevant section in the manual to familiarize yourself with the sequence and logic behind the operation. You can also post questions on the appropriate Triumph Facebook or other internet groups. If you are in any doubt, commission an independent Triumph mechanic to do the job. You can also use a Triumph dealer for work on your T300, but this can prove to be expensive, and lots of dealerships no longer have mechanics that are familiar with the T300 range.

Structuring this book proved to be a challenge. On the assumption that few people will read from cover to cover, some information is duplicated in different sections.

While I have tried to include as many of the jobs required to maintain your T300 as possible, I have not included a blow-by-blow account for everything. So, for example, I have provided some hints and tips on changing the sprag clutch, but not a detailed breakdown or photos of the work.

The writing of this book was inspired by Mark Gaylard, who created a website (mottleybiker.com) that covers some of the maintenance tasks outlined in this book, but I have hopefully taken this a stage further and also detailed the parts that are interchangeable between models. Mark generously allowed me to use some of the text from his website in this book. Having sections describing how to do various jobs was straightforward, but deciding to include upgrades and modifications to the models has opened whole new vistas – there are some incredible bikes out there!

1

the T300 range and the start of Hinckley Triumph

This section is a summary of what I included in the companion volume to this book, *Hinckley Triumph: The First Generation*, which was published in 2012 (and still available from Crowood). This covers each model in detail with all changes and revisions identified as well as the colours used on each bike and details how John Bloor set up the company and created a modern high-tech motor cycle company from nothing except the brand name.

There seemed little point in restating the contents of that first book, so the following is a summary and an update since I finished the previous title.

NAMING CONVENTION

In this book, I refer to 'T300' throughout as T3XX was the code used by Triumph for the range of bikes covered by this book and constitutes the first generation of Hinckley-built motorcycles. So the first machine, the Daytona 750, was given the code TC331 and the numbers increased up to TC399 for the Adventurer. Triumph then went back in the number sequence and used TC301 for the Speed Triple and TC310 for the Super 3. The exception to the T300 rule is the original Tiger, as this is numbered as a T409, but for the purposes of this book it is a T300, as it shares most of its parts with the T300 range.

The second generation of Triumph bikes started with the introduction of the T509 and T595 models in 1997, although T300 bikes of various models were still being manufactured until 2004. From 1997, Triumph started to use the model number in the marketing and naming of the second generation bikes, hence the new Daytona being branded T595.

The use of numbers rather than full model titles makes it easier for Triumph to refer to models.

THE NEW TRIUMPH COMPANY

The original Triumph Motorcycle Company was based at Meriden (near Coventry) and closed down in 1983 after a prolonged decline, both in the face of Japanese competition and a major lack of investment. Many thought this was the end of the marque, but an East Midlands house builder, John Bloor (of Bloor Homes fame), bought the intellectual property rights to the Triumph marque and secretly set about recruiting a small design team to design a new range of bikes. The design team was set up in an anonymous industrial unit near Coventry with the staff sworn to secrecy (so much so that some thought they could still not talk to me in 2010 even though they had retired!). The team included some people who had previously worked at the Meriden plant and therefore knew how to design and package motorcycles.

The new Triumph Company also employed recent graduates with mechanical engineering background and implemented a CAD/CAM software system to replace the paper, pen and drawing boards used at Meriden Triumph. The initial tasks were to identify what was 'best practice' in motorcycle design and there were three aspects to this.

First, there was a need to identify possible suppliers for brakes, front and rear suspension units, chains, wheels and instruments. By the time Triumph started down this path, there were no manufacturers left in the UK who could supply motorcycle parts. The subsequent fact-finding mission included trips to Japan to meet both parts suppliers and the Japanese bike manufacturers.

Second, a range of current Japanese bikes were purchased and analysed for performance and for engineering right down to cutting them up for metal analysis.

Finally, Triumph employed consultants to provide specialist technical advice. As an example, Ricardo helped Triumph to completely understand the thermodynamics of the internal combustion engine.

The net result was that the new Triumph designed a range of engines and bikes fit for the late twentieth century and owing very little to what Triumph had previously produced. There are some urban myths that say the Triumph engine was designed and built by Kawasaki and that Triumph copied the spine frame of the Kawasaki GPZ900, but neither was true – the engines were completely designed and built by Triumph and the GPZ900 actually copied the frames from the last Meriden Triumphs. The spine frame used on the last Meriden bikes was re-engineered and stressed for a heavier and more powerful range of bikes and engines. The whole range of bikes and engines was designed on a brand new CAD/CAM system, which came as a bit of a shock to the ex-Meriden employees, who were used to drawing boards and pencils, but this was all part of John Bloor's concept of the new Triumph as an up-to-date and modern company.

One of the key elements of the design process for the proposed range of bikes was that as many parts (fuel tanks, engines, brakes, chassis, swing arms and running gear) as possible were to be interchangeable, providing economies of scale both for Triumph and for the parts suppliers. This is very useful for those of us trying to maintain the bikes twenty-five years after they were built as we can utilize parts from other models.

In 1988, a 4ha (10-acre) site was bought in Hinckley in Leicestershire (later referred to as T1 to differentiate from later factories in the UK (T2) and abroad (T3, T4), and construction of the new factory commenced. When built, it was one of the most modern motorcycle factories in the world, and continues to keep abreast of the latest technologies. However, at that point the whole project was still a secret until the new bikes were launched on 29 June 1990, when the motorcycle press was invited to the new factory to see both the bikes and new facilities.

The reaction of the assembled journalists was of stunned surprise as they were shown a fully functioning modern motorcycle factory when they were expecting a shed-based operation with three employees. The motorcycle press had already seen some false dawns with the launch of Hesketh and the many attempts to restart Norton, where the products were massively underdeveloped and companies permanently short of cash, lurching from one crisis to another. The new Triumph was in a completely different league. John Bloor invested many tens of millions of pounds to ensure that this was a serious and professional outfit. The pre-production bikes on display for the visit of the journalists included some colour schemes that did not find their way onto production bikes, but were part of the process of getting feedback from all sources.

The range of bikes was launched to the world at the Cologne motorcycle show in September 1990 and John Bloor flew the entire Triumph staff (at that time around fifty) to the show. Research undertaken by the staff on the Triumph stand for the show resulted in further refined colour schemes and models. For example, Triumph displayed a Daytona in an all-white paint scheme but this was not carried forward into production.

THE NEW MODELS

In December 1990, the initial range of three bikes was launched at the International Motorcycle Show at the NEC Birmingham, and in February the first production bikes (1200cc 4-cylinder Trophies) were shipped to the German market, as it was felt that if the Germans liked the quality then the rest of the world would.

Production started at around five bikes per day and gradually increased over the coming months. The initial model range consisted of:

The Trophy (for touring)
900cc triple
1200cc 4-cylinders

The Daytona (sports alternative)
750cc triple
1000cc 4-cylinder

The Trident (roadster)
750cc triple
900cc triple

The range remained the same in 1992, but for the 1993 model year the Daytona 750 and 1000 were deleted and were replaced by the Daytona 900 triple and the Daytona 1200 four, as

An early Trophy 900 in Charcoal Grey Metallic with two-piston front calipers and six-spoke wheels. The exhaust is an aftermarket replacement.

Early Trophy 1200.

A Daytona 1000 in Assam Black with blue stripes; this model was only made in 1991 and 1992.

An early 900 Trident showing the six-spoke wheels and two-piston sliding caliper front brake.

Triumph reacted to customer demand and feedback. The initial range was hedging its bets between the 3-cylinder triples and the 4-cylinder engines, but it was soon clear that the triples were the most popular and were to be the main engine power unit. The 1000cc 4-cylinder engines are quite rare as not many bikes were sold; as a result, the engine was dropped and replaced by the 1200.

Another new model was the Sprint 900, which was in effect a half fairing fitted to the Trident; initially the model was known as the Trident Sprint.

In 1993, another model added to the range was the Tiger, with its enduro styling.

The Tiger set a new trend as it had a plastic tank; Triumph was one of the first manufacturers to use plastic for fuel tanks, followed by Ducati. This was also the first Hinckley Triumph with spoked wheels.

For 1994, a number of new models were announced, including the Speed Triple, Super 3 (with carbon-fibre mud-

A 1200 Daytona.

An early Sprint painted in Caspian Blue with grey engine cases. The exhausts have been replaced on this bike.

A Tiger in Pimento Red. The early bikes had the clutch cover painted the same colour as the body but there were problems with the paint adhering to the cover, so the clutch cover reverted to black.

A Tiger; note the hand guards.

A 1994 Speed Triple in Racing Yellow and a 1995 Speed Triple in Fireball Orange. The orange bike has the original mirrors, while the yellow one has had aftermarket bar end mirrors fitted.

A 1996 Speed Triple with Yoshimura aftermarket silencers.

The Daytona Super 3 was produced over three years and was the same all the way through, except for the change to gold brake calipers for 1996. Just 805 bikes were built. This bike has aftermarket silencers produced in America by D&D.

A Super 3 rear hugger in carbon fibre.

guard, rear hugger) and the Trident Sprint.

The Speed Triple was introduced with a five-speed gearbox, while all other models in the range had six speeds. Many components were also upgraded, so four-piston brake calipers made an appearance along with revised crankcases (eliminating the cover for the sprag clutch) and the three-spoke 17in wheels. The earlier 18in six-spoke wheels continued with some models alongside the new three-spoke wheels.

The crankcases were revised in conjunction with Cosworth, who had expertise in casting aluminium crankcases (Cosworth have their own specialist foundry company) and this redesign saw the demise of the sprag clutch cover. The objective of this redesign was to reduce weight without any detriment to oil-tightness. In October 1994, the oil pickup was modified for the 3-cylinder models. This was owing to some oil starvation issues identified on the Speed Triple Challenge bikes, where pulling wheelies was common, as was the nose of the bike diving under heavy braking, causing oil surge in the sump.

At the same time, the first of the retro models, the Thunderbird, was on display ready for the 1995 model year.

This Thunderbird still has the two-piston caliper fitted to a single disc.

A 1996 Trophy 1200 with revised fairing, complete with pannier set. The control plates to hold the foot pegs were revised for the Trophy and the Sprint Executive.

This was a departure from the previous T300 in that the fuel tank was different and it was the first bike to have a 'retro' feel, harking back to the Triumphs made at Meriden. The engine cases for the Thunderbird (and the later Legend, Thunderbird Sport and Adventurer) were revised with more fins, and the engine covers as well and oil breather system were also revised, identified by the different clutch cover and figure-of-eight covers on both sides of the engine.

This model year also saw the change

from PVL to Gill igniters in an effort to improve starting and lessen any problems with the sprag clutch. The Gill igniter had a revised start voltage and ignition curve and also allowed the engine to spin over twice before attempting to fire the plugs. A different method of connecting the wiring harness was implemented at the same time. The PVL had a detachable connector while the Gill did not.

At the end of 1995, the revised Trophy 900 and Trophy 1200 were announced for the 1996 model year.

The styling for the redesigned Trophy was completely different from the previous version, with a new fairing, twin headlamps and revised ergonomics intended to create a more relaxed riding position, particularly when touring. The revisions included different handlebars with a greater pull-back as well as redesigned foot pegs (and foot peg brackets) and a new instrument panel. The rear light also changed.

The Daytona and Speed Triples also had the calipers changed to a gold finish.

In 1996, another new model, the Adventurer (derived from the Thunderbird), was announced.

The Thunderbird and the Adventurer received oval swing arms. Also for the 1996 model year, the Speed Triple was fitted with a six-speed gearbox (although it is thought that some late 1995 bikes also had this).

However, 1996 was the year that started the end of the T300 range, as the new T595 and T509 models were announced and the transition from T300 to T500 had started. The T500 range had different frames and engines (although the engine internals were very similar to T300s). Nevertheless, the T300 continued on for a few more years.

Shorter front forks (25mm/1in shorter) were fitted to all the Speed Triple and Daytonas in 1996 and the rear shock absorbers were also revised to be lighter and with greater adjustability. The longer forks were retained for the Trophies, Tridents and Sprints as the handlebars were attached to the fork legs above the top yoke. The Tiger gained a new rear rack.

A 1996 Daytona.

A 1997 Adventurer in Amber and Copper. The bike was a development of the Thunderbird and aimed at the cruiser market in America.

The Trophy had revised rear lights from 1996 onwards.

The Sprint Sports was introduced in 1996 in Diablo Black, initially as a limited edition of eighty bikes.

The revised rear lights for the Sprint Sports.

The Sprint Executive, introduced for 1997 and 1998.

A number of run-out specials were also announced at the end of 1996 for the 1997 model year, including the 750 Speed Triple (approximately 300 bikes); this bike was not just a smaller Speed Triple 900 as it reverted to the earlier six-spoke wheels with narrower rims than the 900 version, although it appears that some 750 Speed Triples were built with the three-spoke wheels. The 750 had the shorter adjustable forks as fitted to the 900. However, a new model, the Sprint Sports (a sort of T300 900 Speed Triple but with a Sprint fairing), was also introduced in limited numbers for the 1997 model year (eighty bikes).

Both the Sprint Sports and 750 Speed Triple were intended to use up supplies of T300 engines and components, as the new T509 Speed Triple used the new engine.

For the 1997 model year, the T300 Speed Triple was deleted from the range and replaced by the T509 version. However, bikes were in stock at dealers and were still being registered until 1999! The rear light for the Sprint Sports was also revised from the Trident/Sprint one and was similar to the one used on the revised 900 and 1200 Trophy.

Another version of the Sprint, the Sprint Executive, had revised foot peg brackets, similar to the revised Trophy, and was sold complete with luggage.

For 1998, the Thunderbird Sport was introduced, very much in the café racer mould.

The Sprint Sports was also continued after the sell-out of the 1997 version. It was now offered in black and red and not limited in numbers as its predecessor was. Another variant of the Thunderbird, the Legend, was also announced and was available in 1999.

The Daytona 900 and 1200 were also deleted from the Triumph catalogue as the T300 Daytona 900 was replaced by the new T595 Daytona. Although the standard Daytona 1200 had been deleted, Triumph released a new version called the Dayton 1200 SE. This version was limited to 250 bikes (all with a numbered plaque on the top yoke) and the bike featured Alcon six-piston calipers, gold wheels and black paintwork with gold 'Daytona' on the side. The power for this bike was 147bhp, so it was a bit of a flyer! This was the final version of the 4-cylinder sports bike range.

For 1999, the Thunderbird was deleted from the range, but pressure from the dealers and customers prompted Triumph to reintroduce the bike. Triumph also brought out the Sprint ST, a fuel-injected bike, leading to the deletion of the T300 Sprint and Sprint Sport. The Trophy had further revisions to its fairings and screen to improve comfort as well as a longer side stand and aluminium handlebars, although the weight saving on a bike weighing more than 260kg (570lb) was negligible. The T300 Tiger was deleted and replaced by the new fuel-injected version.

Thunderbird Sport with the original exhausts.

The first version of the Thunderbird Sport, with the twin silencers on the same side.

The Legend, introduced in 1999.

A Legend showing the revised engine cases.

By 2000, the T300 line-up consisted of the Legend, Thunderbird, Thunderbird Sport and the Adventurer, all part of the 'retro' range, and the Trophy 900 and Trophy 1200 as tourers.

The Thunderbird Sport had some revisions, with the silencers now being either side of the bike where previously the twin silencers were on one side only.

Another nail in the coffin for the T300 bikes appeared in 2001 with the new twin-cylinder Bonneville, which was the start of a new 'classic' range. This then extended into a Thruxton model and a number of different Bonneville models, all building on the Meriden heritage. These new bikes were considerably lighter than the Thunderbirds, Adventurers and Legends.

For 2002, the Trophy 900 was deleted (leaving the Trophy 1200), as was the Adventurer.

For 2003, only the Thunderbird Sport (reintroduced after a two-year gap) and the Trophy 1200 were being built, and for 2004, only the Thunderbird Sport was available; at the end of the year they were deleted, ending the production of the T300 spine-framed bikes.

As mentioned earlier, all bikes manufactured by Triumph had been ordered by dealers, so long after a particular model was deleted you could still find one at a dealership. The Daytona 900 that I have converted into a CRK Café Racer was built in 1995 but not registered for the road until 1997, and I am aware of a Speed Triple built in 1996 not being registered until 1999. You could also find one-off paint schemes. The Daytona Super 3 I owned left the factory in Racing Yellow (as were all Super 3s), but sat at the dealer's for a long time; then the first customer had it repainted in black when he took delivery, which confused a number of people. It was restored to Racing Yellow when I bought it. Any Triumph employee ordering a new bike could have it painted any colour, so a number of bikes left the factory in non-standard paint schemes.

The table opposite shows the model years when the bikes were listed, although bikes could be available for a few months before the model year started.

PART NUMBERS

This might seem simple – just find the part number to order the parts and then fit. However, problems can sometimes arise when Triumph modified or upgraded a part (such as the oil feed banjo that feeds oil to the cylinder head) but retained the original part number. In most cases this is of no consequence, as it is an upgrade, but for some parts it is: for example, I ordered some replacement engine bolts for my Speed Triple as the black finish was a bit flaky, but when they arrived they were in silver but with the same part number! The silver bolts had superseded the black ones and only silver was available. So, where there is a superseded part, check that it is exactly what you want.

A Daytona 1200 SE fitted with Alcon six-piston front brake calipers.

IDENTIFYING THE MODEL

At the time of writing, the majority of the T300s produced are over twenty years old, and any individual bike may have had many owners and undergone many changes, as the modular design would enable different bodywork, engines and so on to be fitted. Fairings may have been removed and sometimes bikes try to masquerade

This Thunderbird Sport is the revised model, with the single exhaust on each side.

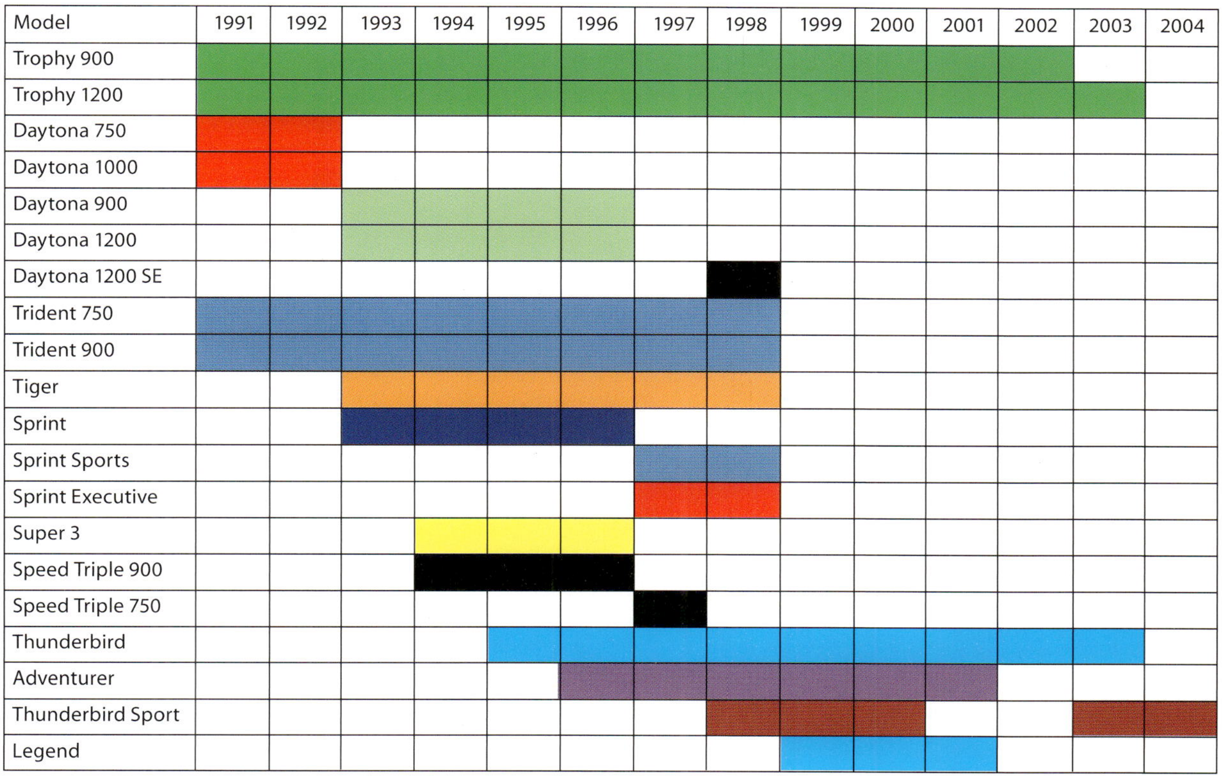

as a different model, the Speed Triple being particularly subject to this type of counterfeiting. In short, it is possible that the bike you may be buying may not be the bike you think it is. I have seen a Daytona with Speed Triple bodywork and the fairing removed, but the VIN number would show its origins as a Daytona. The safest option is to check the VIN number and see if it marries up with the model description.

The easiest way to find the VIN number on your bike is to look at the cross-member under the seat, where there is a metal plate.

The VIN number is also stamped on the front of the headstock but, unless you have removed some of the headlights/wiring, it is very difficult to see and read. This is useful, however, if you buy a bare frame with a V5.

The VIN is broken down into the components listed below, identifying the model, engine, gear ratio and year manufactured.

When ordering parts it may be necessary to give the full VIN number to ensure you get the correct parts.

WHAT DOES YOUR VIN NUMBER MEAN?

Note, only the models covered in the book are listed in the table below, and the VIN numbers are for UK bikes only. The VIN numbers for Triumph bikes sold to other markets across the world are different – for example the Speed Triple is listed as 390 for America and Canada and 301 for the UK market. This can cause complications, as Triumph sometimes brought unsold bikes from, say, America to sell in the UK or offered bikes that were originally destined for a foreign market but remained in the UK.

The VIN number is broken down as follows, using an example of a 1994 Speed Triple with a VIN number SMTC301DMR123456:

The VIN number is also stamped vertically on the headstock, where it is very hard to see!

SM	Manufacturer (Triumph)
TC301	Frame/model (Speed Triple)
D	Engine type (885cc)
M	Final drive ratio (17/43)
R	Year code (1994)
123456	Serial number

The codes relevant to all the T300 models are given below, including different engine horsepower ratings for the same model.

Frame/model

301	Speed Triple
310	Super 3
330	Daytona 750
331	Daytona 750
332	Daytona 750
333	Trident 750
335	Trident 750, 50hp
336	Trophy 900
338	Trident 900
339	Thunderbird
340	Trophy 1200
341	Trophy 1200,125hp
342	Trophy 1200, 100hp
343	Daytona 1000
344	Daytona 1000, 100hp
345	Trophy 1200, 149hp
354	Daytona 1200
357	Daytona 900
362	Sprint
364	Sprint Executive
365	Sprint Sports
396	Legend TT
398	Thunderbird Sport
399	Adventurer
409	Tiger

The VIN number is on a plate under the seat.

Engine type

C	1200cc
D	885cc, 98hp
G	885cc, 115hp
J	885cc, 70hp
K	885cc, 108hp
L	955cc, 108hp
M	955cc, 110hp
N	885cc, 87hp
R	885cc, 83hp
S	599cc, 110hp
T	790cc, 62hp
V	955cc, 149hp
X	955cc, 149hp

Final drive ratio

A	17/52
B	17/50
C	17/48
D	17/46
E	17/44
F	18/45
G	18/43
H	19/43
J	19/42
K	18/48
M	17/43
R	18/44

Year code

L	1990
M	1991
N	1992
P	1993
R	1994
S	1995
T	1996
V	1997
W	1998
Y	2000
1	2001
2	2002

Serial number

100001xxx

2 modular design

One of the key features of the T300 range is the modularity and the sharing of many components across the range. This was driven by the need for Triumph to keep costs down and to have a wide range of models that underneath shared many components. This use of shared parts is of benefit to owners in that many parts are interchangeable, making sourcing them easier. However, there are differences that could trip up the unwary.

FRAMES

While the curved spine frames, made from high-tensile (600MPa micro alloyed) steel and sub-frames are all similar – being an updated version of the spine frames used on the Meriden Triumphs – and while they may look the same, they are not necessarily identical.

The Daytona/Trident/Trophy/Sprint and Speed Triple frames are the same, but the top and bottom yokes have different degrees of offset.

The frames and sub-frames for the Thunderbird/Thunderbird Sport and Legend have different fitting points for the water system header tank, which is located at the top of the spine frame; the Daytona/Trident/Speed Triple/Sprint have the header tank located behind the tank and sitting down inside the sub-frame.

The seat sub-frames are not all identical and vary from model to model, particularly on the Thunderbird/Adventurer/Legend and Tiger ranges.

The rake angle for the forks can also vary – for example, the Adventurer of 1999 had a 27-degree rake angle.

It is an urban myth that Triumph copied the spine frame of the Kawasaki GPZ900. Rather, Kawasaki copied the spine frame from the Meriden Triumphs, and the revised spine frame for the Hinckley bikes had been designed a few years before John Bloor set up Hinckley.

FRONT FORKS

Triumph used two Japanese suppliers for the front forks – Kayaba (early and some later models) and Showa (late) – but all forks share the same 43mm diameter chrome tubes irrespective of which model or supplier, some being adjustable, some not. For 1996, the front forks were shortened on the Speed Triple and Daytona, and models

A bare frame from a Speed Triple showing the spine frame common to all the T300s (with small variations).

The sub-frame on a Speed Triple.

Thunderbird water pump.

Header tank on an Adventurer.

that previously had the forks showing through the top yokes now had the fork tops flush with the top yoke, or with a lower 'pull-through'. The Tridents/Trophy/Sprint and Sprint Sport retained the longer forks for attaching the handlebars above the top yoke.

Kayaba adjustable forks were fitted to Daytona 750/900/1000, Speed Triple 750 and 900, Sprint Sport and Super 3 models.

All non-adjustable models (except the Sprint 900, which was only fitted with Kayaba) had either Showa or Kayaba. All adjustable forks were Kayaba.

Tiger front forks had a different bottom (slider), using longer tubes with the same damper system as other non-adjustable forks as follows; these were Kayaba up to VIN 43523 and Showa from VIN 43523 to VIN 71698 (when the new Tiger 900i replaced the T400).

The Kayaba had 55mm outer seal diameter (originally a smooth dust seal was visible) and these had a larger damper bolt at base. The Showa had a 54mm outer seal diameter (the dust seal originally had an external visible garter spring) and these had a smaller damper bolt at base.

The forks allowed an upgrade from 296mm solid discs to 310mm floating discs by many owners. If the larger discs are fitted then you must fit the later four-piston calipers. The brake caliper fixing hole centres are the same (this does not apply to Tiger 900 and Thunderbird range). It's a good idea also to upgrade the front brake master cylinder from 14mm to $^5/_8$in (15.87mm) to reduce lever travel.

Fitting of 955 Sprint ST bottom sliders allows 320mm discs to be used. All Showa parts have to be used, as these do not interchange with Kayaba. Even the top fork nuts have a different pitch thread – being aluminium alloy and fine threaded, this can lead to a thread crossing mistake, and this can be expensive!

Non-adjustable forks were softly sprung and dive with brake application. Springs can be upgraded (normally with multi-rate springs, but linear springs are always better) and some customers use heavier damping oil, but one change at a time is the best way to progress. The later non-adjustable forks (certainly Kayaba and probably all Showa) reduced the diameter of the damper port hole to restrict damping oil flow.

Fork bushes are not interchangeable between Kayaba and Showa. There is a view that Showa are better engineered apart from having a narrower (15mm) bottom bush. Kayaba use 20mm bottom bushes.

Fork damper holding tool on non-adjustable forks is a 30mm hexagonal nut welded to a long tube. Adjustable forks need a 20mm-long piece of square tubing.

FOOT PEGS AND FOOT PEG BRACKETS

The foot pegs for the rider can be in two positions: a lower one for the touring bikes and a higher one for the

Control plate for a Daytona, with the foot peg in the upper position.

Control plate on a Sprint, with the foot peg in the lower position.

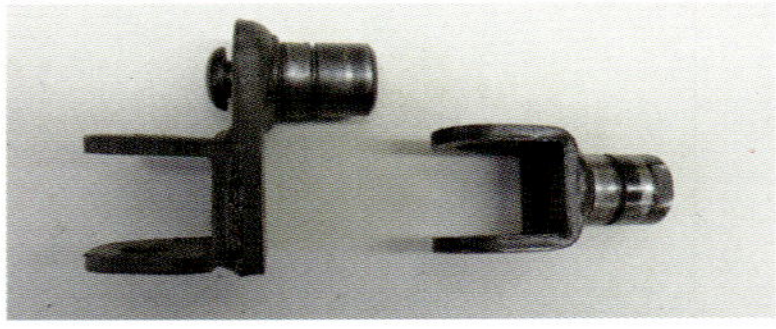

Different types of foot peg brackets.

Daytona and Speed Triple. This is because the control plate to which the pegs are attached can be mounted in two positions. If you want to fit lower rider foot pegs to the Daytona and Speed Triple, the gear linkage and rear brake pushrod will also need to be changed. There are also two types of foot peg, as shown here, which gives four different positions in total – two by the pegs themselves and two on the control plate.

The Trophy foot pegs are wider than those on the Daytona, Trident and Speed Triple.

The rear foot peg brackets are also of two types, depending on what style of exhausts are fitted to the model. The longer ones are for the Trident/Sprint as the exhausts are lower, and the shorter foot peg brackets are fitted to the Daytona/Speed Triple and Sprint Sports, as the exhausts are at a steeper angle.

The foot peg brackets for the later Trophy and Sprint Executive are different to the rest of the range as the control plate is a one-piece casting for both rider and passenger pillion foot pegs.

The rear foot peg brackets and exhaust hangers for the Daytona 750 and Daytona 1000 are different from any of the subsequent models, as they incorporate a welded tube arrangement for the exhaust hanger; the alloy foot peg bracket is only for the foot peg.

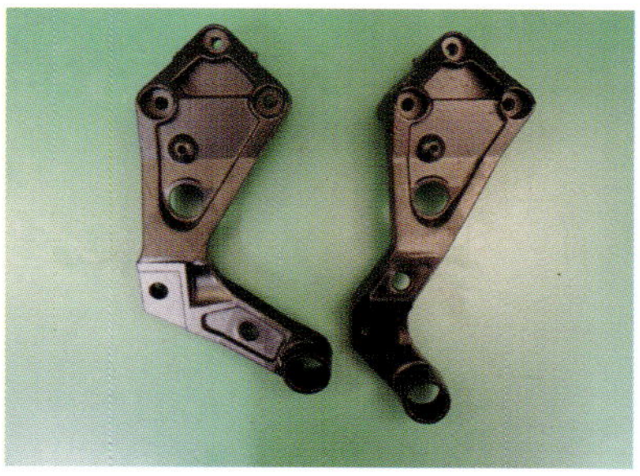

The different rear foot peg hangers depending on which exhaust was fitted. The shorter one appeared on the Sprint, Trophy and Trident, the longer one on the Speed Triple, Daytona and Sprint Sports.

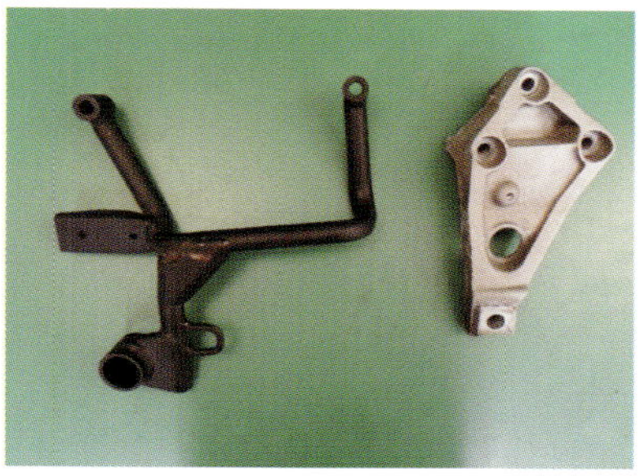

Pillion foot peg brackets for the 1991 and 1992 Daytona 750 and 1000. The tubular frame is the exhaust hanger. Triumph later combined the exhaust hanger and foot peg hanger in one casting.

On later models, Triumph combined the functions so the foot peg hanger also serves as the exhaust hanger.

GEARBOXES

The bikes were originally fitted with six-speed gearboxes, except for the Speed Triple and Thunderbird family, which had five-speed ones. In late 1995, the Speed Triple was provided with six-speed gearboxes, as was the Thunderbird family some time later. The five-speed gearboxes can be upgraded with the additional gear if required, although I have to say I did not notice any appreciable difference between the five- and six-speed bikes under normal riding conditions.

SWING ARMS

The swing arms are made of extruded high-tensile aluminium, welded in a jig and then anodized, either in grey, silver or black depending on which model they were fitted to.

There are a number of variants in the swing arms. The swing arm for the Daytona and Speed Triple has the rear caliper slung under the swing arm, while the Trident/Sprint has the rear caliper above it, so the caliper mounting points and location for the tie bar between the caliper and frame are different. The first generation Trophy and Trident with six-spoke 18in rear wheel and silver swing arm had the rear brake caliper above the swing arm.

Revised control plate on the later Trophy and Sprint Executive.

Control plate on a Triumph Sprint Executive and the revised Daytona.

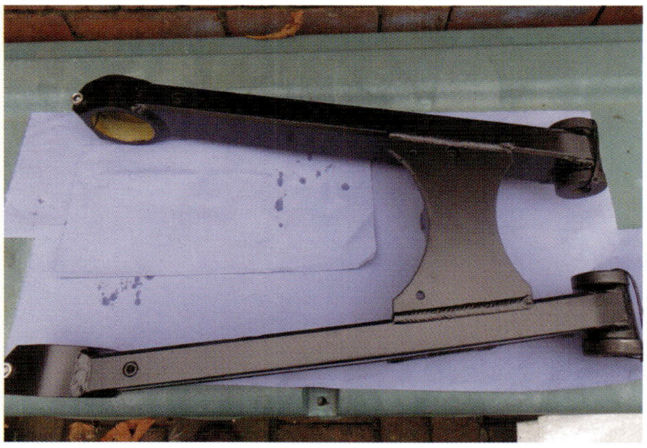

A swing arm for a Daytona or Speed Triple in black. This has been refurbished and powder coated; the factory finish was anodizing. Other models had a similar swing arm but in grey or silver.

Rear brake caliper over the swing arm on a Trident.

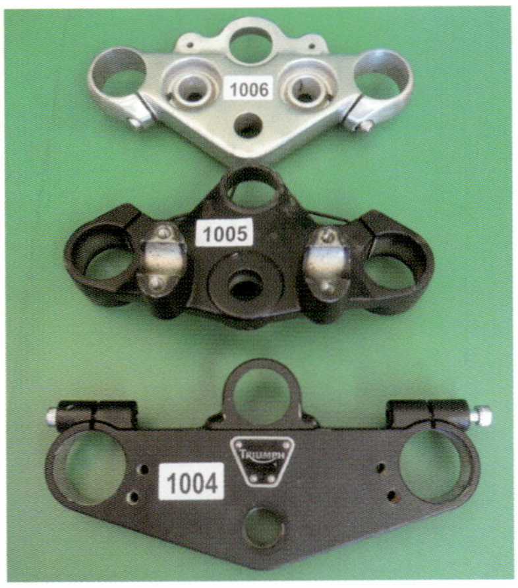

A selection of top yokes: 1004 later Trident, 1005 Tiger, 1006 Thunderbird.

Underslung rear brake caliper from a 1996 Speed Triple in gold.

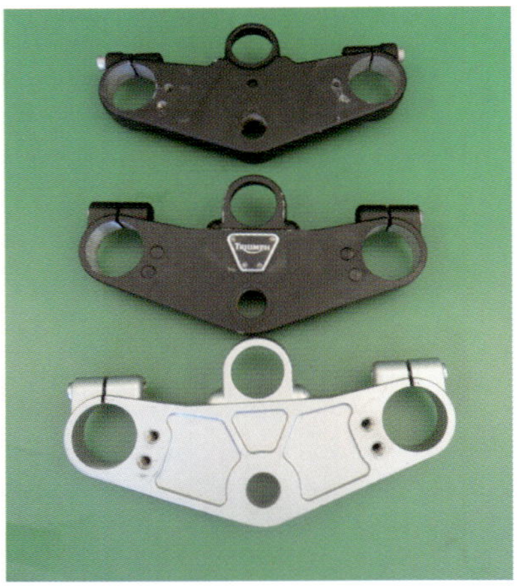

Top yokes: early Trophy at the bottom and Daytona at the top.

A Thunderbird swing arm that has been powder coated.

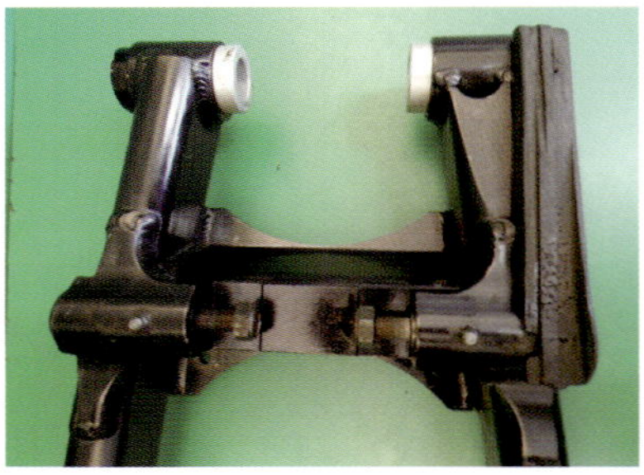

Thunderbird swing arm from underneath.

The swing arms for the Thunderbird/Thunderbird Sport and Legend are different in appearance.

TOP AND BOTTOM YOKES AND HANDLEBARS

The variety of top yokes is considerable, although the majority of the differences are cosmetic, as some are polished and some powder coated black or silver. There are also different offsets depending on the model, so Daytona has a 40mm offset while the Speed Triple has 35mm offset. Some models had the handlebars above the top yoke – the Trophies, Sprints, Sprint Sports and Tridents – while the Daytona and Speed Triples had handlebars below the top yoke, and the Adventurer, Thunderbird and Legend had the top yokes drilled to take clamps to hold the one-piece handlebars.

There is a large range of handlebars fitted to the various models and some can be interchanged between models, as all the forks are the same diameter of 43mm. Some handlebars fit below the top yoke – the Daytona and Speed Triple – and some fit above and are bolted through the top yoke, as on the Sprint, Sprint Sport, Trident and Trophy.

Other models have the bars above the top yoke held by clamps bolted

Sprint Sports handlebars.

Later Trophy handlebars.

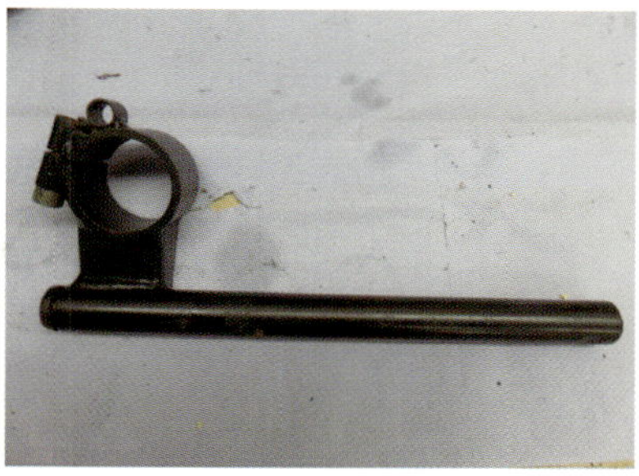

Daytona handlebars. The Speed Triple ones are very similar, minus the little ring welded on the side. These fit under the top yoke.

A set of Trident handlebars.

Thunderbird Sport handlebars.

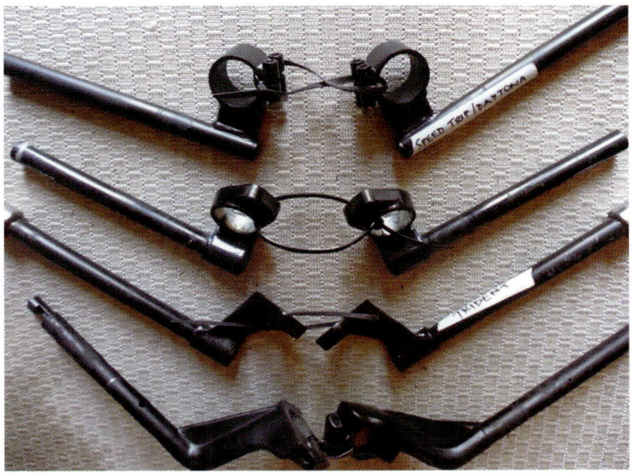

A selection of handlebars from various T300 models.

through the top yoke, as on the Thunderbird and Legend.

One of the most popular handlebars to fit is those from the Sprint Sports (and early Trophies) as they raise the position for a more relaxed ride (on the Daytona and Speed Triple) but give the café racer look. These bars can be fitted to a Daytona as they maintain clearance for the fairing and use the standard Daytona cables, hoses and wiring. The top yoke will not need to be drilled out to take the retaining bolts, as on the Daytona the threaded holes are already there. For a Speed Triple, however, the top yoke will need to be drilled out. If you fit Sprint Sports handlebars to a Speed Triple, the fork tubes will need to be changed to ones from a Trident, as they are longer and fill in the gap where the original handlebars fitted.

Daytona bars have a small ring on the side, the Speed Triple ones do not.

The last Trophies (from 1999) had aluminium handlebars.

The different handlebars also resulted in different bar end weights, so the Speed Triple, Daytona and so on had the bar end weights held to the handlebar by a small Allen-headed countersunk bolt that screws through the bar end weight and into an insert within the handlebar. The early Trophies and Sprint Sports had bar end weights that were threaded and they screwed in the handlebar end. The size

Some of the different bar end weights, depending on the model.

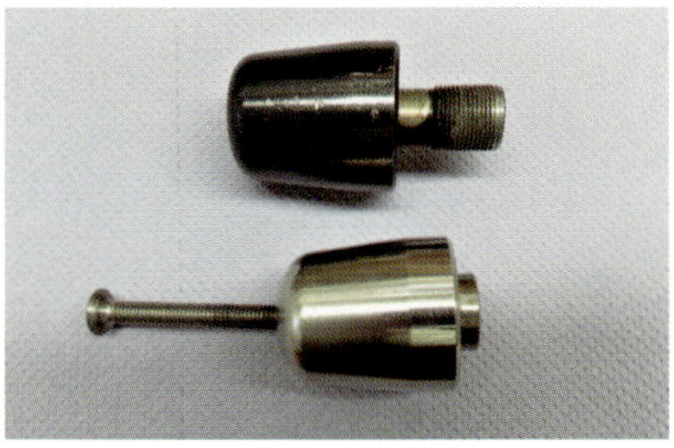

Bar end weights, with two types of fixing; the handlebars need to match the bar end weights.

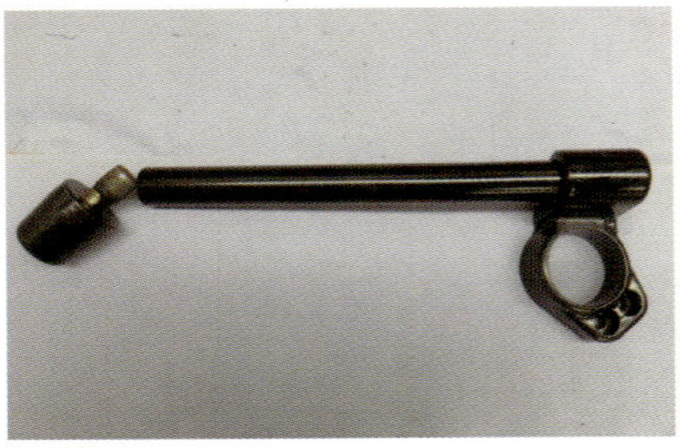

Sprint Sports handlebars and bar end weights.

This was the standard tank except for the Adventurer, Legend and Thunderbird range, which had a different-shaped unit.

Adventurer tank in Amber and Copper.

and pitch of the thread does not allow these to be interchangeable.

The Trophy for 1996 and 1997 had new bar end weights containing 'dynamic vibration absorbers'. These were also seen on the 2002 and 2003 Trophy 1200. The bar end weights for the later models are also physically smaller than the bar ends for the 900.

The T300 range offers an infinite variety of riding position from the 'drop' bars on the Daytona and Speed Triple to the 'comfy' bars fitted to the Trophies, and most things between.

REAR SHOCK ABSORBERS

There are two main types: adjustable ones, fitted to the Daytona (both 900 and 1200), Speed Triple, Trophy (both 900 and 1200) and Sprint Sports; and non-adjustable, fitted to the early Sprints and Tridents. Replacement new rear shock absorbers are no longer available from Triumph and they cannot be rebuilt or refurbished – beware any advert that says that they can. If your rear shock is high mileage then replace with an aftermarket one such as Hagon, YSS or one from a specialist company such as Maxton or Nitron, or one from a race company.

Rear shock absorbers: early Trident (1991 and 1992) on the left, and twin-headlamp Trophy on the right.

Standard rear shock on a Daytona.

The rear shock absorbers came in two lengths, as the earlier bikes were fitted with 18in rear wheels and later bikes were fitted with 17in; so, for example, the Speed Triple 750's were shorter than the 900's as it had an 18in rear wheel. If you change the early 18in wheels for the later 17in type, then fit a longer rear shock to compensate for the difference in wheel diameter in order to retain the excellent handling characteristics.

PETROL TANKS

There are three different fuel tanks in the T300 range. The most common is that fitted to the Daytona, Trophy, Trident, Sprint, Sprint Sports and Speed Triple, which is made of steel.

The underside of a Daytona petrol tank, showing the fuel tap position at the bottom and the fuel sender unit position at the top.

The tank fitted to the Thunderbird, Thunderbird Sport and Legend is different in shape to the Daytona/Trident one and has a smaller fuel capacity, but is also made of steel.

Lastly, there is the fuel tank fitted to the Tiger, which is made of plastic and will only fit a Tiger. Triumph had to have the vehicle regulations changed to allow the fitting of a plastic tank to

The Tiger fuel tank.

Water header tank used on the Thunderbird, Thunderbird Sport, Legend and Adventurer.

Thunderbird Sport water header tank.

Fuel tap in the PRIME position (arrow to the right).

a motorcycle and was the first manufacturer to produce a bike so fitted. Plastic fuel tanks are now common across many manufacturers.

Because the water coolant header (expansion) tank is located at the top of the spine frame on the Thunderbird and Legend ranges, the underside of the Thunderbird tank is a different shape, which makes it very difficult to fit one of the tanks from the Daytona/Trident/Speed Triple/Trophy models as there is no room for the water header tank. This can only be made to fit with considerable modification, involving cutting out the bottom of the tank.

There is one other difference; the fuel tanks for the Daytona/Trident/Speed Triple only have a low fuel light, where the Trophy has a fuel float powering a fuel gauge. This results in different holes under the tank.

FUEL TAPS

The majority of the bikes were fitted with a vacuum tap so that when the ignition is turned off, fuel no longer flows to the carburettor. The fuel tap

Fuel tap on a Tiger. This is a Pingel-style tap and not vacuum operated as on the Trident, Daytona, Trophy, Sprint and Speed Triple.

is visible on the near side of the bike and has a large black knob. The knob has three positions, PRIME, RUN and RESERVE. The fuel tap itself has two connections, one for fuel and one a vacuum hose that connects to the manifold. However, the Thunderbird, Tiger, Adventurers and Legends are fitted with a more conventional Pingel-style tap.

INSTRUMENTS

The later revised Trophy, with a fuel gauge and floats (fuel contents sender) in the tank, has a different connection in the bottom of the tank. The Trident, being the entry-level bike in the range, does not have a fuel gauge.

The early Trophy, Trident, Tiger, Sprint, Daytona and Sprint Sports have a temperature gauge that requires a different sender unit to those bikes only fitted with a temperature warning light. The head temperature sensor (a thermistor) is the same for all models. The change required between temperature gauge and the high coolant temperature warning light is carried out by a specific impedance matching unit (encapsulated circuit board) hard-wired into the appropriate instrument wiring loom.

The Speed Triple, Legend, Adventurer, Thunderbird and Thunderbird Sports have neither a fuel gauge nor a temperature gauge, relying on warning lights instead. Some models also had a clock. The photographs show the different cockpit instrument layouts.

Daytona instruments.

Sprint instruments.

Thunderbird Sport clocks.

A 1998 Sprint Sports.

Speed Triple instruments.

Legend instruments and handlebars.

Trident instruments.

Tiger instruments.

Thunderbird clocks, 2003.

Super 3 instruments.

Trophy instruments.

Revised Trophy instruments.

Trident instruments.

Early Sprint instruments and handlebars.

Sprint Executive instruments. Gordon Smith has added a manual override for the radiator fan.

Late Trident chromed rear indicators.

Front indicators on a Speed Triple.

INDICATORS

The bikes were fitted with a range of indicators, with the later Trident being chromed. The range of indicators fitted to the Thunderbird, Legend and Adventurer were different from the Trident, Daytona and Speed Triple ones.

Late Trident chromed indicators.

A rear indicator on a Trident; these are shorter than the front ones.

Thunderbird Sport front indicators.

GEAR LINKAGES

There are variations in the gear linkages: some are straight, some curved and some have rose joints, depending upon the model.

Straight gear linkage in situ.

Kinked gear linkage in situ.

CARBURETTORS

Triumph carburettor suppliers were Mikuni and Keihin, and they were fitted to the models as follows:

Mikuni carburettors were fitted to Tridents, Sprints, Daytonas, Daytona Super 3, Speed Triples and Trophies (both 3- and 4-cylinder models), while Keihins were fitted to late Trophy 900s, Sprint Executives, Tigers, Thunderbirds, Thunderbird Sports, Adventurers and Legends. The later Sprint Sports also had Keihin carburettors. Some Tigers also had Mikuni carburettors.

All models of carburettor need to be rebuilt with Viton seals to help resist modern fuel problems (ethanol). Float needles are normally Viton-tipped.

Restricted inlet rubbers – presumably to give more bottom end – were used on the Thunderbird 900 for Mikuni carburettor models only, but they can be changed to unrestricted versions fitted to other models. Keihin inlet rubbers were not restricted and remained the same on all models and even the carburettor Bonneville range. Inlet rubbers and airbox rubbers are not interchangeable between Mikuni and Keihin, so if you fit Keihins to a bike formerly fitted with Mikuni carburettors then you will also need to fit the appropriate inlet and airbox rubbers.

Popular opinion is that Keihins may be more economical but Mikunis are better for performance. This may be linked to more restrictive exhaust regulations that were introduced as the T300 progressed.

Mikuni carburettors on a 3-cylinder bike.

BRAKES AND BRAKE DISCS

The early bikes were fitted with two-piston sliding calipers at the front and rear, 296mm fixed discs at the front and a master cylinder of 14mm. These two-piston sliding calipers were common in a large range of Japanese bikes of the period and continued to be used as rear brake calipers long after the introduction of the four-piston calipers in the Triumph range.

The rear calipers could be fitted over the swing arm or under, depending on the model.

Later bikes had $^5/_8$in (15.87mm) master cylinders and 310mm floating discs at the front. The rear brake caliper remained as a two-piston sliding caliper. A worthwhile upgrade is to fit the later $^5/_8$in master cylinder, four-piston

Early two-piston front brake calipers with the 296mm fixed discs.

Rear brake calipers, one over the swing arm and one under.

calipers and the 310mm floating discs to the earlier bikes. If upgrading the calipers to the four-piston type, you must also upgrade to the floating 310mm discs – fitting the four-piston calipers to the 296mm fixed discs (or aftermarket ones) is dangerous and could result in an accident.

The smaller-diameter disc undercuts the outer edge of the brake pad by some 5mm. As the pad material wears down the unused portion 'folds over' the outer edge of the disc, which will increase pressure on the outer edge of the disc, in turn causing it to heat up. In extreme cases, the two fold-over sections will meet, further reducing braking performance.

Upgrading the front brake master cylinder from 14mm to $^5/_8$in will reduce lever travel.

From a cosmetic point of view, the first four-piston calipers were branded 'Nissin' and, from 1995, 'Triumph', but the actual calipers were the same (manufactured by Nissin). From late 1995, the colour of the calipers

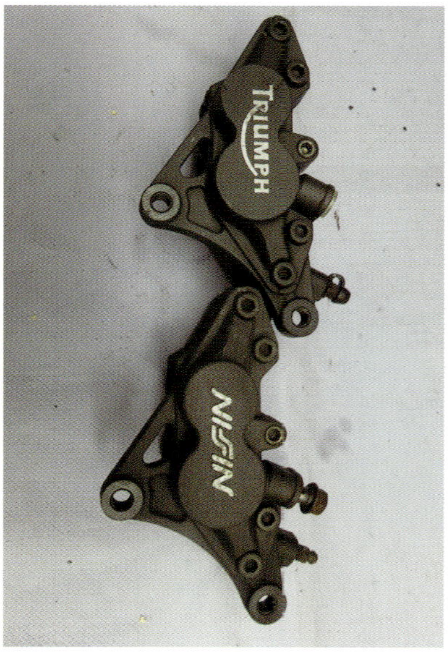

The different branding for the four-piston calipers, both made by Nissin.

Standard four-piston calipers in gold.

Front brake caliper in gold with Triumph branding, fitted from late 1995 onwards.

changed to gold, and the centre of the brake discs front and rear also changed from black to gold to match.

From a durability point of view, the black calipers are preferable because of the way they were manufactured: the black versions were machined and then anodized, while the gold ones were anodized and then machined. This means that the gold ones are prone to suffer corrosion where the seals are located.

SWITCHGEAR

This was common across the range of machines, except for the post-1996 Trophies and Thunderbirds. The Trophy switchgear from 1996 on had a more rounded appearance and the yellow 'cancel indicator' push button disappeared. That function was accomplished by just pushing in the Turn switch. Both types of switchgear are interchangeable.

AIR FILTERS

The air filter on all the T300 bikes is a complete airbox with the filter element contained inside. The 3-cylinder Trophy/Trident/Daytona/Sprint/Speed Triple/Trophy all have the same, but the airbox for the 3-cylinder Thunderbird/Legend/Thunderbird Sport is different, with only one snorkel compared to two for the other models. The airbox for the 1200 4-cylinder engines is the same across all models, irrespective of power output.

The standard 3-cylinder airbox.

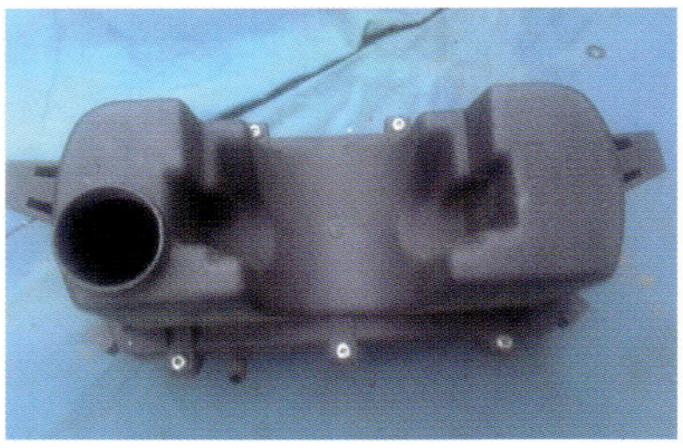

The Thunderbird airbox.

ENGINES

The engines were modular in that they shared many components, such as crankcases and blocks, across the 750 and 900 triples, and they shared a common bore across the entire range.

The long-stroke engines were as follows:

- Daytona/Trident/Trophy/Sprint/Sprint Sports/Speed Triple 900 (actually 855cc) 3-cylinder: 76mm bore × 65mm stroke
- Trophy/Daytona 1200 (actually 1180cc) 4-cylinder: 76mm bore × 65mm stroke
- Daytona 1000 (actually 998cc) 4-cylinder: 76mm bore × 55mm stroke

Sectioned 3-cylinder engine.

BELOW: Bottom crankcase for a 3-cylinder model, in this case a Speed Triple.

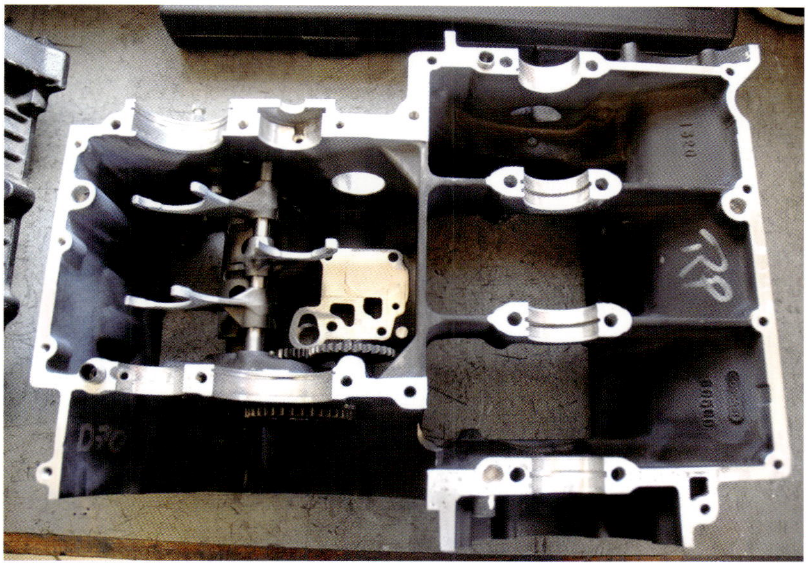

The bore and stroke of all these engines gave 300cc per cylinder.

All had a compression ratio of 10.6:1, with the exception of the Daytona and Daytona Super 3, at 12:1. The Thunderbird was detuned for more mid-range performance and had a compression ratio of 10:1.

The 900 and 1200 engines are similar, the main difference (besides the additional cylinder) being that the 4-cylinder has two balancer shafts in the sump (copying a design from the Lanchester car engine of the 1930s) and the 3-cylinder has a balancer shaft across the front of the engine. The 4-cylinder engine only has two coils, as one coil does two cylinders on a 'spare spark' (wasted spark) system. The camshaft profiles for the Super 3 900 and the Daytona 1200 are the same, and pistons from the 1200 can be used in the 900 to increase compression. The 900 and 1200 both share the same problems with the sprag clutch.

The short-stroke engine, as fitted to Daytona/Trident 750 (actually 748cc) 3-cylinders, has a 76mm bore and 55mm stroke, and a compression ratio of 11:1.

A different crank and pistons were fitted to the 750 engines, and one of the advantages of the modular approach is that you can fit the pistons from the 750 into a 900 to increase the compression ratio and gives around a 10bhp power increase.

The valves are the same across the range, at 32mm inlet and 28mm

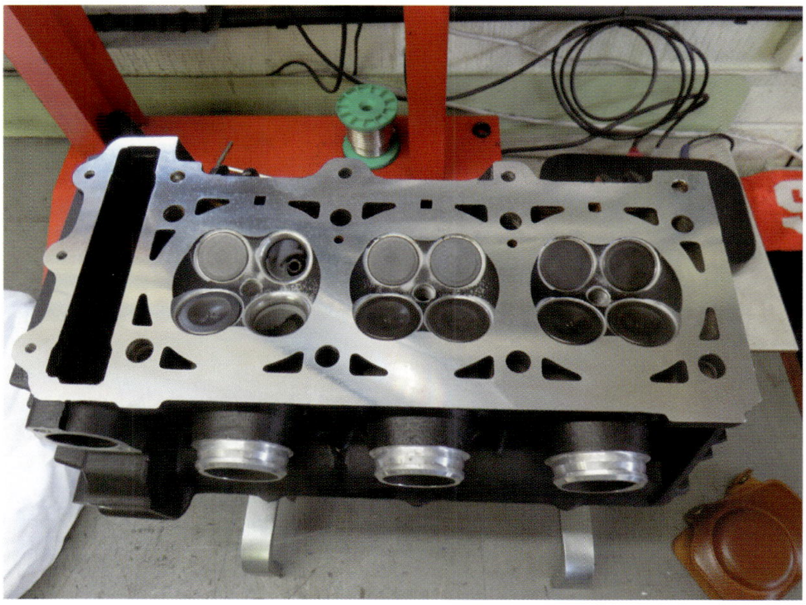

Cylinder head from a Speed Triple/Daytona, showing a newly ground head before being refitted.

exhaust, and the cams are driven by a HiVo chain running at the end (off side) of the engine. This configuration enables the engine to be more compact than placing the cam chain at the centre.

The valve adjustment was by an over-bucket and shim system, which means that they should only require checking every 10,000km (6,000 miles), but after the first 20,000km (12,000 miles) this can become every 20,000km (12,000 miles). If the bike has an unknown service history it's worth checking.

The mounting points on the frame for all bikes in the range are the same, but if you try to fit a Trophy/Daytona/Trident/Speed Triple engine into a Thunderbird – which has the header (expansion) tank under the fuel tank – then you will need to fit the water pump from a Thunderbird/Thunderbird Sport/Legend to the engine, as the water connections and the position of the header tank are different.

The crankcase breathing system also changed with the Thunderbird, Thunderbird Sport, Adventurer and Legend range (and all 1200 engines), and this is identified by the clutch cover being plain with no 'Triumph' name on and the figure-of-eight timing cover. The engine has a rotary breather, which screws into the crank. It is possible to fit the later breather system to earlier bikes but not all cranks have the appropriate holes for the impellor screws, so you need to check before commencing this modification.

A 3-cylinder engine with early flat cover for the sprag clutch.

Oil cooler and mounting used on the bikes with a fairing.

The crankcases were revised in 1994 and the cover plate to access the sprag clutch was deleted.

The faired bikes – Daytona and Trophy – were fitted with oil coolers to ensure adequate cooling in really hot weather. These were not necessary on the naked models.

EXHAUSTS

The exhaust manifolds (headers) on the 3-cylinder engines are all the same – stainless steel, which was then black chromed. However, not all 3-cylinder headers are black chromed; this probably came in with the 'sporty' models. The 4-cylinder bikes' manifolds are made the same way as for the 3-cylinder bikes. For the early 3-cylinder headers, the centre header is separate and is joined to outer headers by clamps below where the oil cooler is positioned.

The link pipes and silencers are different depending on the model and the rear foot pegs fitted. The Trophy/Sprint/Trident have longer pillion footrest brackets so the exhaust sits lower.

The Sprint Sports (and 750 Speed Triple) have an exhaust that looks similar

Thunderbird Sport engine, showing the revised crankcase covers.

Standard 3-cylinder exhaust after polishing, showing the stainless steel used.

Sprint Sports silencers; the ends are not the same as the Speed Triple and Daytona ones.

Standard Speed Triple exhaust silencer.

to the Daytona and Speed Triple, but with a smaller internal bore and end caps. The vinyl finish is also slightly different. The 1200 Daytona SE used the same silencers as fitted to late-model Daytonas.

IGNITERS

The igniters only supply electricity to the spark plugs so in that sense they are not like a modern car ECU, as they are not managing fuelling and are not connected to a raft of sensors. The Triumph igniters are triggered by a crank sensor. The 3-cylinder engines have different igniters to the 4-cylinder engines and they are not interchangeable as the 4-cylinder engines run on a 'wasted spark' principle. The bikes can be fitted with either PVL or Gill igniters, the essential difference being that the Gill ones give the sprag clutch an easier time as it allows the engine to spin over twice before firing the plugs and has a different advance curve.

The Gill igniters have the wiring harness built in, while the PVL has a separate connection for the wiring harness. There were rumours that by changing the wiring harness on the Speed Triple

PVL igniter; note the detachable wiring harness.

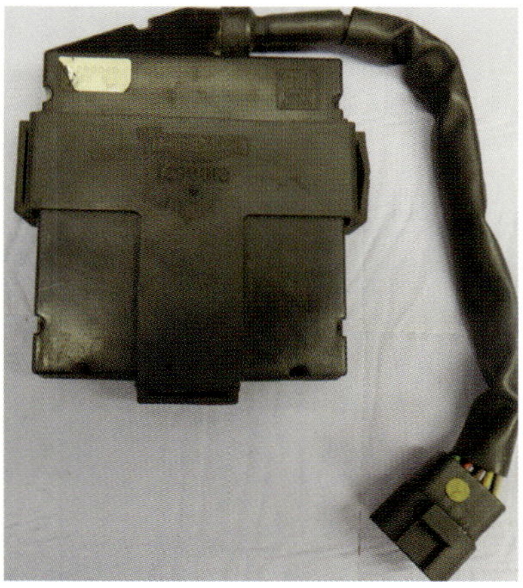

Gill igniter; note the built-in wiring harness.

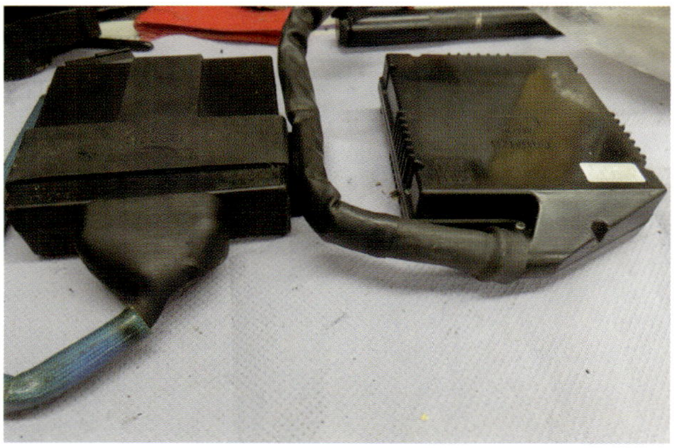

Igniters: PVL on the left and Gill on right. The wiring harness on the PVL is detachable.

Gill spark igniter. The PVL is similar, but the wiring harness connection is different. The name is at the top right.

Super 3 igniter box; note the different colour and the blue lead.

Challenge to one from a 750 Trident would give an extra 1,000 revs.

The Thunderbird range had a number of different igniters, later ones being L-shaped for space reasons.

The revised Trophies also acquired a slim-line igniter after 1997 and the Gill igniter was mounted behind the speedometer.

There are differences between the 1200 igniters in that the T312 Trophy should be high torque (HT) and the Daytona 1200 should be high power (HP). The fully advanced position on the Daytona 1200 is 26 degrees and on the Trophy 1200 is 29 degrees. From experience, the early igniters are a little rougher on pickup from low revs. They will work on both bikes, but it is best to match the model and the igniter for the 1200.

WHEELS

There were only three types of standard wheels fitted to all the models.

The original bikes had six-spoke wheels of 17in diameter for the front wheel and 18in for the rear wheel. They had a 3.5in-wide rim for the front and 4.5in at the rear.

From 1994, some models (Daytona 900 and 1200, Super 3, Trophy 900 and 1200, Speed Triple) were fitted with three-spoke wheels, 17in with 3.5in-wide rim at the front, and 17in with a 5.5in-wide rim at the rear.

The Sprint changed to the new three-spoke wheel in 1996, and the rims were 3.5in front and 5.5in rear. The Sprint Sports and Sprint Executive in 1998 were also fitted with the three-spoke wheels, again with 3.5in rims front and 5.5in rear.

These later wheels can be fitted to the earlier bikes, as the spindle and bearings are the same size; if this is done, it would be worthwhile upgrading the discs and master cylinders at the same time.

The Tiger was fitted with a 19in spoked wheel with 2.5in rim at the front and a 17in wheel with 3in rim at the rear.

The Tiger front wheel had two floating discs and two two-piston calipers.

The Thunderbird and Legend were also fitted with spoked wheels, 18in with a 2.5in rim at the front, and 16in with a 3.5in rim at the rear. The front

The standard three-spoke wheel 17in front and rear.

Six-spoke wheels 17in front, and 18 rear.

The Tiger spoked wheel.

The early square rear light on a Trident, Sprint, Daytona and Trophy.

wheel only allowed the fitment of one brake disc and a single two-piston caliper.

The Thunderbird Sport (introduced in 1998) was fitted with a 17in spoked front wheel with a 3.5in rim, and a 17in spoked rear wheel with 4.25in rim, and two 310mm front discs. These dual-braked, front-spoked hubs are very desirable for the specials builders, particularly those producing CRK conversions.

The Adventurer was fitted with an 18in front wheel with 2.5in rim and a 16in rear wheel with a 3.5in rim; braking was by a single disc and caliper.

The Legend TT was fitted with 17in spoked wheels front and back, with a 3.5in rim at the front and 4.25in at the rear.

SUMPS

Late on in the life of the T300 range, around 1997, there were revisions to the bottom crankcase, whereby the previous 22mm sump plug was replaced by a 14mm one. The early 22mm (metric thread size) sump plug requires the chain eccentric/spark plug 12mm Allen key. The later 14mm (metric thread size) requires a 13mm hex socket. Care should be taken with the correct torque loading – the M22 is 48Nm and the M14 is 28Nm.

RADIATOR FANS

There are a number of different fans fitted to various models, as shown here.

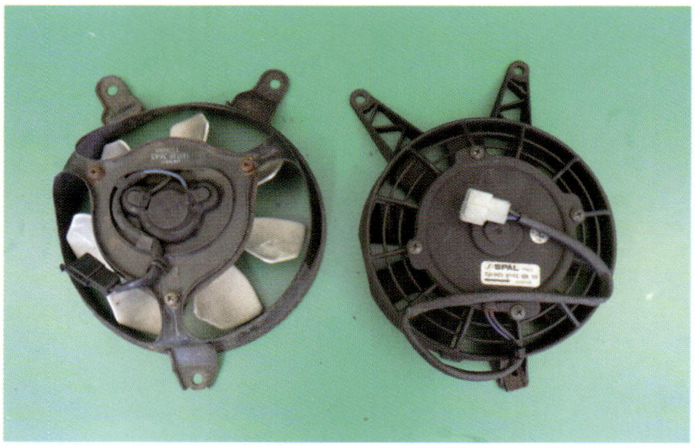

Two different radiator fans.

BODYWORK

The bodywork is held on by a combination of spigots on the body panel pressed into rubber grommets and bolts. Much of the bodywork is interchangeable between models, so for instance Daytona bodywork will fit a Speed Triple (but obviously with colour and decal differences). However, there were changes to the rear lights

Revised rear lights were introduced on the Sprint Sports (1997), Trophy and late Tridents.

(from 1997 with the Sprint Sports and the revised Trophy, and for 1998 for the Trident) and this means that the side panels need to match the rear light assembly. Swapping fairings from model to model will require the appropriate fairing mounting frame and adjustment to headlight arrangements.

Trident side panels with the aluminium inserts have a lower-profile joining piece above the rectangular rear light, which will require some opening-out of the side panel spigot holes.

The Daytona and Speed Triple also had the option of a pillion seat cover (matching the colour of the bike) to give the café racer look. This meant that the seat had two inserts bolted in the side to attach the cover. When the cover was fitted, the pillion grab rail had to be taken off, along with the infill piece. These covers are now sought after and you can expect to pay up to

A pillion seat cover available as an extra for Daytonas and Speed Triples. The cover requires a seat with two captive bobbins in the seat for the cover to be screwed into.

The captive bobbin in a Daytona seat.

Seat with captive bobbins for pillion cover.

£150 or more for one. Sprint Manufacturing makes a glass-fibre copy, but this will require painting and a seat-pad making.

The colour of the Triumph branding on the fuel tanks was determined by the colour of the tank, so, for example, the Caspian Blue Trophy had 'Triumph' written in red edged in white. The 'Triumph' on the black Speed Triple simply had a white outline, but the Racing Yellow version had black lettering edged in white.

Many parts are no longer available from Triumph. The company continued to supply virtually all parts for the complete range of bikes right up the 2000s, but from that point they gradually deleted parts from the parts catalogue. The first parts to go were most body panels, fuel tanks and exhaust silencers. Subsequently, more and more parts have been deleted, including more body panels, brake calipers, carburettors, swing arms and wheels. The bottom line is, go to

Pillion grab rail and insert to fill the gap between the seat and the rear bodywork.

Pillion grab handle fitted to a Speed Triple.

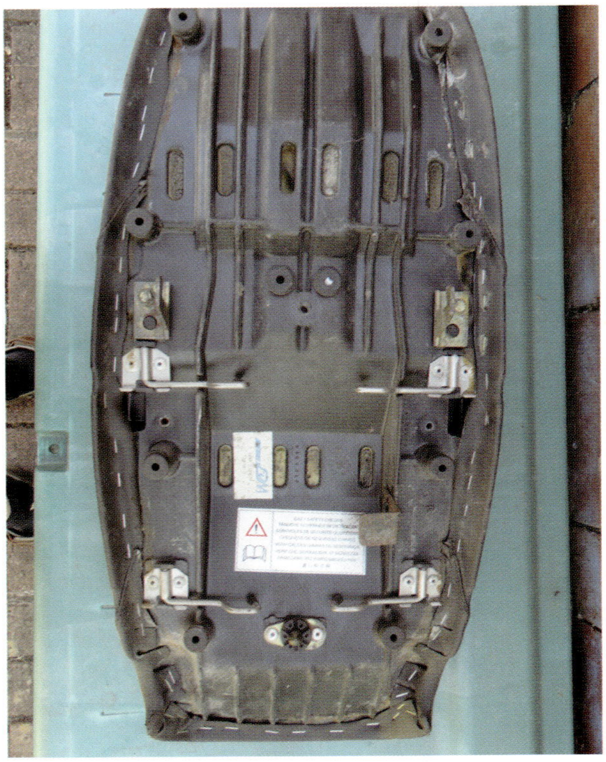

A Trophy seat with fold-out hooks to hold luggage on the rear seat.

Trophy seat with fold-out hooks to strap luggage on to.

Decals on a Volcanic Red background.

Decals for the Super 3.

Decals for an early Trophy 900.

Decals on a Sprint; note the grey engine colour.

Decals for the early Sprint, known then as a Trident Sprint, but later shortened to just Sprint.

LEFT: The decals on a Sprint Sports.

The decals for a black Tiger; the decals for this model are very expensive!

your local Triumph dealer and check to see if the parts you require are available.

There are a number of companies who have online parts catalogues, such as World of Triumph and Fowlers (Bristol Triumph dealers), which are worth looking at, although sometimes they will say parts are available when they are not. I personally go into my local Triumph dealer and have a look at the factory parts list. For mail order, Jack Lilly's (a long-time Triumph Dealer) has a good reputation for prompt delivery.

It must be remembered that when Triumph revised a part, they did not give it a new part number but used the original number, which can cause some confusion.

Sprint Manufacturing can supply many parts no longer available from Triumph sourced from the original manufacturers – for example, they supply Nissin OE brake components and the chain rubbing strip.

For many parts, however, you will have to investigate the second-hand market, which means eBay and other sites such as Gumtree. There used to be a number of specialist Triumph breakers but these have dwindled in recent years and the current 'go to' is Ivan at National Triumph. Ivan is very knowledgeable on the T300 range as well as the later T595 and T509 ranges. I have listed various companies at the back of the book who can provide either parts or services.

3

essential tools and equipment

When carrying out any work on a bike, it is essential that the correct tools are used, both for safety and to prevent damage to the bike (and parts). By trying to use a tool not designed for the purpose you are putting it to will only cause damage (and expense) and increase frustration. If you have bought this book then I am assuming that you already have a decent collection of tools, but the list below will ensure you get it right. As a classic example, I was not aware of the difference between JIS and Philips (and Posidrive) screwdrivers (and screws), but the Triumph range makes liberal use of JIS, and using one for the first time made me realize how much more effective they are.

MANUALS

A full Triumph workshop service manual is absolutely essential. I would not attempt to carry out any work on the bike without first referring to the manual. My copy was bought from eBay at a cost of around £35 and CD copies are also available. It may still be available from the dealers. With my hard-copy version, I have pulled all the pages out of the bindings and put them into individual plastic wallets so they don't get oily finger prints on them when I use it in the garage, and these plastic wallets go into a large ring binder. You will need to look carefully at the date of issue; mine is from 1997 so does not have all the models described in it, but as I am a Speed Triple/Daytona owner it's fine for me as those models are covered.

The Triumph workshop manual.

The original Haynes manual, *Triumph Triples and Fours 91 to 95*, is also a useful addition, and this has now been updated as *Triumph Triples and Fours 1991–2004*, which covers all the Triumph 750/900 triples and fours during that time. The reference number is the same – #2162. The photo sequences can be very helpful, but there are a few errors in the Haynes manual (for example it only lists Mikuni carburettors as being on all the models), so I would always use the Triumph workshop service manual as a first point of reference, and use the photos in the Haynes manual to help in visualizing what needs to be done.

Another Haynes publication that goes into a lot of detail is *Motorcycle Workshop Practice Manual* by Pete Shoemark. This makes excellent bedtime reading!

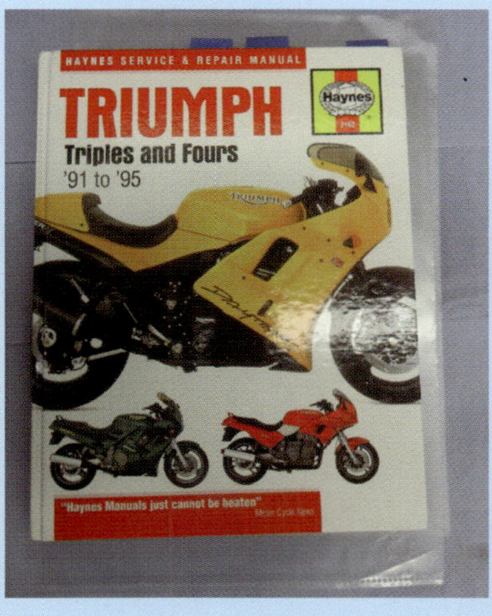

The Haynes manual for T300. This has now been updated to cover all models from 1991 to 2004 under the title Triumph Triples and Fours 1991–2004.

Haynes's other companion manuals *Motorcycle Carburettor Manual, Motorcycle Basics Manual* and *Motorcycle Electrical Manual* will all give you a good background in motorcycle maintenance and help you in performing the necessary tasks.

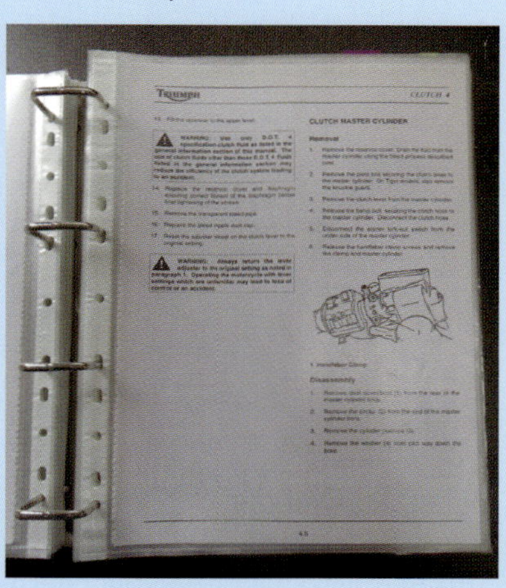

The Triumph workshop manual split into individual pages and placed in plastic sleeves and a ring binder. This prevents oily finger marks on the original pages.

Haynes' Motorcycle Workshop Practice Manual, *a useful introduction to understanding the basics. This has been updated.*

The standard Abba stand frame, which will require specific bobbins.

Abba stand bobbins, which are made to match up with different manufacturers and models.

An excellent guide to workshop practice as well as modifying your bike is *Customizing your Motorcycle – Shed-Built to Show Bike* by Chris Daniels, published in 2018.

I cannot emphasize enough the importance of not starting any work on the bike without reference to the Triumph workshop manual backed up with the relevant Haynes manual. It is essential that you familiarize yourself with the job you are about to carry out before you begin. If you are in any doubt consult someone with experience.

BEFORE YOU START

After you have read all the relevant manuals, prepare a checklist of what parts you are likely to use and have them to hand. Then it is vital to identify what tools you will require. The list below will allow you to work on the bike safely and without causing damage by using the wrong tools. I am particular when it comes to tools and try to buy the best (within reason), as cheap tools can break or are not accurately sized. Gordon Smith reports that he had to file down the Triumph damper rod tool on each flat to get it to fit properly; it was approximately 0.05mm oversize. Cheap Torx bits are almost guaranteed to break.

You are likely to be spending a fair bit of time on your maintenance and restoration projects, so make sure your garage or workshop is as conducive to this as possible, with good lighting, heating, storage and workbenches. A fire extinguisher is essential, and it must be big enough – should you have a fire, you don't want to run out of the extinguisher agent before the fire is out!

Tidy up the workspace to ensure you have room to strip things down. I clear the workbench and put down sheets of newspaper and have a roll of kitchen towel to hand. If necessary, have some metal trays to place items in so that liquids don't go everywhere.

SUPPORTING THE BIKE

One of the key things to remember about the T300 range is that they are very heavy, the lightest model being in excess of 210kg (463lb) and the heaviest 232kg (511lb) – both dry weight – so supporting the bike properly and safely is critical both for the bike and for the person working on it. Removing the swing arm creates a problem as supporting the bike without being able to use a paddock stand can create issues. Putting a car trolley jack under the sump is a recipe for disaster, and there have been examples of bikes falling over, with serious results not only for the bike but also for the person doing the work. I know of one person who had to give up riding motorcycles because of serious back and hip injuries he suffered when a bike fell on top of him. I once tried to take the front forks out of my ex-Racing Speed Triple by doing this and the bike fell over; fortunately it was standing next to a wooden fence so did not fall very far, but it did £100 of damage to the seat hump, which had to be resprayed.

My solution is the Abba stand, which I now consider an essential piece of kit, and this fits into the bike's frame using adapters. The Abba stand frame is standard but you will need to buy a separate fitting kit specifically for the motorbike range you are working on. The basic superbike stand is around £100 with the fitting kit around £20. Abba now do an extension to the original stand that allows the front wheel to be raised from the ground; effectively the bike then pivots around its centre, allowing either the rear or the front wheel to be raised above the ground with the front lifting arm. This costs around £50.

I supplement the Abba stand with a front paddock stand from Chris Foxley (Foxley Starters), which fits through the headstock. Fortunately, Triumph used the same-sized hole in the headstock for later bikes, so it fits into my Thruxton as well. Chris makes these to order, as the hole in the bottom of the headstock varies with manufacturer.

Abba also make a Sky Lift, which can raise the whole bike in the air and takes up considerably less room in the garage than the traditional bike lift.

An Abba stand in use, with the extension to allow the bike to rock. The front of the bike is held with a front paddock stand.

An Abba Sky Lift with Mark Gaylard's Speed Triple receiving attention. The Sky Lift can be folded up when not in use.

It's not cheap, at around £440 (sometimes available on a special offer), but if space is at a premium in your garage or workshop then it may fit the bill.

Go to the Abba stands website to see videos of the various bits of kit being demonstrated. I am a satisfied customer and have found the service excellent, but there are other companies who offer similar stands.

A 'bump stop' fitted to a standard-style motorcycle bench; this holds the bike up until a paddock stand can be placed under the rear wheels.

I have a motorcycle bench modified with a 'bump stop' that holds the front wheel in place on the stand, and I then put a paddock stand under the rear to raise the rear wheel off the ground. If I take the engine out, I have a heavy-duty scissor jack (not a car jack!) that sits on the bench and can go under the engine; I can disconnect everything and then lower the engine. I have also used this scissor jack on the motorcycle bench to remove the swing arm (the front wheel captured in the bump stop and the jack under the engine). For safety, it is also a good idea to use ratchet straps to secure the bike to the motorcycle bench to stop it from falling over.

To keep the bikes standing in a more upright position when in the garage, I

Heavy-duty scissors jack for use on the bike bench.

Side stand puck with wooden packing.

use a side stand puck screwed to a block of wood.

CLEANING

Ultrasonic cleaner This piece of kit is useful for cleaning carburettors, although in the most common sizes you can only place one carburettor in at a time. Gordon Smith has an ultrasonic cleaner that will take a full set of three carburettors suitably stripped with the individual jets in a small wire basket (or sieve). With a set of four he does them in pairs.

The cleaner will remove the crud and dirt inside the carburettor, but parts like jets and pilot jets will need to be cleaned with copper or brass wire as the ultrasonic cleaner will not get into the inside of the jets. If you leave the jets without cleaning them the bike will not run correctly. I would always recommend washing as much external dirt and debris off a bank of carburettors with something like white spirit before putting them into an ultrasonic cleaner.

After an hour or so at 50°C (122°F), remove and blow off any excess cleaning solution with compressed air (carefully). Then spray all the external parts with a protective spray, such as Motorex Moto Project. Finally, have a closer look with a jeweller's eyepiece, loupe or magnifying glass for final cleaning with carb cleaner for stubborn stains, before reassembling.

Occasionally you can find cheap ultrasonic cleaners in places like Aldi and Lidl. If you don't want to buy one, though, get the carburettors cleaned by a professional outfit (such as Paul Barnett at Triumph Motorbike Spares).

Parts washer I have a small one and use the recommended fluid, but a plastic washing up bowl, a stiff paintbrush and some paraffin will do the same job, if not quite as neatly. I would definitely not recommend petrol for cleaning parts because of the fire risk; petrol vapour can travel just above the floor and be ignited some distance from where you are. My brother's MGB car was destroyed in a fire at a restoration company for that very reason. Petrol is not very good for the skin either; it's only place is in a fuel tank!

HAND TOOLS

Spark plug socket One of the side effects of using a large-diameter spine frame is that there is very restricted clearance above the centre spark plug, and the holes through the cam cover for the spark plugs are quite narrow so a standard spark plug socket (18mm) will not fit! A thin-walled plug spanner is required and, as the spark plug rises out of the hole, the ratchet will have to be removed (as it hits the spine frame); once the plug is loose, a piece of rubber hose placed over the spark plug will enable you to get it out of the hole. As part of the standard tool kit for the bike, Triumph supplied a thin-walled plug socket, but most of these

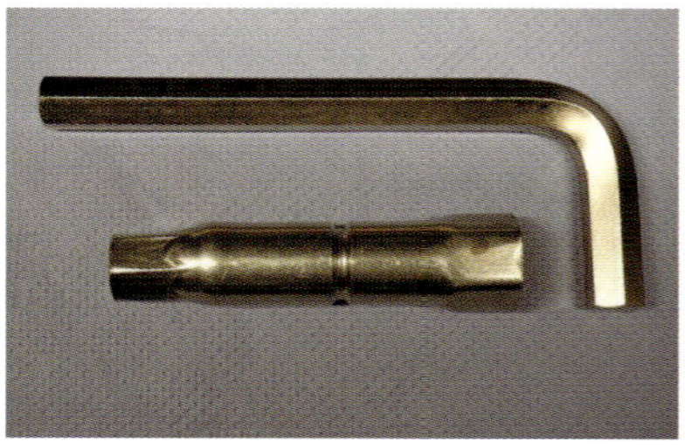

The spark plug spanner as supplied by Triumph in the under-seat tool kit.

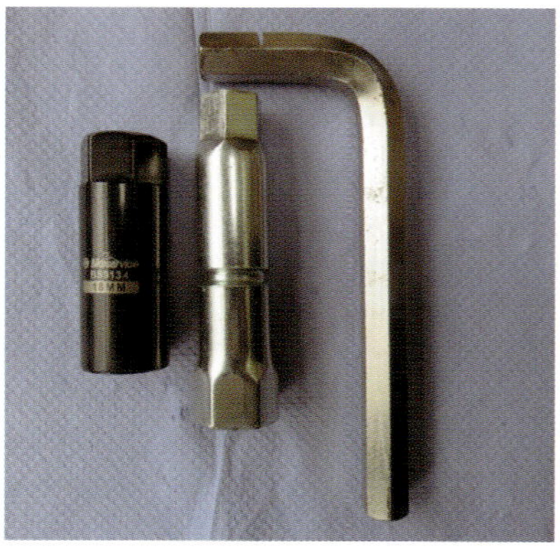

Spark plug spanners: on the left is an aftermarket 18mm one, and on the right a plug spanner.

have disappeared and they are much sought after second-hand. If you can't find one, then buy a thin-walled plug spanner and make sure it has a rubber plug inside to make extracting the spark plug easier. I found one for around £10 on eBay and is of a good quality. I have found that if you shorten the Allen key that fits into the plug spanner it will fit under the spine frame.

Standard socket set A $^{3}/_{8}$in drive will suffice for most jobs but some additional sizes will need to be bought – a 36mm is required for the front sprocket nut and I would use a ½in drive for this with an extension bar. Some different-length extension bars and fixed bars are also needed. I always undo nuts/bolts with a fixed bar and then use the ratchet to reduce the risk of damaging ratchets if you are undoing tight nuts/bolts. I also have a ½in drive fixed bar (sometimes called a breaker bar) if really needed!

I would also have more than one 10mm socket and 10mm spanners, as this is the most common size used on motorcycles (and they seem to disappear into a garage black hole never to be seen again). I have lost track of how many 10mm sockets I have lost. Don't stint on the quality of sockets and spanners, as cheap ones can break and split. When this happens knuckles

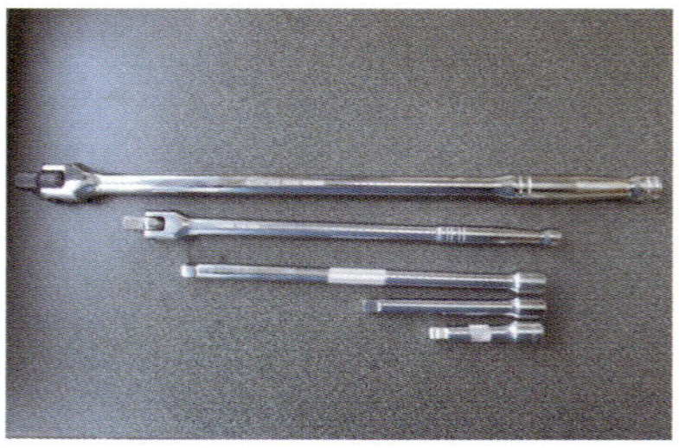

Breaker bars and socket extensions. The ½in drive is at the top, the rest being $^{3}/_{8}$in size.

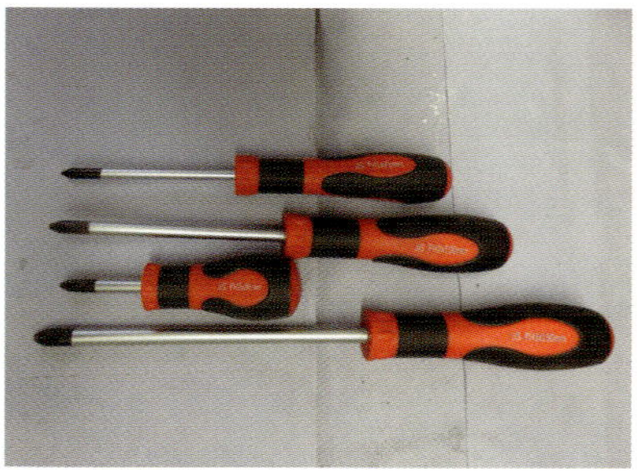

JIS screwdriver set, essential for any work on a T300.

get bashed and you can't finish the job until a replacement tool is obtained. You don't need to buy the most expensive but I have found the Halfords Professional range good value and decent quality; I also have Teng and Facom tools (I bought some of the Facom when Halfords stopped stocking them and sold off the existing stock at half price). Be very wary of buying tools at auto jumbles or bike shows as very often these are of poor quality. If you want to maintain your bike properly then invest in good tools.

Torx sockets (bits) A number of the bolts on the T300 range have Torx heads, up to and including T55. I would recommend getting a set of quality ones as the cheap ones have a habit of breaking.

JIS (Japanese Industry Standard) screwdrivers A set of these is also vital if you want to remove the screws that hold the brake and clutch master cylinder covers. JIS screws are also used on the carburettors and, again, if you try to use a Phillips screwdriver you will certainly chew up the head and make removal very difficult. Sizes 1 and 2 will suffice, but I bought a quality full set on eBay for around £25.

Torque wrench This is absolutely essential for carrying out some of the maintenance tasks on the T300 (and any bike). The consequences of not using the correct settings can be very expensive. I actually have two, one with a range of 10Nm to 50Nm (this allows the sensitivity for the smaller range around the 10Nm figure) and a second one with a range of 20Nm to 100Nm. It is vital that the torque wrenches are recalibrated on a regular basis, particularly the ones at the lower end of the ranges. Don't be tempted to buy cheap Asian imports; I use Norbar ones, which are made in the UK.

Impact driver A $^{3}/_{8}$in size fitted with a number of different bits is useful. I also have an electric version, which is more than helpful when removing the front sprocket retaining nut (which is torqued down to 132Nm). The alternative is a length of scaffold pipe on a ½in drive extension!

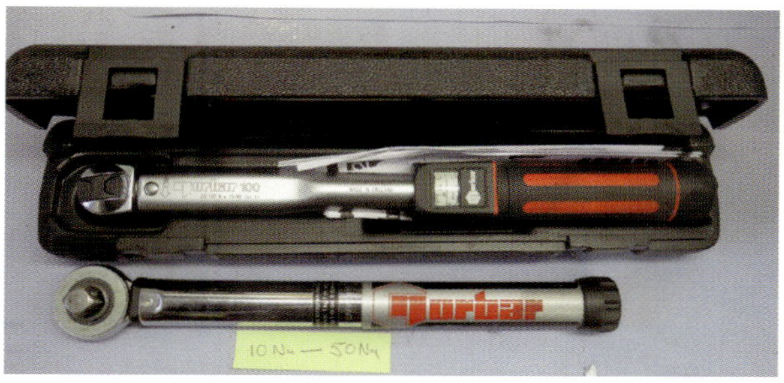

A pair of torque wrenches with different maximum ratings, one lower than the other.

Selection of picks.

A $^3/_8$in impact driver.

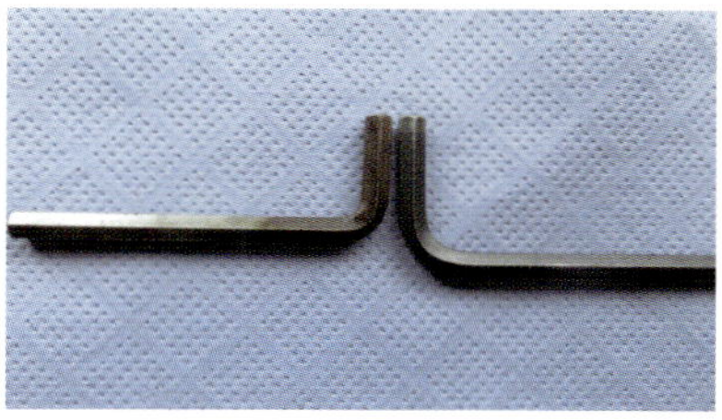

Modified Allen key for cam cover bolts; a standard one is on the right.

An electric impact driver.

Allen key set Having a set is essential, but I would have more than just the bent bar type. I also have a T-handled set and one that fits into a ½in drive socket extension. A $^3/_8$in version would also be useful!

Access to the two bolts under the spine frame holding the cam cover on is extremely limited. A standard Allen key is a really tight fit under the frame. To make access easier, shorten the end of a 9mm Allen key.

Circlip pliers A decent set of inside and outside circlip pliers will be required, particularly if you are going to overhaul the brake and clutch master cylinders. I find a set of picks a useful addition for removing circlips.

Picks A set of picks comes in handy, particularly when trying to get the small circlips out of brake and clutch master cylinders. Using these is better than ruining the tips of small screwdrivers.

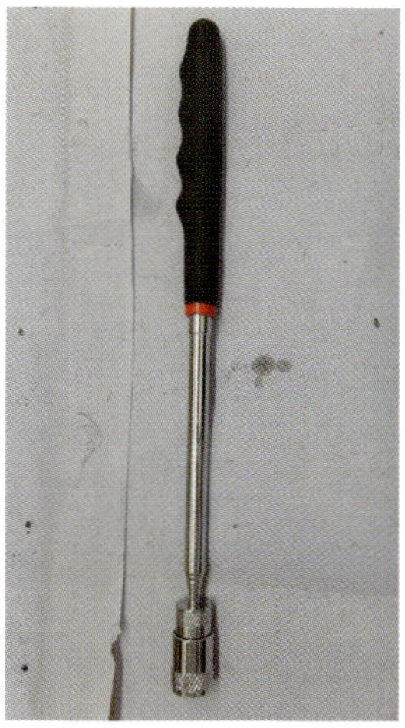

Telescopic magnet with a light at the end.

Telescopic magnet tool This is used to lift out the shims and is also really useful for retrieving stray nuts and bolts. I once dropped a nut into an engine; fortunately it was visible and I could reach with a magnetic tool that had a telescopic extension – a real lifesaver, as otherwise I would have had to dismantle the engine. The magnet tool I have has a light built into the end so when peering into the gloom of an engine I can see what is going on.

Assorted hammers I have a hide and copper, a rubber and a conventional steel hammer; all have their uses. Using a steel hammer can cause damage to components, however. The one I use the most is the hide and copper one.

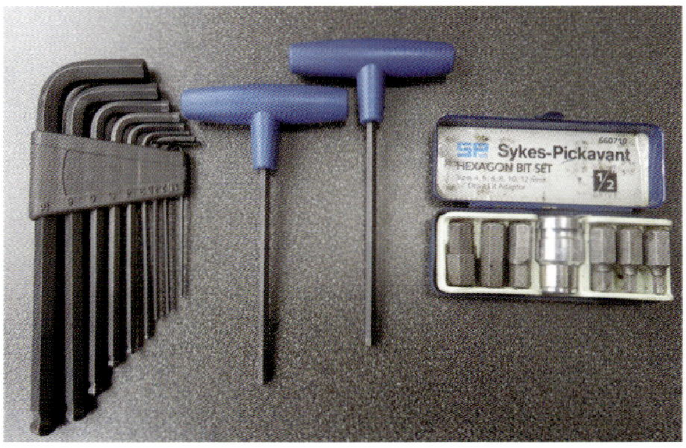

LEFT: Allen keys of various types.

RIGHT: A selection of hammers: rubber, copper and hide, and steel. All have their uses in maintaining a motorcycle.

A chain press.

Metric tap and die set Make sure you buy decent quality, as these can save the day in cleaning up clogged or damaged threads.

Chain press This is essential for riveting a new link when changing the drive chain; I am not a fan of the sliding link, as they can come off.

MEASURING INSTRUMENTS

Micrometer If you are going to check the shims, then this is essential. Buy one with a range of 0 to 25mm. This will also come in handy when checking the thickness of brake discs as well; you can't use a vernier caliper gauge for this as there is usually a small ridge or lip at the edge of the disc, which would give a false reading.

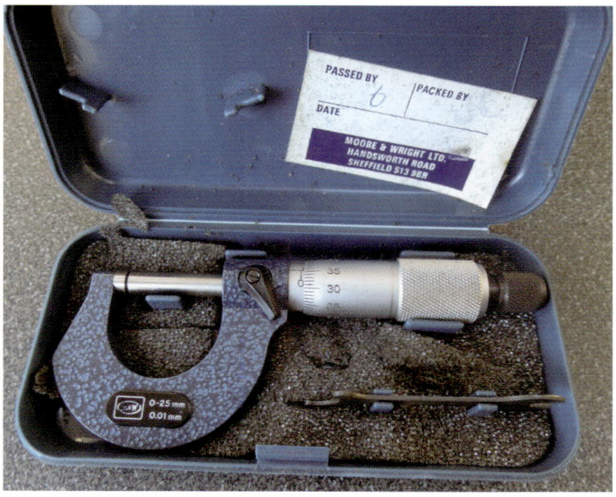

A micrometer. This was purchased second-hand on eBay for £30, but is a quality item.

Multimeter This will allow you to see if the alternator is working properly and the voltage flowing into the battery. It can also be used to test for resistance on coils and the crank sensor.

A digital one is far more accurate than the moving coil analogue type, but there are some cheap and nasty ones out there. Before doing any resistance checks, you should always short the two test leads together (on the resistance range) to see if it indicates 0 ohms (0.0), or very close to it. If it does not, then check the test leads or change the internal battery.

Feeler gauges For adjusting the shims and the crank sensor air gap, you will need a set of feeler gauges. You can get a full set, or buy individual ones, colour coded for each size.

Thermal strips/temperature sensing guns These are useful for recording peak temperatures on radiators and engine cases. In recent years, temperature sensing guns have become widely available and are not expensive.

Compression tester This is an invaluable tool for diagnostic purposes. It will show if there are problems with either the piston rings or the valves not sealing properly. Compression readings for the 1200 should be in the range 180–220psi with no more than 25psi difference between cylinders. For the 900 it is 140–185. Always carry out a compression test with the throttle fully open otherwise you may get a false reading. Anything around 100psi indicates a very worn motor.

A multimeter.

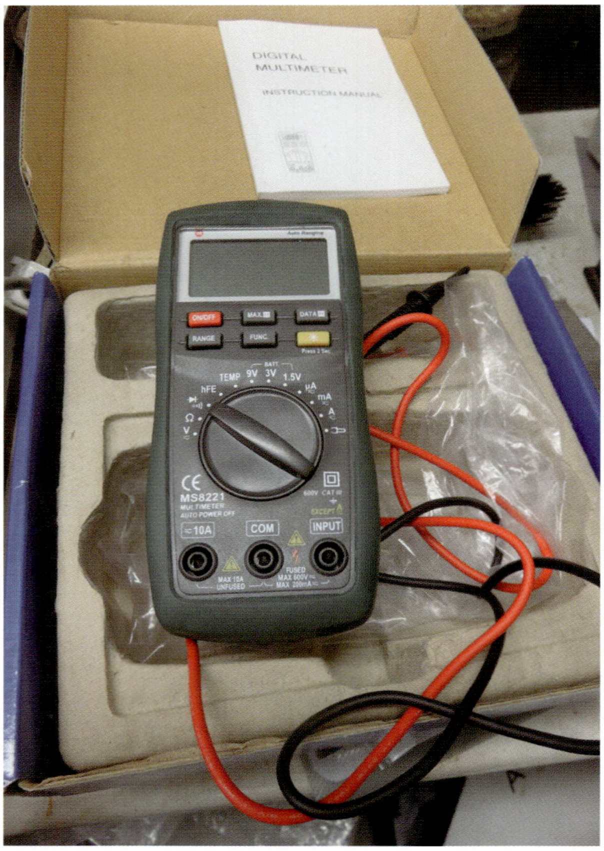

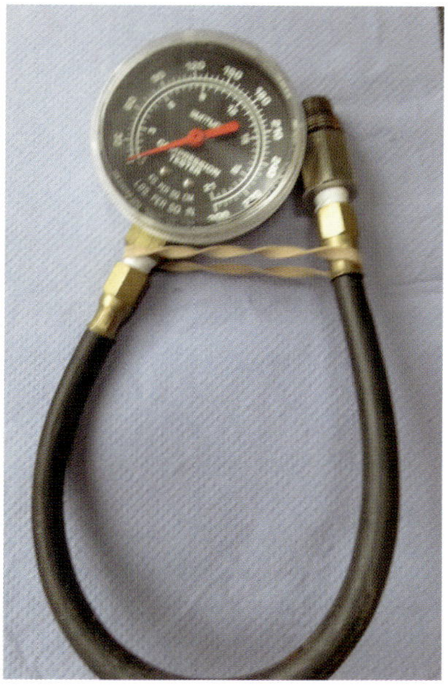

Compression tester.

The key measurement is not necessarily the maximum reading but that there is not more than 25psi difference between the cylinders.

Tyre gauge and foot pump Don't underestimate how badly a bike will handle if the tyre pressures are not correct, so check regularly. The majority of the bikes run with 36psi front and 41psi rear, but check the handbook.

EXTRACTION TOOLS

Stud extractors These are a useful addition to the tool kit, particularly if trying to get cylinder head studs out.

Valve shim tool If you intend to check your valve shims, then consider buying a dedicated valve shim tool. This is no longer available from Triumph but you can still get aftermarket ones. Expect to pay around £60.

Brake piston extractor tool Brake pistons can be really difficult to remove, so to make life easier and avoid mangling the pistons by gripping with a pair of pliers, use a proper extraction tool.

Spring puller Some aftermarket exhausts require the sections to be joined by springs, so a proper spring puller is helpful.

Heat gun This is a useful tool to have where there are components that have seized up. A blowlamp or gas torch is far too hot and is more likely to damage aluminium components. I have a paint-stripping hot air gun that does the job. You only need to warm things up, not melt them!

Freeze spray This can be very helpful when trying to get seized studs or pilot screws out of carburettors or the fork adjusters at the bottom of the forks. The technique is to warm up with a heat gun and then use the freeze spray: the expansion and contraction can sometimes be enough to free the seized component.

BLEEDING AND DRAINING

Hand pump This is essential for draining the fuel tank. If you have ever siphoned petrol by sucking on a pipe then you do not want to repeat the process! This is even more relevant in the current environment, as modern fuels have a vast range of additives, most of which are dangerous to your health if ingested. I find the hand pump shown here is very effective at getting most of the petrol out of the tank in a safe way. The only issue I have is that it has quite a high pumping capacity so it is very easy to overfill the petrol cans. I have two 5ltr (1gal) plastic petrol cans to put the fuel into (and store away from the garage). I try to drain fuel outside so that any spillage quickly evaporates and does not represent a fire risk.

The weight of a petrol tank when full is significant so I always drain of as much fuel as possible before removing the tank to reduce the risk of dropping it. Refitting the tank is also much easier if it is empty. Most of the T300 range has a fuel capacity of 25ltr (5.5gal) –

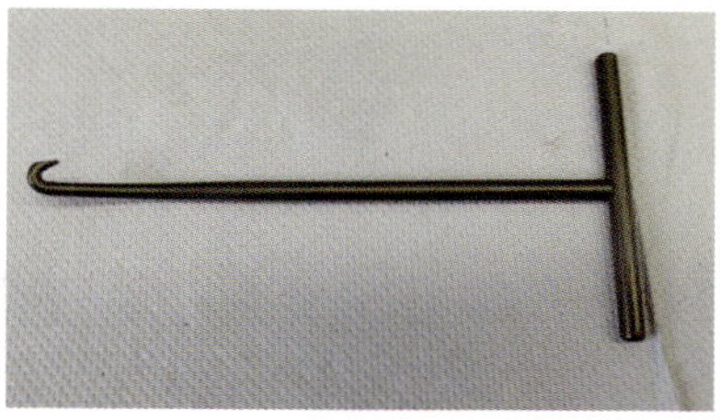

A spring puller, essential for fitting exhaust springs.

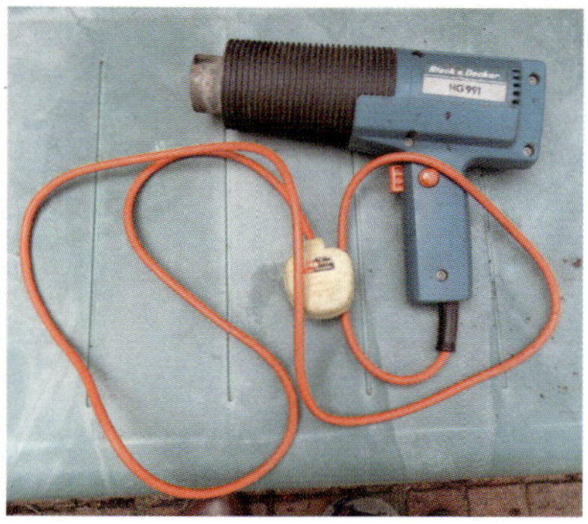

A heat gun.

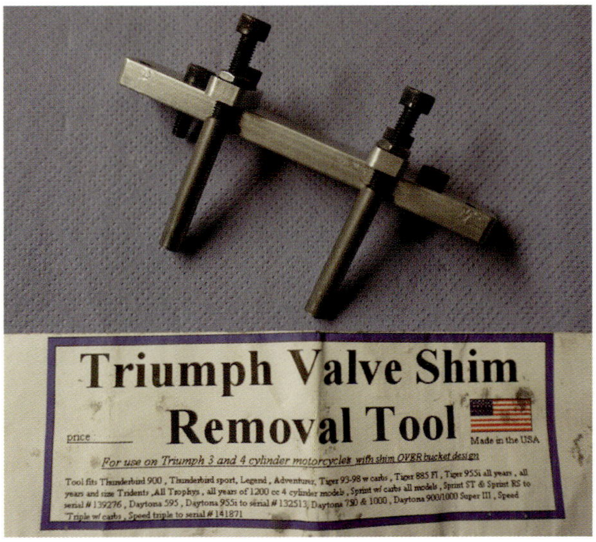

Valve shim tool. This is not the official Triumph tool (T3880012), as this is no longer available, but an aftermarket version.

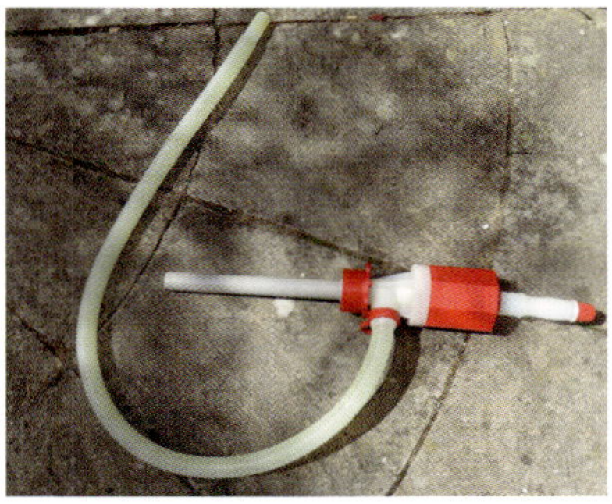

Hand pump for draining petrol from a fuel tank.

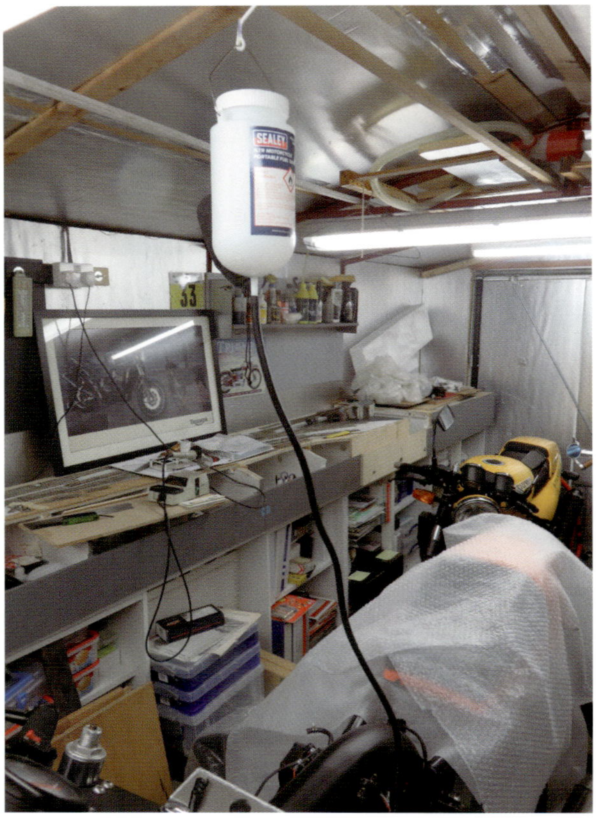

Portable fuel tank.

the 1200 and 900 Daytonas, Speed Triples, Tridents, Tiger and so on – while the Thunderbird/Adventurer have a 15ltr (3gal) capacity; 25ltr weighs 19kg (42lb)!

Dummy fuel tank Given that the fuel and vacuum connections for the tank are not the easiest to access, it is easier to test the engine without the tank. I use a dummy fuel tank so I can start the engine and check out the operation of the throttle and chock cables without the fuel tank, and check for leaks from the cam cover. Always hang the dummy tank from a secure hook above the bike; it is gravity fed, so crack the lid open to prevent an air lock and fuel starvation on extended engine runs when synchronizing the carburettors or checking the cooling fan operating temperature. They are not expensive; I paid around £25 for mine and it is well worth the money.

Mityvac pump As recommended by Mark Gaylard, this is ideal for bleeding the brakes and clutch system. It creates a vacuum in the system so fluid flows from the master cylinder into the relevant caliper. I have found this far more effective that the traditional jam jar and rubber pipe set-up.

LUBRICATION

Oil can Still an essential tool!

Grease gun Triumph are one of the few motorcycle manufacturers to incorporate grease nipples in their models (rear suspension linkage only, not the swing arm). Only use quality grease, preferably molybdenum disulphide. However, this is not very resistant to water, so a lithium-based high-melting-point grease (LM2) should be used.

Red rubber grease and brake cleaner.

Red rubber grease This is a must for any work on the brake calipers, front and rear. Copper slip has its place but not on any rubber components, as it makes the rubber swell.

Copper slip This is an anti-seize compound for use on threads only – not rubber seals or O-rings, as they will swell.

Ceramic paste This can be used on exhaust studs and the exhaust manifold and has a higher temperature rating than copper slip.

Penetrating fluid Use a proper penetrating fluid and not WD40, which is

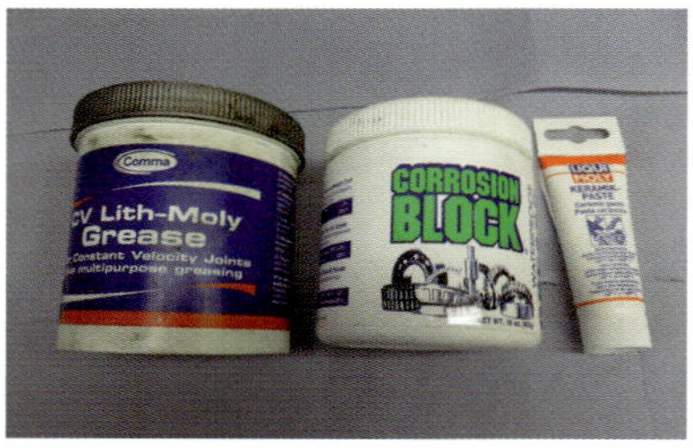

Molybdenum grease, ceramic paste and corrosion block.

Penetrating fluid and engine polish.

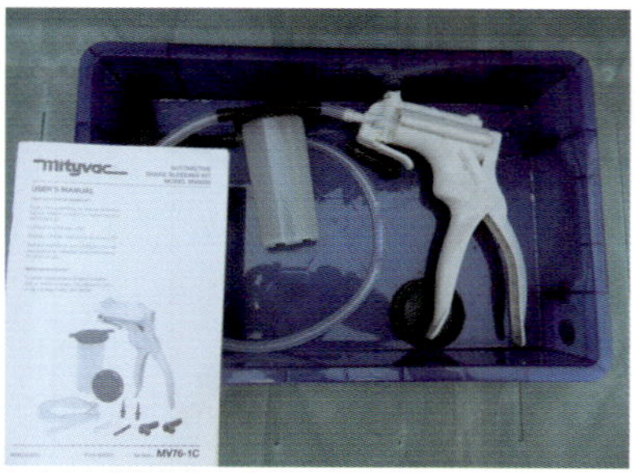

Mityvac brake and clutch fluid bleed system.

Oil can.

a de-watering compound (WD stands for water dispersant) and was not designed to be used as a penetrating fluid. There are lots of brands of penetrating fluid on the market; just buy a reputable one.

Contact cleaner Again, use a proper contact cleaner to clean contacts rather than WD40 and always go for a good brand.

Corrosion block (waterproof grease) This is used in the wiring connectors to prevent corrosion.

OTHER USEFUL ITEMS

Digital camera or phone I have found that taking lots of photographs of the bike and its parts when dismantling comes in really useful when reassembling the bike, particularly if the reassembly takes place many months after the dismantling. Sometimes the factory manual is not always as clear as it might be, so taking photos as you go can be really helpful.

Sandwich bags/sealable plastic bags When dismantling parts, it is essential that all the parts are kept together, so plastic sandwich bags (which can be sealed) are a good idea; the bag should be labelled with the identity of the parts inside. Using these sealed bags will ensure that the small nuts and bolts don't go walkabout. Bagging parts up is essential if a complete restoration is being undertaken and it could be many months between dismantling and rebuilding. I store the bags in plastic crates, which I also label up, making life easier when the rebuilding commences.

Paper towel rolls While I sometimes reuse pieces of fabric like old T-shirts, disposable paper towels have the advantage of being pristine, and using them to lay your parts on will help to ensure cleanliness. The last thing you want is bits of grit from oil-stained rag contaminating clean engine parts with expensive consequences.

Head torch A light is invaluable when peering into the murky depths of the motorcycle, and one worn on your head keeps your hands free. A head torch is also useful when searching for lost nuts and bolts on the garage floor. They are readily available from motor factors and places like Screwfix in a range of sizes and power.

Sweeping the floor at least once a week will also make finding dropped components easier, of course – and possibly that missing 10mm socket!

Dremel/small drill and small wire brushes This is an excellent way of cleaning aluminium corrosion from things like brake master cylinders and any other small alloy parts. I use small brass wire brushes as they are less aggressive than steel ones.

Triumph swing arm tool The swing arm needs to be taken out to change the chain rubbing block, but can be a pain to put in again as the shaft has to go through the frame, swing arm and engine plates. Triumph had a special tool that fits in the end of the shaft and guides it through. This is no longer listed by Triumph but is worth seeking out. I have included a schematic drawing alongside a photo of the tool itself so that you can get a tool turned up at your local engineering company.

Triumph used to supply the dealers with a board on which they could place the special tools needed on the T300 range. At one time you could order any of these special tools, but sadly they are no longer available. Sometimes they come up at auto jumbles, so keep your eyes peeled.

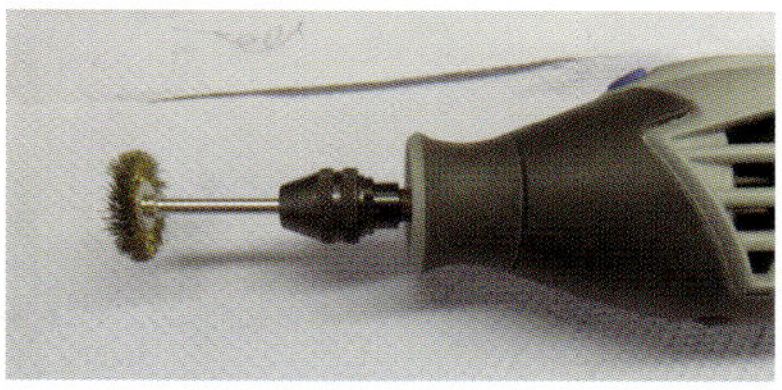

Dremel mini-drill and small wire brushes.

Triumph tool for inserting the swing arm shaft.

A board of the Triumph service tools for the T300 range. Unfortunately the service tools are no longer available from Triumph but can be found online.

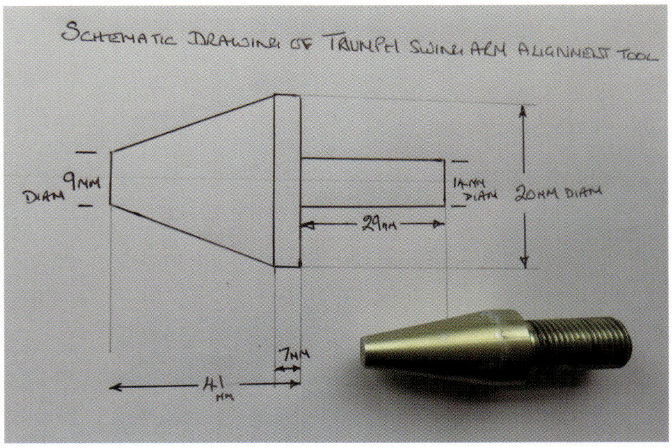

Triumph swing arm tool and schematic drawing, if you want to get one made!

4

common problems

The T300 bikes were well designed and built, incorporating 'best practice' of the time, and so are pretty bomb-proof; but, as with all makes, there are some common problems, the majority of which are the result of bikes now being over twenty years old and suffering from poor maintenance. If bikes are not serviced regularly and properly then expect to find problems, which are not the fault of the design team at Triumph or the manufacturing process, but neglect.

Bikes left sitting around and not being used is another cause of problems; they need riding on a regular basis. Being left outside for long periods is not going to be a good base for reliability either!

As a general rule, if the bike is not running well then start by looking at the carburettors, then the plugs, followed by plug leads, the ignition pick-up and finally the coils. This chapter aims to identify the common problems that you are likely to find and the resolution to those problems.

STARTING THE BIKE

This may seem a strange item to include in a book on maintaining T300s – surely it's just a case of a bit of pull on some choke, press the starter and away we go? Not quite.

Triumph has incorporated a vacuum system for most of the T300 range (except the Tiger and Adventurer/Thunderbird/Legend models, which have a Pingel-style tap below the fuel tank) into the fuel system so that when the engine is stopped, no fuel will flow into the carburettors. (With the Pingel system, common to most other bikes, you have to remember to turn to the OFF position if the bike is to be parked up for long periods of time.)

The use of the vacuum tap means that if the bike has been left standing for some time, the carburettors will be empty of fuel. This means that the engine has to turn over many revolutions to fill the carburettors with fuel, which runs the risk, with a low battery, of damaging the starter sprag clutch. If the starter sprag clutch fails then it is a very expensive repair on post-1994 bikes, as the engine will need to be removed and the crankcases split to change the sprag clutch.

Therefore, before starting, make sure the battery is fully charged and in good condition. Then the fuel tap needs to be set to PRIME and pushed in for 30 seconds; this allows fuel to flow into the carburettors (if you listen carefully you can hear it) so starting should be easy.

Once the carburettors have been primed with fuel then the fuel tap knob can be returned to the RUN position.

As an aid to starting, Triumph modified the sprag clutch to spin the engine over faster (by increasing the number of teeth to fifty-three) and the igniter was also modified (Gill) so that the engine would turn over a couple of revolutions before the igniter sent a spark to the engine; the initial voltage was also different, as was the advance curve. The Gill igniter is a direct replacement for the earlier PVL one.

If the bike is out on a run and is left in hot sun for a few hours it is possible that fuel has evaporated from the float bows so it is prudent to use PRIME before setting off to ensure that the float bowls are full.

Remember that if the side stand is down, the bike will not start until the side stand is moved up (there is a switch activated by the side stand) and the clutch needs to be pulled in as well to activate the switch on the clutch lever. On the early bikes the engine will not run with the side stand down but this was changed on later bikes.

SWITCHES

Side Stand Switch

This is located just in front of the side stand under a cover and, if the bike is stored for long periods, the contacts inside the switch can corrode; it does not help that the position of the switch is close to the road so it gets covered

Fuel tap in the PRIME position, with the arrow on the bodywork on the right.

Fuel tap in the RUN position, with the arrow on the bodywork on the right.

The side stand switch is located under the plate and has a plunger.

The side stand switch is under the cover on the revised side stand bracket.

in muck. As the side stand has to be up when starting the bike, this will then prevent the bike from starting. A squirt inside with contact cleaner will help. Work the side stand backward and forward to clean up the internal contacts. If that fails, replace the switch. The plunger has a rubber boot protecting the plunger from moisture migrating upwards, and a blob of grease on the plunger should help prevent this.

Some early models had the side stand relay incorporated within the PVL igniter. Later the side stand relay was mounted on the fuel tank support bracket. Later still, the side stand relay was not fitted, presumably being reincorporated within the Gill igniter.

On later bikes you can start the bike with the side stand down but with the clutch pulled in.

Clutch Switch

Again, if this is faulty it will prevent the bike from starting. The switch is located underneath the clutch reservoir (and not the easiest to get access to) and, like with the side stand switch, the internal contacts can corrode, so again a squirt inside with a contact cleaner and work the clutch lever in and out to clean up the contacts. As a last resort, the switch can be removed and dismantled and the contacts cleaned up.

Pickup sensor adjustment.

PICKUP SENSOR

This is located behind an engine timing cover on the offside of the engine (140mm/5.5in in diameter, secured by seven cover bolts) and is normally reliable. However, over time the electrical resistance starts to break down due to heat; the engine will fire up with no problem, but 15km (10 miles) into your ride, when the engine gets hot, it starts to cut out. If left for half an hour the bike will start again, but as soon as it gets hot it will cut out again. Unfortunately, once the pickup sensor starts to fail, it cannot be repaired.

Gordon Smith did some investigative work and found that micro-arcing occurs at the solder joints between the winding wires and the output terminal posts (where the output lead is

Clutch switch viewed from underneath.

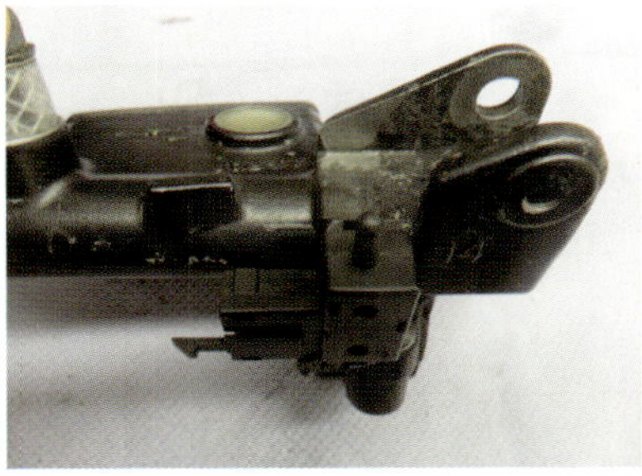

Clutch switch.

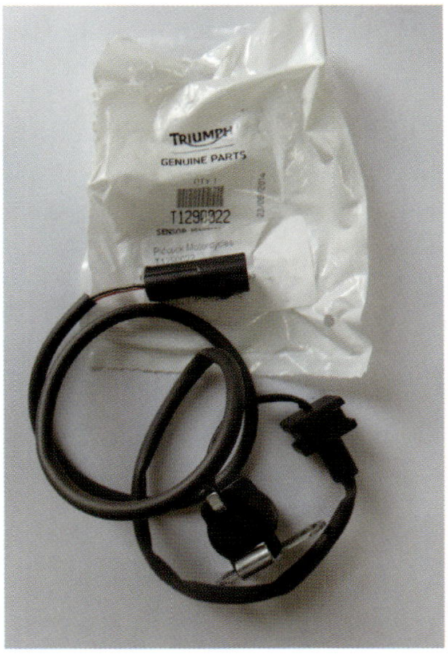

Replacement crank sensor.

connected). Over time, repeated temperature cycling (getting very hot then cold) causes the resistance to increase and the output pulse seen by the igniter to decrease to the point where a spark is no longer generated. When this happens it may recover with cooling, but eventually the failure becomes permanent. One way to avoid this is to carry out regular resistance checks of the crank sensor and the coils.

The only solution is to replace the pickup sensor, ensuring that the air gap is set to 0.6–0.8mm. Triumph later allowed for an air gap to be set at 1.0mm. PVL crank sensor resistance is 530 ohms plus/minus 10 per cent. Early Gill crank sensors were also 530 ohms but lately the Gill specification has been changed to 600 ohms plus/minus 10 per cent.

The price from Triumph for this part seems to have risen considerably recently and is now over £100, but Sprint Manufacturing can sell you the same part as an alternative. When changing the pickup, don't forget to order a gasket for the cover as well.

PLUG LEADS

The plug leads sit in a hot zone above the engine and under the fuel tank and will gradually fail. If tested, the leads should give a 4–6 kiloohm resistance. Remember that the plugs should have the screwed top removed from the top of the plug otherwise the plug leads won't fit! There should be a distinct click when the lead is pushed onto the plug.

If the plug leads and/or coils need replacing, then consider replacing both (HT leads and HT coils) with stick coils provided by Paul Messenger, thus removing the need for HT leads altogether (*see* Chapter 7). This will improve both starting and running.

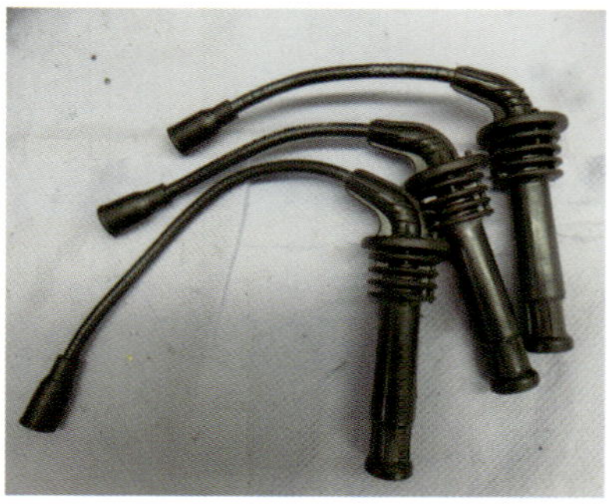

Plug leads.

Paul's 'Coil on Plug' kits are only available for the 3-cylinder engines, as the 4-cylinder engines work on a 'wasted spark' ignition. I have them on both the Speed Triple and CRK (Daytona) and they are simple to fit.

FUEL STARVATION (THUNDERBIRD AND ADVENTURER)

When some owners reported that they were suffering a fuel starvation problem, Triumph suggested that the internal seal be replaced with a different part (T2400175). I would assume that most bikes have had this done under warranty.

COILS

The coils are numbered, so that #1 is on the nearside of the bike, #2 the middle cylinder and #3 mounted on the offside of the bike.

The coils are pretty reliable, but over time, sitting in the hot area over the engine and under the fuel tank, they can start to degrade (and the bikes are all well over twenty years old) and cause a misfire. As with the igniters, there are two brands – early bikes used PVL and later bikes used Gill. It is not a good idea to mix the two brands on the same bike as they have different internal resistances. It is not a problem, however, mixing coils and igniters from the two manufacturers, so PVL coils with a Gill igniter will work fine and vice versa.

If you are electrically minded, you can check the resistance in the coils. Triumph and the Haynes manual give the readings as follows: primary (LT) resistance is approximately 0.6 ohms and the secondary (HT) resistance 10K ohms. However, PVL list the secondary reading as 8.7K (HT).

Due to the method of manufacture, the internal connections between the terminals and the windings are not

Coils on the off side of the bike.

Standard coils.

proper full soldered joints, so there is a tendency for at least one joint to fail over time. When this happens, the higher voltage can jump across the microscopic gap across the connection, but over time the joint 'soots up' and the (spark) voltage can no longer jump the gap. Sometimes a coil will give the required resistance but a small sideways pressure to the large HT terminal will cause the reading to fluctuate considerably.

If you have a suspect HT coil that seems to be OK on the resistance test, then swap it out for a known serviceable item to confirm the diagnosis.

The wiring code for the coils is as ollows:

Red	Common
Green/grey	#1
Yellow/blue	#2
Brown/yellow	#3

A worthwhile upgrade for 3-cylinder bikes is to replace the standard coils with the stick coils sold by Paul Messenger.

BATTERY

When built, the bikes were all fitted as standard with a conventional lead acid battery, but many similar batteries available over the last decade have not have been of good quality, particularly cheap Chinese imports. Not only do these cheap batteries not last more than a year or two, but they can lead to a significant drop in cranking capacity, critical in starting the bike. If the battery is not in tip-top condition, then the sprag clutch can be damaged on starting, resulting in a very expensive repair.

It is better to pay a little more for a recognized branded battery, as the few pounds saved buying a cheap one will be nothing compared to the cost of replacing the sprag clutch. Also be aware that there are counterfeit branded batteries around on the internet; Yuasa seem to be the favourite to copy. Only buy branded batteries from recognized suppliers. The copies are next to useless and usually fail very quickly. Check the crank amperage quoted for the battery (it needs to be more than 200 CCA) as well, as the cheaper batteries don't have high enough cranking capacity.

I always prefer to go with Yuasa for batteries. They now do an absorbed glass matt (AGM) battery, which has a higher cranking amperage (210 CCA) so should spin the engine over better; the code for the T300s is YTX14AHL-BS. AGM batteries are sealed and have lower internal resistance and can therefore deliver a higher current, and they also charge faster than a traditional battery.

Lithium-ion batteries are now available, with a saving in weight of around 3.4kg (7.5lb), but some require a separate dedicated battery charger, so ensure that if a lithium-ion battery is fitted that the correct charger is used. Gordon Smith has been using lithium iron phosphate (LiFePO4) batteries in all his fleet of T300 bikes since 2013, along with a dedicated lithium charger. LiFePO4 is a type of battery, now called lithium polymer (or LiPo), which is not the same as the older original lithium-ion (Li-on) type. The early Li-on types were prone to catching fire through over-voltage from the alternator, at anything over 14.8v. Later types of LiPo are fitted with internal battery protection circuits to protect the cells.

Before fitting any LiPo, ensure that the alternator output (regulator) is working correctly and does not exceed 14.8v. Similarly, check the battery negative, frame and alternator earths are the same potential – a quick resistance check between these three should have a resistance reading of close to 0 ohms, though up to 0.2 ohms is acceptable.

The lithium battery is a great improvement over the standard lead acid types. The higher nominal terminal voltage of 13.8v also overcomes any 'wiring losses' in the wiring harness, which can lead to there being as little as 10v available at the HT/LT terminals at tickover with lead acid types. This is a great boon in avoiding those involuntary 'topples' in a car park or slow-moving traffic, where the engine suddenly dies! Lithium batteries do require a wake-up on a cold winter's morning, but a quick flash of the headlights before pressing the starter button is all that is required. They hold their charge extremely well, only needing charging if some work has been done on the lighting and the terminal voltage has dropped a bit.

There has also been debate about whether the standard alternator will properly charge a lithium-ion battery, but a survey of T300 bikers revealed that there are no problems fitting one. Under no circumstances puncture a lithium-ion battery case, as this will set of a chemical reaction that you can't put out and gives off toxic fumes.

Fitment of spark plug stick coils from Paul Messenger will also aid starting and running (only available for 3-cylinder engines).

REV-COUNTER

These are generally reliable, but the ones fitted to the Speed Triple seem to suffer with age and give widely different readings, with the needle bouncing around. This is not a problem for models such as the Daytona as there are lots of them around, but Speed Triple rev-counters are rare and will cost over £200.

If the rev-counter needle is erratic or dies, check the three-pin block connector at the rear of the instrument, clean the contacts and use waterproof grease to stop water ingress.

The rev-counter is driven from the #1 coil, and if the needle moves around and the engine is stuttering, then it may be because the coil is breaking down.

Clutch assembly.

CLUTCH

The clutch is generally reliable, but if bikes are left standing for a considerable time it is not unknown for the clutch plates to weld themselves together so that when fired up you can't engage first gear without an almighty clunk or the engine stalling. Where there has been a cylinder head-gasket failure, this increases the chance of the friction plates welding themselves to the steel plates (due to water contamination in the oil); on my CRK (built on a Daytona 900 base), more than half the plates had bonded themselves together due to corrosion.

The consequence was that if the bike was left for a week or two then, when it started, it would stall when selecting first gear. In my case, a complete replacement of all the clutch plates was required after I had solved the problem of the liners leaking water into the sump!

Both friction plates and steel plates are available from Triumph as well as secondary suppliers such as Sprint Manufacturing.

Changing the fluid in the clutch system is something than can also be forgotten and may lead to poor clutch operation. Like with the brakes, the

Old clutch plates showing corrosion on the steel plates through lack of use. Once they end up in this state, you will probably have to replace them.

Clutch basket ready for plates to be fitted.

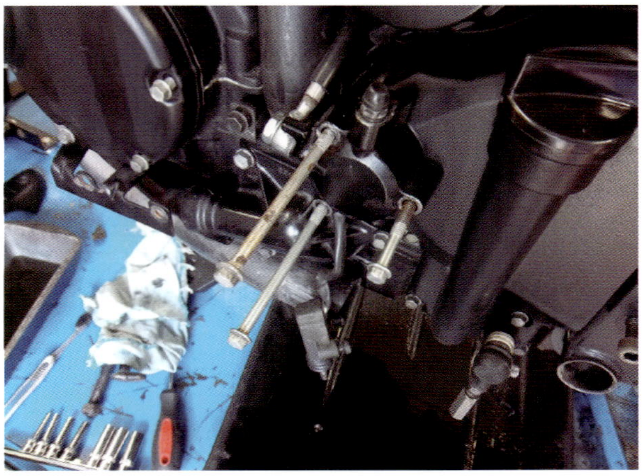

Clutch slave cylinder removal. Note the different-length bolts and put them back in the correct hole.

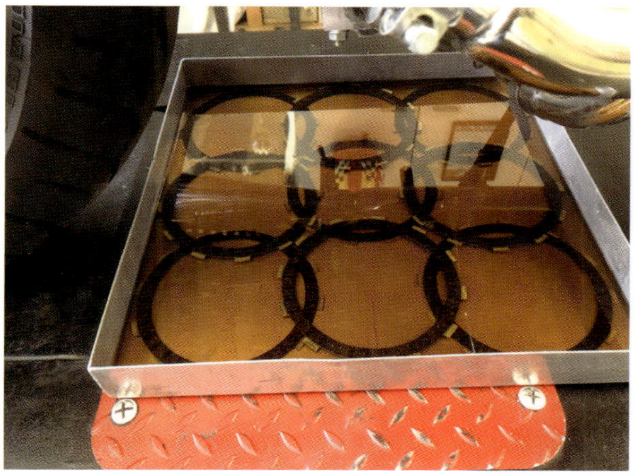

Friction plates soaking in oil for 24 hours.

A new part ready for installation.

fluid is hygroscopic, absorbing water, and it also degrades over time, so change it at the same time as the brake fluid. The first time I overhauled a clutch slave cylinder, the fluid resembled brown tar.

New clutch basket in place.

Be very careful when tightening up the clutch basket bolts, as they will snap off if over-tightened, giving you another job to do! They should be torqued down to 10Nm. If in doubt, replace.

The clutch slave cylinder is also very reliable, but, again, on a twenty-year-old bike it's worth replacing the seals and spring, or replacing with a new slave cylinder (*see* Chapter 5). Remember that the clutch slave cylinder has different-length bolts, so be sure to put them back in the correct places.

The front sprocket, clutch pushrod and seal (upper left just in front of the chain). The gearbox shaft is at the bottom right. The retaining washer on the sprocket is the old type, since superseded.

You will need to buy a special tool to hold the clutch basket when tightening up the bolt.

It is important that the friction plates are soaked in clean engine oil for at least 24 hours before fitting.

Under no circumstances should car oil be used in the bikes. This can cause clutch slippage because car engine oil does not have to lubricate the gearbox, as in motorcycles.

OIL WEEPING FROM THE SPROCKET COVER

Sprocket cover removed.

At first sight, this can be alarming, but it is not usually a major problem although it needs investigating. There may be a number of different causes.

First, there may be an excess of chain lubricant built up behind the sprocket cover and, when hot, this may have started melting and leaking out.

Front sprocket removed. The sprocket shaft seal is behind the sprocket shaft.

Clutch shaft seal.

Front sprocket retaining ring. This version replaces the earlier type. Never reuse the old one – always replace with new.

The sprocket cover also covers a couple of seals into the engine and gearbox that can fail with age. These are the clutch pushrod seal and gearbox output shaft seal (hidden behind the front sprocket). The gearchange shaft seal seems to wear more, so, as a modification, you can add a suitable-sized O-ring to the gearbox shaft (just past the splines) so that when the sprocket/dipstick cover is pressed home the O-ring sits flush up against the rear of the gearchange shaft needle roller bearing.

To check both these seals, you need to remove the combined oil filler and sprocket cover as well as the clutch slave cylinder. Unfortunately, removing the sprocket cover requires the oil to be drained from the bike first.

You can lean the bike against a wall but this is not very secure, especially when trying to remove the front sprocket (given the torque required to disconnect the sprocket retaining nut) so I would not recommend it.

Once the cover is removed, the pushrod for the clutch can be slid out, revealing the seal. The seal can be replaced by one from Triumph; however, this is a twin-lipped seal designed for rotary motion rather than an in-and-out motion. The seal can be replaced by a four-lipped mini fork seal (8X16X9 TC4, metric fork and damper nitride) at a cost of around £4.

Sprocket shaft seal.

Sprocket shaft seal front.

Just remember to lubricate the inside of the seal after fitting and before sliding the clutch pushrod through.

The clutch pushrod can wear and start leaking oil, so it is a good idea to take it out and clean up where it goes through the seal. Use a very fine wet and dry, say 1500 grit, to clean of any wear mark. It is also possible to reverse the rod.

The gearbox output seal is hidden behind the front sprocket, so the sprocket will have to be removed first to gain access to the seal.

Given the effort required and the low cost of the seals, it is sensible to change them when the front sprocket needs changing, combined with an oil and filter change.

The sprocket retaining tab washer has now been superseded (as seen in the photograph) and you should never re-use the old retaining washer – always fit new.

CLUTCH AND BRAKE MASTER CYLINDERS

Standard screws in the reservoir top.

New master cylinders for clutch and brake are no longer available from Triumph but overhaul kits are available.

The first problem is with the two countersunk screws that hold in the cover plates on the master cylinders, which can be an absolute pain to remove. If they have not been removed for some time (and were over-tightened the last time they came off), they can seize up, and it is very easy to mangle the heads as they seem to have been made of some metal with the consistency of cheese.

Once the heads are chewed up, drilling out becomes the only solution. This needs to be done with care. Make sure that the reservoir is completely cleaned out so no swarf remains to destroy the seals in the master cylinder.

The removal of the cover screws is not helped by the fact that the natural tendency would be to use a Phillips (or Posidrive) screwdriver, but the screw heads have been made to JIS standard from Japan (not surprising, as they come from a Japanese manufacturer, Nissin), and this is not the same as a Phillips screw head. It is essential that a correct JIS screwdriver is used, which should make removal much easier. I find putting my full weight onto the screwdriver with both hands before turning helps. Do not be tempted to replace the old screws afterwards; either use new ones or replace with stainless steel with an Allen key head, size M5 × 0.8 × 15mm. The Triumph part number for new screws is T2020166 (screw reservoir).

Comparison of master cylinder reservoir screws: standard on the right, stainless steel on the left.

I also put a tiny bit of copper slip under the countersunk heads of the screws and don't tighten them down too much.

There are two sizes of brake master cylinders, 14mm and $^{5}/_{8}$in, and the larger size ($^{5}/_{8}$in) is a worthwhile upgrade. The clutch master cylinder only comes in one size.

Overhauling the brake and clutch master cylinders is covered in Chapter 5.

Indicator stalk on a Speed Triple.

BREAKING INDICATOR STALKS

The indicator stalks on most of the models are quite long and, over time, become brittle and start to droop or even snap off. Brushing past the bike can have fatal consequences for the indicators.

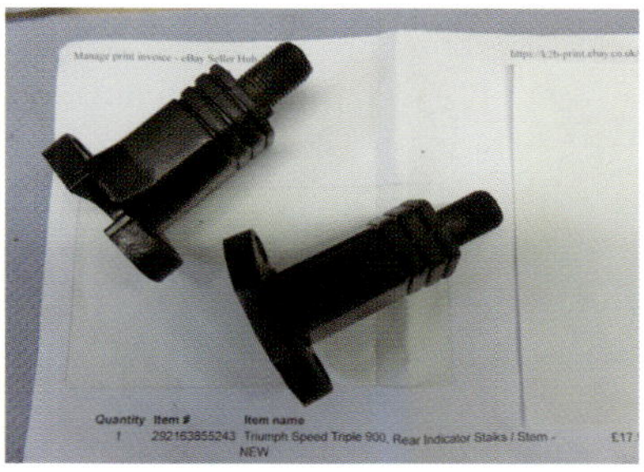

Replacement rear indicator stalks from Sprint Manufacturing.

Again, these are no longer available from Triumph but stalks can be bought from Sprint Manufacturing or second-hand ones can be sourced – although these may also be old and brittle.

The indicators are fixed to the stalks by two screws at the back of the indicator. The lens is fixed to the lamp unit by a single screw from the back of the lamp unit.

These indicators were also used on some Japanese models so some searching may reveal alternative parts.

Replacement screws in the reservoir top.

LOOSE GEAR LEVER AND REAR BRAKE LEVERS

I think the classic phrase is 'they all do that, sir,' and this certainly seems to be true on the T300s. There is a thin-

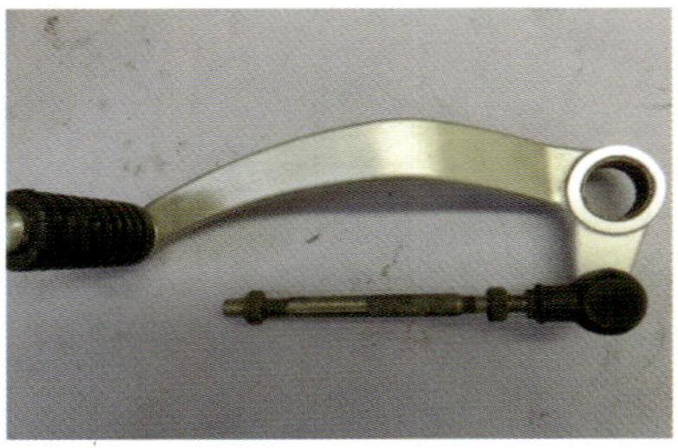

Gear lever and bush.

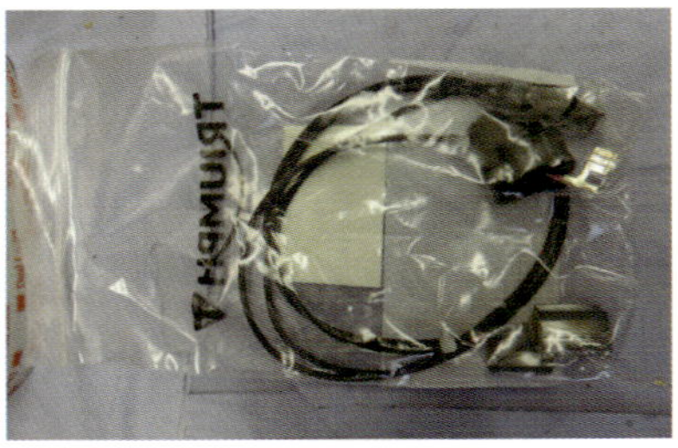

Replacement neutral light switch and cable.

walled bush available from Triumph that can be used as a replacement – simply press out the original bush and press in a new one. However, in my experience replacing the bush inside the gear lever hardly seems to make it better. I have done this twice and not noticed any difference!

NEUTRAL LIGHT

The bikes are now over twenty years old and one of the most irritating faults that develops is that the neutral warning light decides either to only work intermittently or not at all. Talk to any T300 owner and they will have experienced this. The light on the dash is triggered by a brass plunger switch, which is screwed into the nearside of the engine between the water pump and the sprocket cover and can be removed using a 14mm socket. Over time, particularly with limited use, contaminants in old oil cause a surface patina to build up on the selector drum, which interferes with the electrical contact on the brass plunger. The neutral switch contact spring can also be gummed up; wash it out to free it up.

Remove the plunger switch (when the bike is in neutral) and use a thin screwdriver to scrape and clean the selector drum, then refit the switch.

When the switch is replaced, do not refit the washer between the switch and sump but use a small amount of silicone sealant to provide an oil-tight seal. Deleting the washer allows the brass plunger to press harder on the selector drum and hopefully improve the electrical contact. On all the T300 bikes that I have owned (and that's five of them) the light sometimes works and sometimes not, so I have learnt to live with it.

FUEL SYSTEM

The fuel tap has three connections to it, two being for fuel and one being the vacuum pipe; check that the vacuum hose has not split or cracked with age, as this will prevent it from holding a vacuum and operating the tap properly.

There are two potential problems related to the fuel tap. First, the plastic circular knob on the outside of the bike can fracture with age as the plastic goes brittle; partly this is caused by the part actually connected to the internals of the fuel tap being relatively small. It is also the result of the tap not being used, so it seizes up. I use the PRIME position every time I start the bike (*see* Chapter 4, Starting the Bike). One solution is to fill all the spaces at the rear of the plastic tap with 24-hour Araldite to reinforce the central part. If you really want to go upmarket, Sprint Manufacturing can sell you a very nice CNC aluminium knob.

The second problem is with the internal part of the fuel tap, which can leak petrol. If you discover fuel under the bike then it will have filled the gearbox. Under no circumstances attempt to start the bike, as this could cause a hydraulic lock and severely damage the engine. First, check the oil level, as petrol can have found its way into the sump and contaminated the oil (a good sniff should confirm any petrol

Location of the switch for the neutral light, just to the right of the water pump

Fuel tap on a Daytona, Speed Triple or similar.

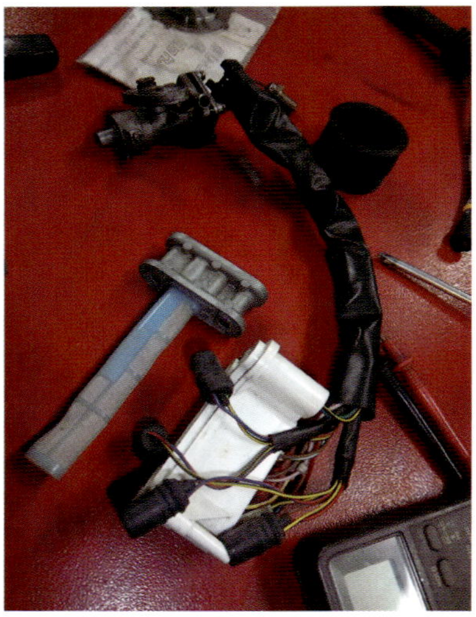

Fuel tap internals.

Fuel tap with the back filled with epoxy resin to reinforce the plastic.

The vacuum pipe goes to the back of the fuel tap.

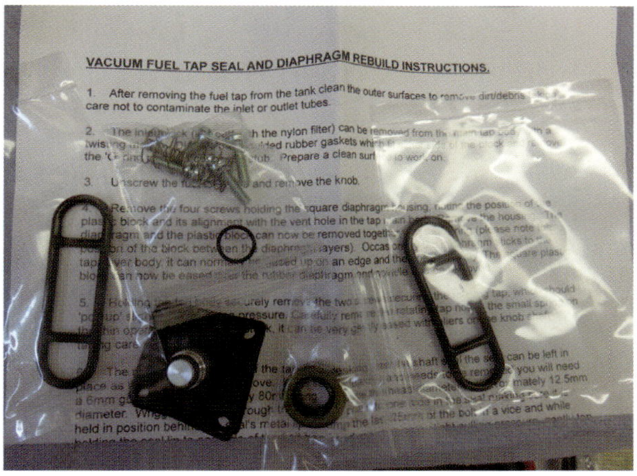

A fuel tap rebuild kit.

Propping up the tank to check the routing of the vacuum and fuel pipes.

contamination). If petrol is in the oil, disconnect the fuel tank, fix the fuel tap (or, even better, replace it) and then drain and replace the engine oil and filter.

There is an overhaul kit available for the fuel tap internals but this seems to be a very hit-and-miss affair in terms of solving the problem – many owners who have used the repair kit have reported failure after a relatively short space of time, while others have had no problem. I suspect the issue is with screwing the two halves of the body together so that there is consistent pressure on the rubber seal. A full replacement of the tap is the only guarantee of success.

The fuel pipes supplied by Triumph have been pre-curved, as it's a bit of a tight fit around the tap, with the limited space under the tank; these preformed pipes are expensive, at approximately £45, but are considerably less work than making up a pipe yourself. The fuel piping is an 8mm fuel hose if you want to make up the hose yourself. The vacuum pipe is $^{3}/_{16}$in and the fuel pipe is $^{5}/_{16}$in.

When refitting the tank after changing or overhauling the fuel tap, it is very easy to get either the fuel tap pipe or the vacuum pipe kinked when the tank sits down on its mountings. Check that the wiring harness has not slipped down the spine frame and is interfering with the run of the vacuum pipe. I find that resting the rear of the fuel tank on a block of wood makes it easier to check everything before finally lowering the tank and bolting down.

Using the PRIME and RUN positions regularly will ensure the internals of the tap don't seize up.

CARBURETTORS

With regard to jetting, the centre jet is always smaller than the outer ones as the airflow is slightly less in the centre of the airbox. The usual jetting would be two 150s with the middle one 125. Appendix V gives the standard jet sizes for most of the models. Later models of the Trophy (from 1997 onwards) used the same main jets for both 3- and 4-cylinder engines.

The screws holding the tops are JIS heads, not Phillips, so use the correct JIS screwdrivers to avoid chewing up the heads.

The pilot screws can seize in the carburettor body and be a real pain to remove; try the usual methods, but remove the carburettor from the bike first.

To remove a seized-up pilot jet, try heating and then freezing with a freeze spray, repeating two or three times. When heating, do not use a naked flame source but a heat gun, to prevent the carburettor from getting too hot. Then use a screwdriver that is a really good fit into the screw head. Once it's removed, do not be tempted to put the old pilot jet back in – get a new one! An overnight soak in penetrating fluid may also help.

The inlet rubbers can harden and crack, which can result in erratic running as this lets air into the intakes, so these inlet rubbers must be replaced.

The 1200 engines were originally prone to intermittent fuel starvation as the fuel tap was switched to RESERVE and so Triumph issued a revision to the fuel pipes feeding the carburettors. Two balance pipes were added so two new T-pieces (T3620266) were inserted, along with a new balance pipe (T3620257) between the two T-pieces.

Various brands of fuel stabilizer.

EXCESSIVE OIL CONSUMPTION

This is not really a common problem as the engines are quite capable of doing 10,000–16,000km (6,000–10,000 miles) before needing a top-up. However, it is very easy to overfill the engine with oil. To check the oil level, the bike needs to be level so not on the side stand; if it is on a centre stand, place some wood under the front wheel to level it. The dipstick needs to be taken out, wiped and then screwed all the way back in and removed again to see the oil level. If you just place the dipstick resting on the top face of the filler to take the oil level this will give you a false reading and you will put in more oil; if you overfill then the excess will be burnt off. The difference between the high and low levels on the dip stick is 0.5ltr (0.1gal).

Another possible reason for burning oil could be the valve stem seals having become hard due to either the bike being stored for a long time or not used regularly with the appropriate oil and filter changes. A compression test will show if there is a problem with the rings. On a bike that has been stored for some time, do a compression test and then remove the spark plugs and drop in a few tablespoons of diesel oil in each of the bores and leave overnight (or a couple of days if you can) without the plugs in. Still with the plugs removed, spin the engine over (putting a rag over the spark plug holes to stop the diesel going everywhere) and then redo the compression test to see if there is any difference in the compression values.

LOOSE FOOT PEGS

The foot pegs are secured to a control plate (which is then bolted to the frame) by a domed-head bolt from the back, and these can become loose. To fix, the gear linkage or brake linkage will need to be removed to allow the control plate to be removed; the bolt that holds the foot peg to the control plate can then be tightened. It is helpful to note and mark the position of the foot peg in relation to the ground and the control plate before removal so that when it's been tightened and the control plate remounted, the foot peg is in the correct plane. The domed-head bolt can be replaced by an Allen-head bolt (or a standard bolt head), and a star washer and a thread locking compound can be added. I prefer a standard bolt head, because then, if the foot peg comes loose again, you won't need to remove the control plate, just slip an open-ended spanner onto the bolt head.

ETHANOL DAMAGE

The bikes were designed in the early 1990s, before the use of ethanol became commonplace. However, in the last few years, ethanol has been added to fuel to produce cleaner emissions, initially at 5 per cent concentration, but then increasing to 10 per cent in 2020 and 15 per cent from 2021.

Ethanol is created from agricultural products such as grain and sugar beet and is added to most petrols. Why should this be a problem?

Ethanol reacts with some metals, polymers and natural rubbers and basically rots them! It is also an effective paint stripper. It is also hygroscopic, which means that it extracts moisture from the atmosphere, so if you leave your bike stored over the winter then the water absorbed by the fuel will settle to the bottom of the tank, which means when you come to start the bike it will be trying to start on water. The water separating out can also lead to rusting at the bottom of the tank and leave a nasty residue in the carburettors as they dry out.

There are two solutions to this. First, if the bike is to be stored over winter, drain the tank and the carburettors. Given that modern fuels contain a number of highly volatile elements, these would evaporate away anyway, leaving the fuel less effective than it should be.

Second, you can add a fuel stabilizer to prevent the hygroscopic effect. There are a number on the market, such as Sta-Bil and Star Tron from the USA (among others). If you live near the sea, then ship's chandlers can supply you, as the issue with ethanol also affects boat engines. Millers Oils' Tank Safe is another good product. There are also many available online. I run with fuel stabilizer all year round. If you go touring, take some with you in small plastic bottles – say 50–70ml (around 2fl oz), which takes up less space than a full 250ml (half-pint) bottle.

For a period of time, the Super Unleaded petrol above 97 octane from BP and Esso did not contain ethanol (although unavailable in Devon, Cornwall, Teesside or Scotland), but with the advent of 10 per cent ethanol the situation is likely to change and you will need to check. The situation in Europe is different, so, again, check before travelling.

There are also kits available to remove the ethanol from petrol but this should be done carefully as handing petrol is dangerous and should never be done inside a garage.

Blistering on the Tiger Tank

Ethanol not only plays havoc with fuel lines and carburettors but also with the plastic fuel tanks fitted to the Tiger. The symptoms are blisters forming on the tank like a severe rash. Also you may find when the tank is removed, it will be impossible to get it to fit back on the bike as the tank has swelled and is now out of shape. All of this damage has been caused by ethanol; the type of plastic used when the bike was designed did not anticipate having to cope with ethanol in the fuel. The same problem occurs on Triumph T595 tanks and other manufacturers' bikes who switched to using plastic tanks at the same time, particularly Ducati.

The problem of the tank not fitting when you try to put back on the bike can be resolved by draining it and leaving for a few weeks with the fuel filler open; the tank will then regain its original shape and can be refitted but the blisters will remain. As an alternative, Denis Fitch found that if you put the empty tank in the fridge for an hour, the mounting holes all line up again. You need a large fridge or a chest freezer to do this and a very understanding partner!

The problem of the blisters is not easily resolved, as this is caused by the ethanol leeching its way through the body of the plastic. They can be rubbed down and the tank repainted but this is not always successful. The only solution is to try to find a used tank without the blistering, but they are in high demand as many owners are looking for them. The demand for the T595 tanks is such that it is almost impossible to find a decent one second-hand.

I can only reinforce the message to use a fuel stabilizer all year round to prevent the problem occurring in the first place.

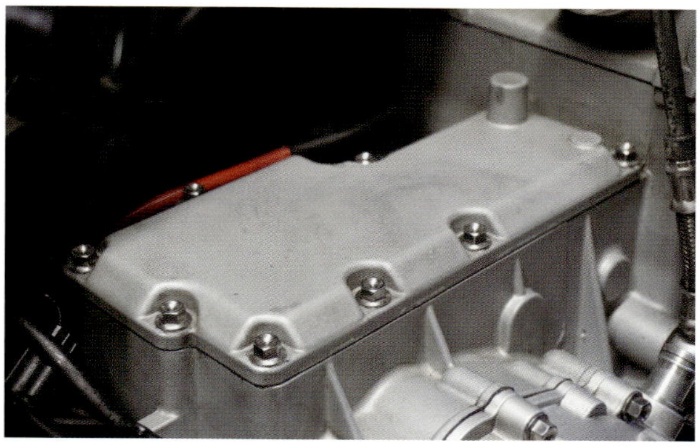

Cover plate to access the sprag on pre-1994 engines.

Trophy with original-style sprag clutch cover.

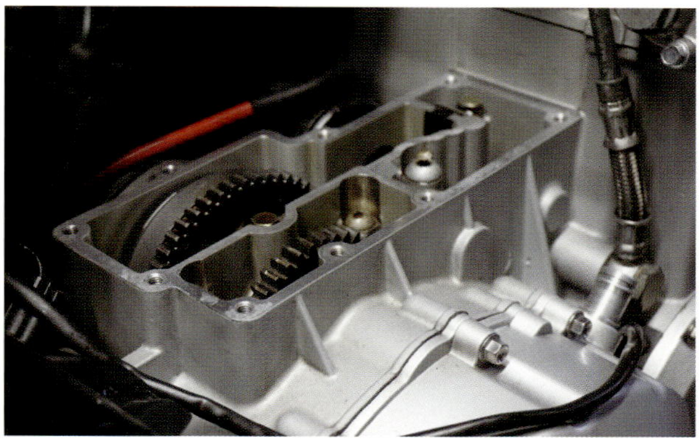

Sprag clutch with cover plate removed.

Sprag clutch.

IN-LINE FUEL FILTERS

The fuel system has very small in-line fuel filters that fit into the T-pieces near the carburettors. On a 25-year-old bike these will need changing, as they are likely to be clogged up and could restrict fuel flow. These two 'witch's hat' filters can be removed, dried out and then given a 'flick' so that most of the debris falls out. What remain are often manmade fibres, which can be removed using an eyepiece or magnifying glass.

Don't be tempted to fit large, bowl-type filters as the fuel system is essentially gravity-fed, and these large bowls don't fill properly so will create erratic running. If you have find lots of sediment then the issue is with the tank, not the in-line filters.

SPRAG CLUTCH

This is the starter clutch and engages when the starter button is activated; once the bike has started, it disengages when you stop pressing the starter button. As mentioned earlier, if the battery is not in tip-top condition and the float chambers are empty (because the PRIME position on the fuel tap was not activated), there is a danger that the engine will spin over more slowly, take longer to attempt to start, and then suddenly stop with a clunk – that's the sprag clutch gone! Once this happens the sprag will need to be changed.

Up to the 1994 model year, the sprag clutch was covered by a rectangular plate behind the cylinder block

Crankcase split.

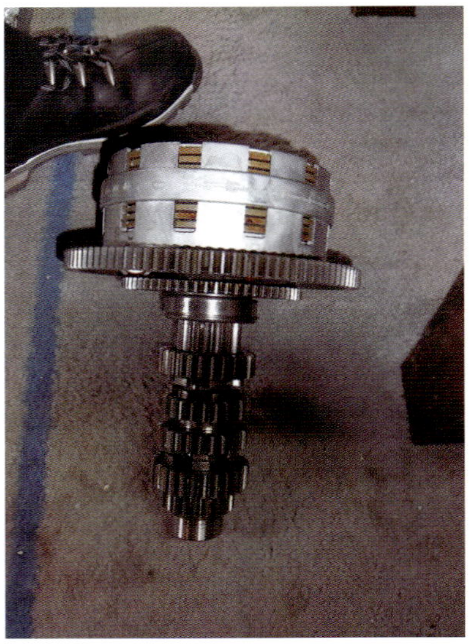

Clutch basket removed.

Clutch and gearbox removed.

and was easily accessible in the event of failure; this cover could simply be removed and the sprag repaired or replaced with the upgraded sprag (*see* below).

From 1994 onwards, the crankcases were revised and the square cover plate was deleted, so to gain access to the sprag clutch the engine has to be removed and the crankcases split, an expensive job if given to a dealer or garage. The job will require the engine to be taken out of the frame, placed upside down on a sturdy bench – these engines are not light! – and the sump removed, followed by the lower crankcase. The clutch assembly and the gearbox can then be removed. The sprag gear is mounted on the back of the clutch assembly.

In September 1995, a service bulletin was issued from Triumph detailing changes to the sprag clutch and the changing of some parts; this changed the number of teeth for the sprag from fifty-one to fifty-three, which enabled the engine to turn over faster when starting. Presumably this upgrade was fitted to bikes manufactured at the back end of 1995.

As part of the upgrade process, Triumph also provided a special tool to mill out part of the internal corner of the crankcase to allow for the slightly bigger upgraded sprag clutch gear wheel. This milling tool is no longer available from Triumph dealers (none of the special tools for the T300 range are), but judicious use of a mini drill and abrasive grinding stone will create the clearance required. To prevent swarf and debris from this process going into the gearbox, use plenty of wadding and grease. It will take multiple test fittings of the revised sprag until there is sufficient clearance. I don't know of a specific 'clearance' figure, but Gordon Smith allowed 2mm to cover for the heating-up of components.

The original sprag/idler gear tooth count was 51/15; the upgraded sprag is 53/13.

Sprag clutch showing clearance.

The sprag clutch early and revised; note the slightly larger diameter of the revised gear wheel (top).

Alternator in the foreground and the starter motor immediately behind the engine block.

As there are two different sets of teeth for the small idler gear, different sprag assemblies are required:

Thirteen-tooth starter idler gear
sprag assembly T1221030

Fifteen-tooth starter idler gear
sprag assembly T1221025

These sprag assemblies come as complete kits as above.

As part of the upgrade process in curing any sprag clutch issues, Triumph also changed the igniter to a Gill one. This allowed the engine to turn over twice before attempting to fire and the advance at starting was also changed. The list of replacement igniters is as follows:

Model	**Replacement igniter part**
Trophy 1200 to VIN 4901 (not French market); Australia and Germany to VIN 9082	T1290071
Trophy 1200 from VIN 4902 (all VINs for French market); Australia and Germany form VIN 9083	T1290071
Trophy 900	T1290060
Sprint 900	T1290060
Daytona 1200 (except French market)	T1290071
Daytona 1200 for French market (all VINs)	T1290070
Daytona 900	T1290060
Daytona Super 3	T1290062
Daytona 750	T1290080
Daytona 1000	T1290105
Trident 900	T1290060
Trident 750	T1290080
Tiger	T1290061
Speed Triple 900	T1290060

The sharp-eyed reader will have noticed that the Thunderbird is not listed as, at the time of the change above (September 1995), the Thunderbird already had the revised igniters.

It is essential to have a fully charged battery, use the PRIME position on the fuel tap (not forgetting to push in for 30 seconds) to minimize the potential for damaging the sprag. A set of stick coils from Paul Messenger will also help starting.

ALTERNATOR RATTLE

There are a number of issues around the bolt that holds the paddle drive for the alternator. The fault manifests itself with a ringing rattle, which seems to ease if the lights are switched off. The cause of the problem is the impeller becoming loose on the shaft even though the bolt that holds it in has had threadlock applied. The solution is to remove the alternator, remove the impeller and, if the splines of the impeller are worn, replace it. It is a good idea to replace the cush drive rubbers at the same time. In some cases, the bolt head has sheared off and the remains of the old bolt will need to be removed. If the bolt has seized then the shaft within the alternator will need to be replaced, although it's probably easier to buy a second-hand alternator complete.

There were reports that for a short period incorrect bolts were supplied to Triumph and these can be identified by having no markings on the head at all; if you have these fitted, they should be changed. The correct bolts have '10.9' marked on the head. I would assume that most have been replaced under warranty.

To remove the alternator, follow the steps below:

1. Remove the clutch slave cylinder.
2. Remove the cover plate for the cooling pipes (known as 'Billy the Fish').
3. Remove the three bolts holding the alternator.
4. The alternator is difficult to get out as there is not much to grip, so carefully insert a 150mm ¼in extension bar through the vents in the cover to help you rock the alternator out of its housing.
5. Disconnect the electrical connections.

One tip when removing the alternator is to give the three bolts that hold it to the crankcase a sharp tap with an

Alternator cover removed.

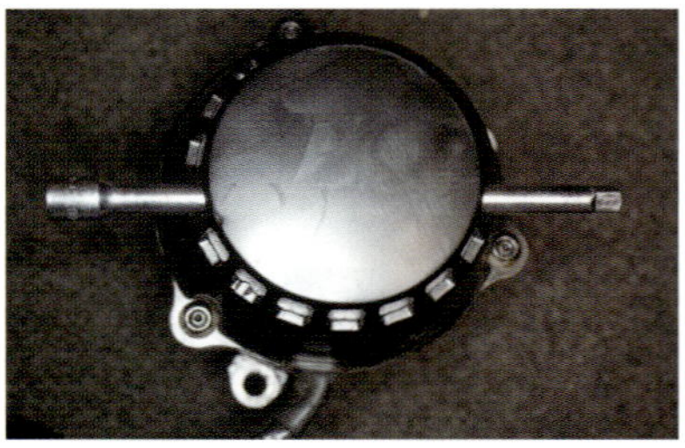

Using a socket extension bar to help remove the alternator.

Alternator drive of the later type, through-bolt and nut.

The early type of alternator drive, with two short bolts from each end. There is not a hole completely through.

impact driver, as the heads of the bolts tend to rust themselves to the body of the alternator. The threads themselves are normally not seized. When reassembling, use a little grease to hold the cush drive rubbers in place and wipe some oil around the O-ring. Remember to attach the earth ring and block connectors. It is a good idea to clean the contacts in the block connector with proper contact cleaner (not WD40) and use some corrosion block into the terminal block to keep out moisture.

Mark Gaylard went one step further and increased the size of the bolt holding the impeller in to an M8, but this involves drilling out and tapping the impeller shaft to the larger size. This will require a good pillar drill and a means of clamping the alternator.

The alternator is driven by a splined shaft that is powered by the starter clutch assembly, and this splined shaft runs through the engine into the other half of the cush drive cup – one half is in the alternator and one half is in the crankcase. The drawback of this set-up is that the clutch has to be removed to replace either the splined shaft or the bolts.

There are two different methods for fixing the crankcase end of the drive.

Retaining nut on the alternator.

The original method was for a bolt into a blind hole at each end of the splinned shaft, but this was subsequently modified to a hole through the splined shaft with a long bolt holding the half of the cush drive cup with a bolt head at the clutch end. The through bolt nut is at the alternator end. This was fitted from VIN number 056685 onwards.

To change to the revised part (through bolt) is as follows:

1. Remove the clutch.
2. Remove the alternator.
3. Do not remove the splined shaft but push the replacement shaft against the old one (at the clutch end) and slowly push the old shaft out at the alternator side. The inner part of the cush drive impeller can then be fixed to the shaft and the nut tightened at the clutch end.
4. Replace the clutch and refit the alternator.

Voltage Regulator

This is housed in the back of the alternator (under an easily removable alternator cover) and is pretty reliable. As an alternative source from Triumph for these, they are the same as used on the Suzuki Mk 1 Bandit, both 600 and 1200cc.

The voltage on the bike's system should not exceed 14.5v otherwise it will fry the battery.

If the regulator appears to have failed, don't assume it is the regulator! First, check all the connections in the circuit.

1. Undo and tighten the four Phillips screws inside the alternator cover.
2. Disconnect and spray every electrical plug connector with a proper contact cleaner (not WD40) and then plug them back together .The connectors are under the seat and under the fairing inserts of the steering head (for models with a fairing).
3. Check and clean all earthing points.
4. Spray contact cleaner into the ignition switch and operate a few times.

Only when all the above steps have been taken should the voltage and regulator be checked again.

SWING ARM CLAMP

The adjuster to move the chain is clamped into the rear of the swing arm and has a specific torque setting of 36Nm, and no more!

Unfortunately lots of owners fail to check what the torque setting is (or don't use a torque wrench) and then over-tighten the bolt that clamps the adjuster, with the consequence that the swing arm clamp cracks and breaks – and once this happens, the swing arm is scrap! Triumph can no longer supply a new replacement swing arm, so the second-hand market will have to be investigated, and finding good swing arms is difficult; even if you do find one, it will probably require refurbishing.

Changing the swing arm is a major job, so to make life a little easier, clean the underneath of the bike before starting and take the opportunity to change the chain rubbing block and clean up the suspension linkage and regrease at the same time.

The key tool when changing the swing arm is tool no. 3880060, which fits into the end of the swinging arm spindle and allows the swing arm, spacers and frame to line up. This tool is no longer available from Triumph but I have provided a drawing – *see* Chapter 3 – so one can be made.

Trying to line up all the holes (frame at each side, two engine plates, swing arm and so on) to knock the swing arm spindle through is difficult without this tool to guide the swing arm spindle.

This where the swing arm can crack if the clamp bolt is over-tightened.

The revised suspension linkage with a grub screw rather than a clamping bolt.

SUSPENSION LINKAGE DRAG LINK CLAMPS

The original design for these had a clamping arrangement with a bolt that was tightened to grip the shaft for the linkage. Like the swing arm clamp,

An original-style drop link that has cracked. This is not repairable.

this requires a specific torque setting (8Nm); too much, and the clamp will break and this cannot be repaired. The torque setting for this clamping bolt is below the lowest setting on the smaller torque wrenches (which usually start at 10Nm), so be very careful indeed when tightening this bolt.

The linkage was subsequently revised in March 1995 (from VIN 29156), when the clamp was eliminated and a grub screw used instead.

When I came to change the rear shock absorber on my 1994 Speed Triple, I found one clamp completely broken and the other one with a large crack in it, so the whole assembly was replaced with the later type. I would suggest that if you have recently bought a T300, then you should check the linkage as a safety precaution. Many owners have reported the cracking of the suspension linkage drag link clamps so it is a very common problem.

FRONT FORK ADJUSTERS

The bottom fork compression adjusters tend to be left for years without being moved and as a consequence they can seize up, particularly as they are in a very wet and dirty position. The

Compression damping adjustment.

Preload adjustment.

Rebound damping.

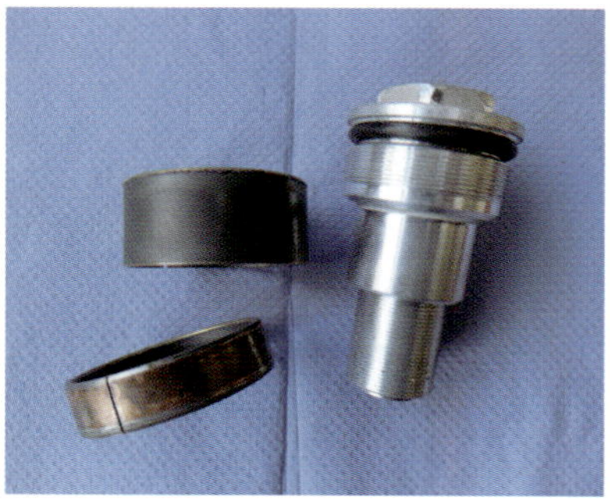

Adjustable fork top removed from the forks.

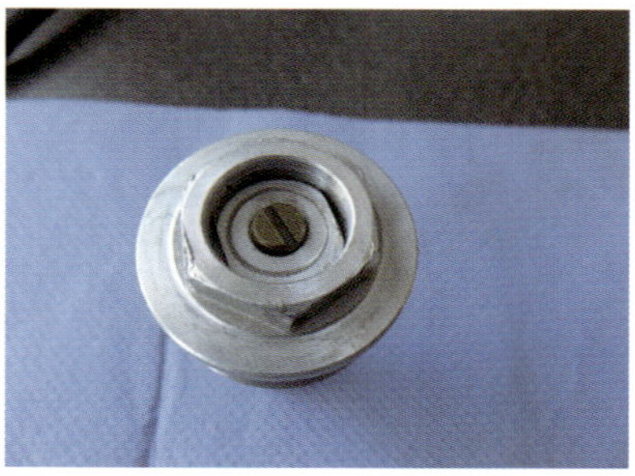

Adjustable fork top showing damage to the corners.

top rebound adjusters can also seize up with lack of use. Both of these can be a real pain to rectify, usually requiring the forks to be taken out of the bike and stripped and rebuilt – not a cheap option.

The second problem is that the nuts for adjusting preload at the top of the forks often seem to have been attacked by some gorilla with the incorrect-sized spanner and this has rounded off the corners. Again, the forks will have to be taken out to replace the adjusters. Triumph can no longer supply the fork top adjusters (I had the last set!) but the same top adjusters were used on some Japanese bikes, such as Kawasaki. As an alternative, a specialized suspension company may be able to rebuild them if you take the fork legs.

To prevent the bottom adjusters from seizing up, click them fully in and fully out regularly (annually), and do the same with the top rebound adjusters. More details on suspension setting and overhauling the fork legs is covered in Chapter 5.

OIL FILTER BOLT

The oil filter on the T300 range is not of the cartridge type but an old-style paper filter element that fits inside a housing in the sump, which then has a cover plate. There is no inherent problem with the design but the bolt that retains the cover plate has a specific torque setting, and over-tightening this bolt can have dire consequences as it cracks the housing in the crankcases. If this happens the crankcase is scrap. The torque setting for this bolt is 18Nm.

CARBON REACTION ON SUPER 3

The Super 3 was in effect a 'blinged-up' Daytona 900 with a modified engine (high-compression pistons, different cam profiles), six-piston calipers and some carbon-fibre parts. The carbon parts, particularly the hugger bolted to the swing arm, can create some problems.

Where the carbon-fibre hugger is bolted to the swing arm, minute 'fretting' can occur, which rubs through the microns-thick anodizing on the swing arm and sets off corrosion due to the ingress of moisture. If corrosion

The bottom of the crankcase showing the hole the oil filter goes in, which is then covered by a plate. The bolt goes down the middle. Just above is the bridging pipe for bikes without an oil cooler.

is present, rectification can be quite difficult as the chemical treatment needs to be in two parts, first to 'kill' the corrosion and then to provide a base coat. When I stripped my newly acquired Super 3 to give it a good clean I removed the hugger and found massive corrosion on the top of the swing arm, a horrible white powder, which, when cleaned off, revealed a big hole in the swing arm.

This corrosion caused by carbon fibre is a well-known problem in the aviation industry and was explained by a friend who is an engineer for an aeroplane manufacturer. They have a dedicated team to go out to customers who have planes a few years old where this problem has been identified, and they remove the outer carbon panels and treat the corrosion on the aluminium airframe.

You can buy the required chemicals from specialist aviation companies but it is very expensive.

Replacing the swing arm and putting some thin rubber pads between the swing arm and hugger would be the preferred solution.

Corrosion on a Super 3 swing arm caused by the carbon-fibre.

Corrosion on a Super 3 swing arm caused by a reaction to the carbon-fibre hugger.

ALCON SIX-PISTON CALIPERS – THREAD DAMAGE

The Alcon calipers fitted to the Super 3 and the Daytona 1200 SE (as well as being sold as an accessory by Triumph) are cast in alloy, and there is a tendency for the threaded bolt holes for the steel caliper mounting bolts to 'pick up' and damage the thread in the caliper body. The only solution is for a steel helicoil insert to be put in the mounting holes. Chris Foxley says that every set of these calipers he has seen have all needed helicoils, and that included the set of my Super 3.

RADIATOR CAP AND FAN SWITCH SENDER UNIT

The radiator cap should be replaced regularly, because if the cap fails it can contribute to overheating problems.

The fan sender unit is housed at the back of the radiator some 12.5cm (5in) below the radiator cap. To check the operation of the fan, just short the two terminals at the back of the switch (with the ignition turned on) and the

Radiator fan switch.

fan should trip in. If it does not operate then replace the sender unit.

To test the fan switch, you need to remove it and immerse it in water, with a multimeter on resistance connected across the terminals (not shorted by the water), and bring to the boil. Using your best jam thermometer, check to see if the switch short-circuits between 94 and 105°C (201–221°F). As an alternative to boiling water, use a heat gun. Always take the switch out to test it and always replace the rubber seal.

BRAKES

Brake Pipes

Some of the very early T300 range have plain rubber brake hoses, such as the Trident and the short-lived 750 Speed Triple. The later bikes were fitted with braided steel hoses covered in rubber. The earlier all-rubber versions can swell with age, which leads to poor braking; these should be replaced with the braided steel hose. All hydraulic hoses have a limited life, and Triumph recommend replacing every four years.

Front Brakes

These are very reliable but on bikes more than twenty years old they may require a strip down and overhaul, and this is covered in Chapter 5. The front caliper bolts are M10 × 1.25 pitch and should not be over-tightened (beyond

Front brake caliper with the pad pin removed.

40Nm), as this can strip the threads on the caliper. If you fit four-piston calipers to a bike previously fitted with the two-piston type, you will find the bolts are too long, but if you shorten them then there is not enough thread at the end (there was previously a spacer). Replace them with the bolts that match a four-piston caliper.

For the four-piston calipers, the usual issue is that the brake pad retaining pins can seize up and be difficult to remove. If the internal part of the pin is damaged then the next step would be to hammer in a Torx bit and then try to unscrew. Also consider using a proper penetrating fluid, but if it is seized solid then careful drilling out will be required. Always have a set of new pad pins to hand before stripping the calipers for the first time.

Regular cleaning of the caliper and slackening and tightening the brake pad retaining pins should reduce the chances of the pin seizing up. Don't over-tighten the pin either. Check the discs for cracks on a regular basis.

With the floating discs, it is possible for the discs to no longer float if there is a build-up of brake dust in the disc bobbins. Use a penetrating spray with a small nozzle to blast out any residue. If you leave this problem unattended, there is a possibility that the discs will warp because they are no longer floating, which will then cause excessive run-out and be felt as juddering at the lever under braking.

The two-piston brake calipers fitted to the front brakes of the early Trophy, Trident and Sprint are similar to the rear caliper, and their overhaul is covered in the next chapter.

Rear Brakes

The major problem with the rear brakes is that, as they work on a sliding pin arrangement, they can seize up as the pins corrode. If the caliper is partially seized, it can lead to overheating of the rear brake disc and consequently warping, so the disc will need replacing. Being located where they are, they can be covered in road dirt and debris,

Underslung rear brake caliper.

which does not help. The same problem that occurs with the front calipers of the brake pad pins seizing also happens with the rear caliper – even more so because of its position. Again, as part of the preventative maintenance schedule, regularly slacken and retighten the pins. I deal with the caliper overhaul in Chapter 5.

EXCESSIVE LEAN

If you find that the bike has an excessive lean when it is on the side stand then it is certainly a problem with the side stand bracket or excessive wear where the bolt passes through the side bracket. The side stand legs are generally fine, but, if abused, can lead to the bracket holding the side stand arm to the bike bending or twisting and therefore increasing the lean angle of the bike. Dropping the bike on that side can also lead to the bracket bending, as can turning the bike by pivoting it around the side stand. These bikes are certainly not light; the dry weight of a Trophy 1200 is 235kg (512lb); add another 20kg (44lb) for oil and fuel and you get over 250kg (550lb), so the side stand is taking some punishment.

There are two types of bracket attaching the side stand to the bike, and it is the earlier one that can twist and bend. Triumph introduced a revised bracket from 1999, which is less prone to distortion. The original bracket, when twisted or bent, then hits the cover for the oil filler/sprocket cover and leaves a mark. If the bracket is hard up against the oil filler casting then the bracket needs replacing, either with a new original type or preferably with the revised bracket. On my Speed Triple the original bracket was bent and when I removed the bracket there was a 'witness mark' on the oil filler/sprocket cover casting; I replaced the bracket with the revised type.

This bending of the bracket manifested itself particularly on the Trophies when fitted with loaded full luggage systems (panniers and top box), which massively increased the weight of the bikes. Sitting on the bike when it is on the side stand does not help either. To rectify this, from 1999 Triumph introduced on the Trophy 900 and 1200 as standard a revised bracket and arm (and for a short period offered a revised

Revised side stand bracket.

Original side stand bracket.

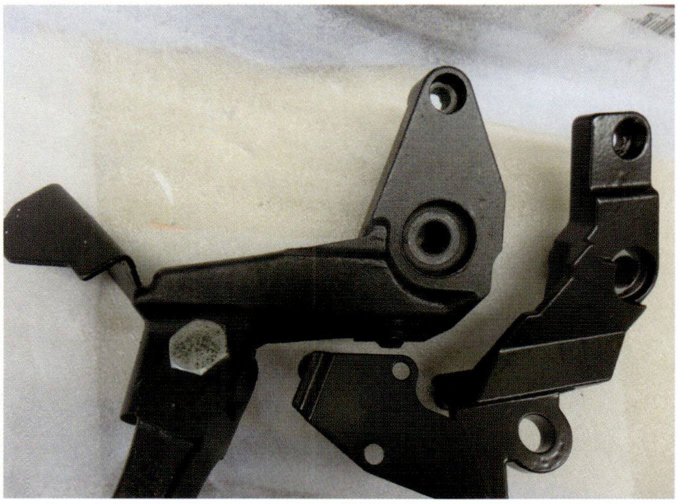

Comparison between the original side stand bracket (left) and the revised bracket (right).

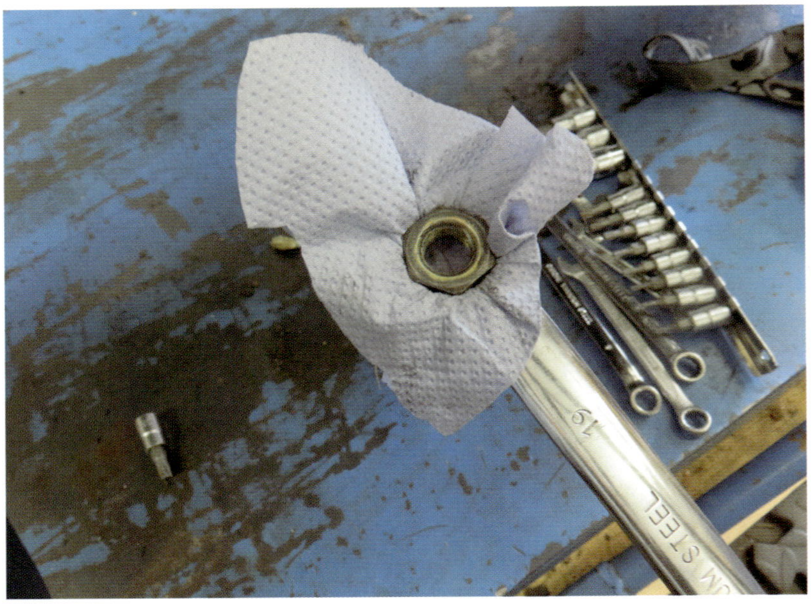

Holding the nut that goes inside the frame where fingers can't reach!

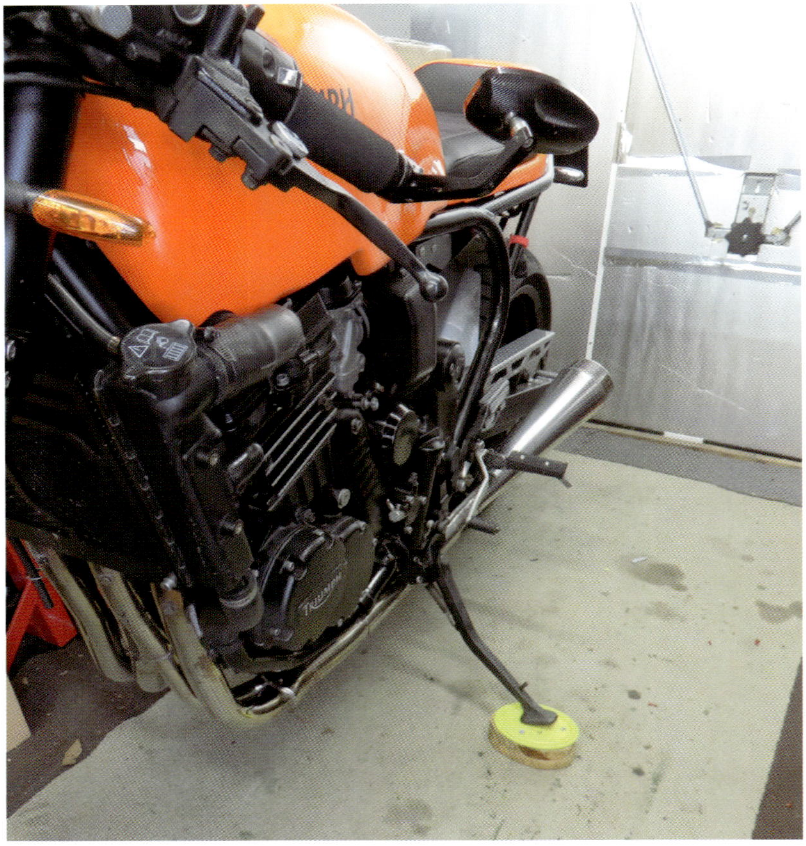

Side stand puck screwed to a block of wood to solve the excessive lean.

side stand kit as an aftermarket option, which incorporated a revised bracket and a longer side stand). This centre stand upgrade kit had the revised bracket and a longer side stand, with the number 2080204 cast into the arm (although there seems to be a different number on another long side stand arm – 2080424). These longer side stands are much sought after and they are as rare as hen's teeth!

The bolt going through the revised bracket and stand screws into the rear of the side stand so once you have taken the nut off the back don't be tempted to try and knock the bolt through. The nut holding the Torx bolt that holds the side stand bracket is tucked away underneath the bike and access is really difficult. When refitting the side stand bracket put some tissue into the ring spanner to hold the nut whilst you turn the Torx bolt.

When I asked Ivan at National Triumph if he had one of the longer side stand arms, he went through his box of stands and out of the fifty he had in stock, only one was the longer side version. Needless to say I bought it to rectify the lean angle on my CRK, but even this did not fully resolve the problem as the bracket was twisted, so I also had to change that to the later type.

It is not recommended to sit on a fully laden bike on the centre stand either, as this can damage it. If fitting a centre stand to a bike not previously fitted with one, don't forget to get the handle that bolts just above the rear foot peg on the near side, as this will help get the bike onto the stand. On my Super 3, I could not get the bike on its centre stand without using this handle. Also remember to fit the rubber stop that protects the exhaust.

I have a side stand puck screwed to a thick piece of wood to give the bike a more upright stance when it's in the garage – a simple measure to counteract excessive lean.

5

maintenance and care of the bike

CLEANING AND GENERAL CARE

When the bikes were supplied new, Triumph recommended a Motorex product to spray on the powder-coated engine cases. Motorex still do the same product, though it is now called Moto Protect, and is thoroughly recommended; I use it all the time and the crankcases on my bikes, which are now twenty-five years old, are in excellent condition. Other long-term owners also report that it keeps the powder coating in fine shape. Spray on and wipe off two or three times a year, or after cleaning the bike.

When cleaning the engine with commercial detergents, be careful with products containing bleaching agents, which, when dried, can leave streaks on the engine cases that can be difficult to remove.

For bikes such as the Thunderbird and Adventurer that have a lot of chrome plating, I would use a fine chrome polish such as Mothers (an American brand), or the fine version of Solvol Autosol. The standard Solvol Autosol can be a little coarse for the crankcases and leave scratch marks.

Moto Protect silicone spray by Motorex, as recommended by Triumph.

For protection, if the bike is used over the winter and bad weather, then ACF 50 is recommended, though it is quite expensive; it was originally developed for protecting helicopters when in storage. Apply with a small paintbrush or put on a cloth and wipe it over the area to be protected. Triumph recommended that WD40 should not be used on chrome surfaces as it could cause some discoloration.

STORING THE BIKE

If the bike is taken off the road over winter then there are some precautions you should take:

1. Drain the carburettors of fuel.
2. Drain the fuel tank (or at least put in fuel stabilizer and run it through the carburettors by starting the engine).
3. Over-inflate the tyres by 15psi; this will help to prevent a flat spot developing. It is also helpful if the bike can be moved on a regular basis. Remember to check the tyre pressure when the bike comes out in the spring and return to the correct pressure.
4. If the storage facility is damp then spray the bike with AC50 or WD40 to protect the surface over winter.
5. Place a paddock stand under the rear wheel to keep the bike upright. If the bike is left on the side stand it puts extra weight on the nearside fork leg, which could lead to premature failure of the fork seal. If you don't have a paddock stand spare (for example, if you have more than one bike), then screw a side stand puck to a block of wood so that the bike is in a more vertical position.

I also like to power up the bike on a monthly basis (first having put the battery on charge) until the engine gets really hot (the thermostat needs to open and the water circulate through the radiator). This ensures that any condensation that might have formed inside the engine and exhaust system (unless you have a heated garage) evaporates off.

SERVICE INTERVALS

For readers who don't have a Triumph handbook to hand, these are the main elements of regular servicing:

Spark plug replacement: 20,000km (12,000 miles)
Valve clearance check: 30,000km (18,000 miles)
Air cleaner change: every 40,000km (24,000 miles)
Brake fluid change: every two years
Engine oil and filter change: every 10,000km (6000 miles)
Fork oil change: 20,000km (12,000 miles)
Grease rear suspension linkage: every 10,000km (6,000 miles)
Coolant change: every two years
Lubricate headstock bearings: every two years
Replace caliper seals: every two years
Replace clutch/brake master cylinder seals: every two years
Lubricate swing arm bearings: every three years

FRONT FORK 'PULL-THROUGH'

The recommended amount by which the front forks are above the top yoke (known as 'pull-through') varies from model to model. This is important, as in 1996 Triumph introduced shorter forks on some models, and some of these have a reduced pull-through or even need to be flush with the top yoke. The VIN number will indicate what the pull-through should be.

Fork pull-through, in this case 28mm.

Depending on your riding style, you may want to deviate from these standard Triumph recommendations. For example, the standard pull-through on the Speed Triple is 28mm, but if you want to sharpen up the steering then the forks can be pulled through by a few more millimetres; just be aware than any changes from the Triumph recommended settings are carried out at your own risk. Triumph invested a lot of time and effort and employed some excellent test riders to arrive at the settings below.

The pull-through is measured from the top of the yoke to the top of the fork up to the point where the fork top has what looks like a large washer.

This table lists the recommended settings:

Model	Pull-through (distance above top yoke)
Trophy up to VIN 29155i	25mm
Trophy from VIN 29156	20mm
Daytona, Super 3, Speed Triple up to VIN 29155	28mm
Daytona, Super 3, Speed Triple from VIN 29156	Flush with top yoke face
Sprint up to VIN 29155	25mm
Sprint from VIN29156	20mm
Trident up to VIN 29155	25mm
Trident from VIN 29156	20mm
Tiger, Thunderbird, Thunderbird Sport and Adventurer and Legend TT	Flush with top yoke

SUSPENSION ADJUSTMENT

The Triumph handbook issued with each bike has a section on how to adjust the front and rear (where adjustment is fitted) suspension, and I have included the details here for those who don't have access to the original.

Before covering the suspension adjustments, as part of the regular maintenance the spring preload adjuster and compression damping screw should be screwed all the way in, then all the way out and then set to the preferred setting. This ensures that all the screws remain free and do not seize up, saving a considerable amount of grief and expense. There are twelve 'click' positions, with 1 being fully screwed in (and the hardest setting); all counts are from this no. 1 position, so count each click as you unscrew. Don't do this with the radio on in the garage as you won't hear the clicks, although you should feel them.

Always use a screwdriver that is a good fit (not too slack, but a nice tight fit) into whatever you are screwing/unscrewing, as this will reduce the chances of damaging the screw head. Use a large screwdriver, particularly with the bottom adjuster.

Front Suspension

Rebound damping (at the top of the fork) This is changed using a screwdriver, and you should be able to hear the screw click. First screw all the way in (clockwise) and then all the way out (anticlockwise) to check that the adjustment is free. Then screw all the way in again and unwind the screw, counting the clicks to the setting indicated in the chart below. Remember position 12 is the minimum effective damping.

Compression damping (at the bottom of the fork leg) Again, the screw should be fully screwed in (clockwise) and then screwed out (anticlockwise) until the required setting is found.

Spring preload adjuster The preload adjuster requires a 17mm open-ended spanner. Again, rotating the adjuster clockwise screws the preload in and anticlockwise screws it out. There are eight bands on the outside of the adjuster, with position 5 being pre-set by the factory. This is where a decent-quality spanner counts, as it will be a better fit.

The front suspension settings are shown in the table opposite.

Rear Suspension

The reality is that most T300 bikes will have had (or should have had) the rear shock absorbers replaced, as the Triumph rear shock absorbers are not rebuildable, despite what you may read in adverts. Triumph no longer supply replacement rear shock absorbers, so an aftermarket one may now be fitted. For completeness, I am including a table showing the settings for a Triumph rear shock absorber, but

Rebound damping.

Compression damping adjustment.

Front suspension settings

Loading	Spring preload	Rebound damping	Compression damping
Solo standard	5	6	6
Solo softer	6	9	8
Solo firmer	4	4	3
Rider and passenger	4–5	4–6	3–6
Rider/passenger/luggage	1–4	1–4	1–3

if you have fitted an aftermarket one, you will need to refer to the settings included with that. If you are buying a new replacement aftermarket rear shock absorber, enquire about any variations in damping before fitting. You can also ask if the rear spring can be better matched to your weight and the weight of the bike. I fitted a Hagon Daytona rear shock to my CRK and found that as the CRK weighs nearly 30kg (66lb) less than the Daytona, the rear suspension is too hard.

The standard Triumph rear shock absorber has the spring preload adjuster under the seat, and there is a hexagonal nut on the top with an indicator window on the side. Adjustment is made with a 10mm socket or ring spanner. To increase the spring preload, rotate the hexagon nut clockwise, and to reduce turn anticlockwise. The window indicator has five numbers – 1 to 5, the minimum being position 1 and the maximum 5. The Trident 750 is only adjustable for spring preload.

The damping adjustment is made by turning a large circular adjuster with four numbers on it and an arrow mounted above. Setting 1 is the softest and 4 the hardest. The adjuster must only be rotated anticlockwise, and after position 4 it goes back to 1.

The rear suspensions settings are shown in the table below left.

I must admit I found very little difference changing the damping on the original rear shock fitted to my Speed Triple. Changing a 24-year-old standard rear shock with 77,000km (48,000 miles) on the clock to a new aftermarket one, however, showed just how saggy the old unit was, and the new rear shock transformed the handling.

Rear suspension settings

Loading	Spring preload	Damping
Solo standard	3	2
Solo softer	2	1
Solo firmer	4	3
Rider and passenger	3–4	3–4
Rider/passenger/luggage	3–4	3–4

Preload adjustment.

Triumph rear damper adjustment.

Spring pre-load adjustment.

Grease Nipples

One of the really good things about the T300 range is that the rear suspension linkage is fitted with grease nipples, which, if looked after, will ensure the rear suspension works effectively. This is quite unusual on motorcycles. Neglect, however, can lead to seizure of the linkage and some expense. If seizure has occurred then it is a bit of a struggle to remove the pins in the linkage.

I use molybdenum-based grease on the bike yearly; Triumph recommended every 5,000km (3,000 miles). Gordon Smith suggests that as molybdenum-based grease is not waterproof, an alternative should be used when greasing up the pin that goes through the suspension linkage.

When greasing the drag link spindle, undo the 8mm clamp bolt (or grub screws for the later type) and rotate the spindle. It's the areas of the spindle that pass through the four 'fingers' of the drag link that never get greased, so rotating the spindles regularly keeps them from seizing up. Don't forget to re-tighten the clamp bolts/grub screws, but take care not to over-tighten the clamp bolts, as they are only 8Nm.

It is a good idea to remove the grease nipples regularly and check that they work properly; if not, replace.

BODYWORK

The bodywork is held onto the frame by a combination of bolts and spigots, which push into rubber grommets. It is not unknown for the plastic spigots on the bodywork to break off, and if that happens they need to be plastic welded back on. When taking the bodywork off the bike, two things will help to avoid breaking off the lugs:

1. Grease the lugs and the rubber grommets with red rubber grease every time they are removed.
2. Rather than pull on the bodywork, try to press on the end of the lug and push it through the grommet, taking it gently. Just giving a hard pull is guaranteed to break off some lugs. Red rubber grease is your friend not only for brake overhauls but also for bodywork.

When bolting down bodywork try to avoid bolting down too tightly, as this will crack the panels.

Remember that Triumph can no longer supply new bodywork, so treat it gently. You may be able to find replacements on the second-hand market but it will probably be the wrong colour so a respray is then required and the decals may not match. The Speed Triple, for example, has a Union Jack flag on the tailpiece.

Bodywork grommet.

Bodywork spigot.

Speed Triple rear bodywork and decals.

FLUID CHANGES

Brake Fluid

Triumph recommends that the brake fluid should be changed every two years. This is because it is hygroscopic so absorbs moisture from the atmosphere, and over time this reduces the efficiency of the brakes. As all the bikes are now over twenty years old, it would be wise to also remove and clean out the brake 'splitter' below the headstock where the brake pipes to the two front calipers output from.

If you are overhauling the brake master cylinder and there is evidence of sludgy brake fluid residue then this splitter will also be filled with sludge. The bolts for the splitter seem tight at 14mm and too slack at 15mm. A $^{9}/_{16}$ AF spanner seems to fit really well. Just refilling with new brake fluid will not cure the problem, however.

I have always found bleeding the brakes a bit of a pain until Mark Gaylard suggested using a Mityvac system and I now use this with both brake and clutch fluids.

Clutch Fluid

This tends to be overlooked until the operation of the clutch becomes problematic, but should really be done at the same time the brake fluid is changed. Again I use the Mityvac pump to bleed.

Coolant

The recommended interval to change the coolant on these Triumphs is two years, irrespective of mileage. Many people who only do a few thousand miles a year (or less) might think they can leave as long as they like if the bike is garaged over the winter. The problem with this approach is that it ignores the fact that the coolant not only provides antifreezing properties but also anti-corrosion inhibitors. Given that the engine has a mixture of both aluminium and steel components, it is essential that the coolant is replaced regularly, as the corrosion inhibitors degrade over time.

I use the standard Triumph coolant, HD4X OAT (part number A9610046A), which is pre-mixed to the correct strength. There has been considerable debate on various forums and Facebook pages regarding alternatives to the Triumph product, particularly with regard to possible cylinder head gasket failures, but I have not experienced any issues so continue to use Triumph's coolant.

Nissin-branded calipers.

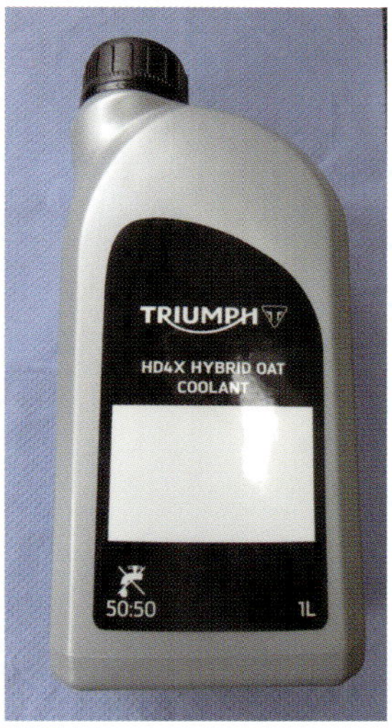

Triumph coolant.

Cylinder head Once aluminium in the cylinder head starts to corrode, it can lead to the water passageways becoming restricted, which will lead to reduced cooling to the cylinder head. I once owned a Lancia Beta engine intended to go into a Lancia Stratos replica; these alloy cylinder heads were notorious for internal corrosion and restricting water flow, and indeed on test, the cylinder head would not flow water so had to be scrapped. Coolant is your friend in keeping corrosion out of your engine. Gordon Smith reported that on one of his Trophy 900s he had to scrap the cylinder head and crankcases as the internal corrosion was so bad water would not circulate properly.

One of his other bikes, a Sprint Executive, had similar problems. Following a cylinder head gasket failure, he discovered large deposits of limescale that resisted all attempts at flushing with Coolant Systems cleaning solutions. This is evidence that previous owners had used tap water in the engine, which had then led to the build-up of limescale. Under no circumstances should tap water be used except in an emergency (but then needs draining out and replacing at the earliest opportunity). If you mix your own antifreeze, only use distilled water. Gordon eventually cleaned up the internals of the cylinder head by taping over the water holes and filling the head with Harpic Power Plus for thirty minutes, then flushing out the head. This eventually got rid of the limescale build-up and allowed the head to be reused.

Cylinder head bolts These are through-bolts that go through the head and then the crankcases and are surrounded by the coolant. If the antifreeze is not changed regularly, they can corrode to the point where they will break when being removed, leaving a stub inside the bottom crankcase. I rebuilt an ex-Speed Triple Challenge bike in 2010 that appeared never to have had antifreeze (race bikes are only allowed to use plain water) since it was built in February 1994; when the cylinder head was removed, two of the bolts snapped off, requiring the crankcase to be sent off and the remains of the bolts spark eroded out. This then required an insert for both holes. The remaining bolts exhibited severe wasting and all had to be replaced.

If the antifreeze has been changed regularly, the bolts should be inspected and, if in good condition, they can be reused. It had been thought that

Corroded cylinder head bolts caused by not changing the antifreeze regularly.

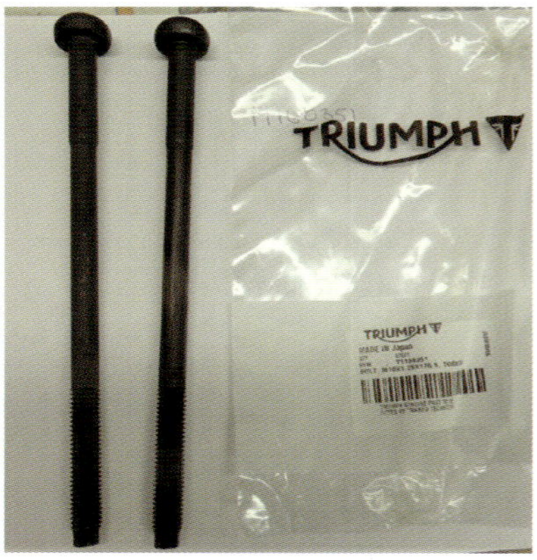

New cylinder head bolts.

these bolts were one-time use only as they would 'stretch' over time, rendering them unusable. However, this has turned out not to be the case. Check that the underside of the head of the bolt is free of corrosion to ensure that when they are torqued down the pressure is equal on all bolts. If in doubt, replace the bolts. They are not expensive to buy, being around £90 for a full set.

Water pump The water pump can also suffer from the same internal corrosion as the rest of the engine.

Changing the coolant If the bike has an unknown service history, before filling with fresh antifreeze, drain the coolant, then flush out with a garden hosepipe before refilling. The expansion tank should also be taken out and flushed out. The best way to clean the sediment from the expansion tank is to put a couple of small bolts into the tank and give it a good shake before finally flushing out.

When draining the coolant, ensure that the water is drained from the following points:

- Drain plug on the side of the engine
- Drain plug in the water pump
- The radiator pipe. Undo the short piece of hose on the radiator pipe and allow the water to drain out. Undo the radiator cap as well to ensure that all the coolant can drain out of the engine.

I can't emphasize enough how important it is to change the coolant every two to three years, irrespective of mileage, particularly given the modest cost of replacing the antifreeze. It really is a false economy not to do so. As many owners have discovered, saving a few pence on coolant has resulted in a blown head gasket and the cost of getting the head cleaned up as well as new gaskets (a new cylinder head gasket is around £100).

Triumph gave the coolant capacity on all the models (including the Thun-

The drain plug for the engine block.

The drain plug for the water pump.

The radiator drain point. Disconnect the rubber pipe, pull off the metal pipe and water will come out.

Expansion tank pipe.

derbird/Thunderbird Sport/Adventurer) as 2.8ltr (100fl oz), except for the Super 3, which is listed as 3ltr (105fl oz).

Airbox and snorkels.

AIR FILTER AND AIRBOX

Triumph designed the air filter and airbox as one assembly, and the complete unit should be changed every 40,000km (24,000 miles), although in dusty climates this should be done more frequently. Forgetting to do this can lead to erratic running, as the air/petrol mixture will be affected. One of the downsides of the design is that the complete airbox assembly can only be changed by removing the carburettors as well. To put it mildly, this can be a right fiddle! Because of the complex nature of an airbox change it is not unusual to find that the filter is completely clogged when you acquire a bike that is over twenty years old.

The photos show the state of an air filter on the Daytona I bought for my CRK conversion. As covered later in this chapter, if you remove the airbox you can replace the air filter element with an aftermarket one (such as Pipercross) and, if the back of the airbox is cut in half, the filter can then be removed and cleaned without the need to remove the carburettors the next time the filter needs attention.

Clogged air filter.

Airbox opened up to show the original air filter.

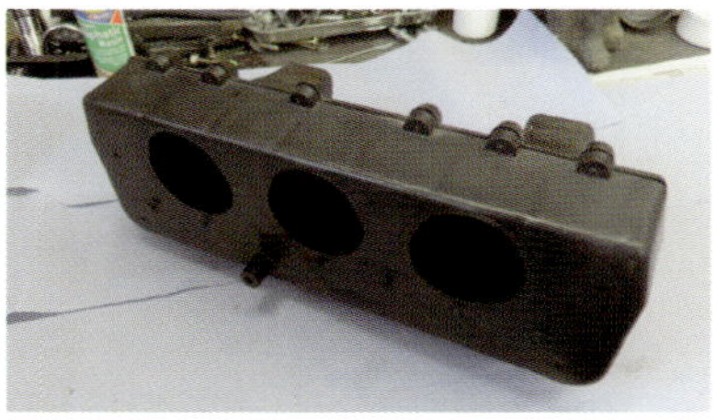

The 3-cylinder airbox.

THERMOSTAT

If you are new to the T300 range, you may at first be mystified as to where the thermostat is hidden, as Triumph placed them inside the water hoses. On the Thunderbird range, it is housed under the fuel tank, just behind the radiator pressure cap. On all other models, it is housed inside the hose just behind the radiator pressure cap on the radiator. The Triumph handbook says that the thermostat should open at 83 degrees.

When replacing the thermostat, make sure that it goes into the hose in the correct orientation, so the large end faces the radiator and the hole is at the top. The more recent thermostat supplied by Triumph does not have a hole in it (to allow bubbles of air to pass through), but it seems sensible to drill a small hole similar to the original.

Radiator top hose with thermostat hidden inside!

Old-style thermostat (left) and new (right). Note the hole in the old-style thermostat.

Old-style thermostat (left) and new (right).

ENGINE

The engines are very reliable if maintained properly with regular oil, filter and coolant changes. The only issue on some early engines was premature crank failure, but Triumph resolved this by changing the oil feed banjo to the cylinder head, thereby increasing oil pressure at the crank.

Before removing the engine from the bike, if you are going to split the engine cases, remove the front sprocket while the engine is still in the frame and the chain is still attached. The nut for the front sprocket is at 132Nm (and needs a 36mm socket) and is difficult enough to remove anyway – even more so if the engine is out of the frame.

To help remove the front sprocket, one technique is to pass a large baulk of timber through the rear wheel (with cloth padding to avoid marking the spokes of the wheel and the swing arm) and then use a scaffold pole (on a ½in drive socket) to loosen the nut on the front sprocket. A powered impact driver makes life much easier. This can sometimes take two people hanging off the end of the scaffold pole! Gordon Smith reported that the front sprocket nut on his 1992 Trophy 900 had Loctite in the back of the nut and on the threads and it required a meaty (1,000W, 450Nm) electric impact gun to get the nut off.

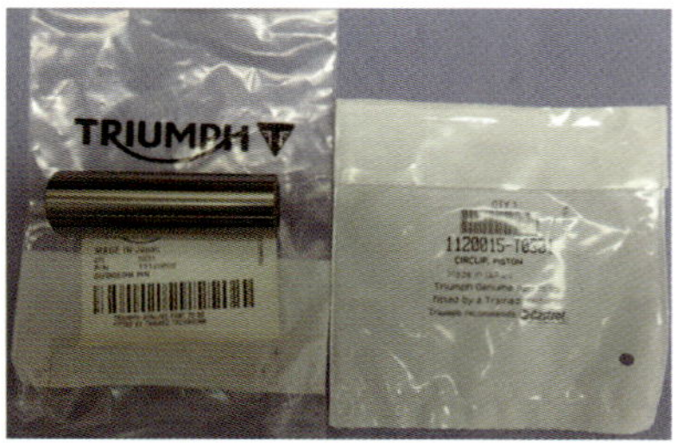

Triumph gudgeon pins and circlips. The pins are sold as a set of three.

Remember that these engines are heavy – a 900cc triple engine weighs around 70kg (154lb) and a 1200 4-cylinder weighs 78kg (172lb), dry and with carburettors, so you need help to move it once out of the frame.

It is also advisable to check the compression before any attempt to take the engine out. Compression readings for the 1200 should be in the range 180–220psi with no more than 25psi difference between cylinders. For the 900, it is 140–185. Always carry out a compression test with the throttle fully open otherwise you may get a false reading. Anything around 100psi indicates a very worn motor.

If the cylinder head has been removed, it is essential that the liners are taken out and the seating cleaned. The wet liners need to go back in the correct place: the #2 liner is a selective fit and is marked with a green dot on early engines and a letter B on later engines, and also needs to go back in the correct position in relation to the front of the engine.

The process of replacing the cylinder liners is covered later in this chapter.

The rubber parts inside the engine covers are for sound deadening purposes and can be removed if required.

Small End Piston (Gudgeon) Pins

On high-mileage bikes these can wear and could cause a catastrophic failure, so if the engine has been stripped down for an overhaul (or a head gasket change) it's a good idea to replace the gudgeon pins with new ones, along with new gudgeon pin circlips.

Mark Gaylard has found a way that the gudgeon pins can be changed in situ once the cylinder head has been removed. Remove the circlip holding the pin into the piston and then insert into the hollow gudgeon pin one of those expanding plugs used in hanging hooks (these can be found at your local DIY store). Insert, expand and then slowly withdraw the pin.

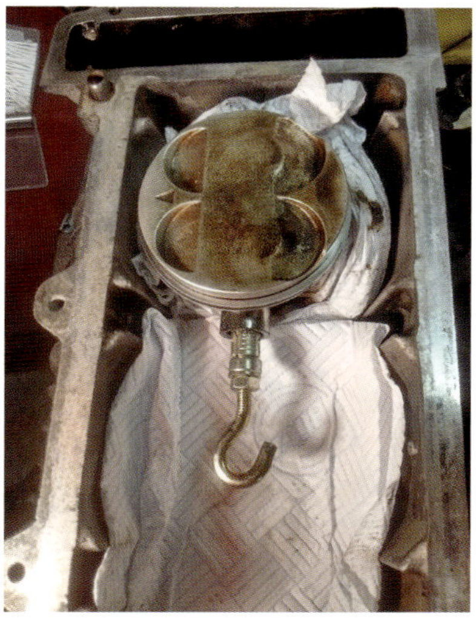

Changing gudgeon pins in situ using an expanding plug.

Camshafts

There are different cams fitted to the various models and each is given a colour code, which should be visible as a blob of paint at the end of the camshaft, but over time it can be difficult to identify the colour. The colours were:

Green: fitted to the Trophy, Tridents, Daytona, Sprint Sports and Speed Triple.
Blue: fitted to the Tiger, Thunderbirds and Legend. These are milder than the green cams, with less lift and less duration.
Red: fitted to the Daytona Super 3 and Daytona 1200. These have a higher lift and duration than the green camshaft.

Cams can be swapped between models (obviously not between 3- and 4-cylinder engines), but if this is done then the jetting for the carburettors will need changing, preferably on a dynamometer.

When dismantling an engine and taking out the camshafts, remember that camshaft caps holding the camshafts in are line bored when the head was manufactured so they must go back in the same place. Therefore it is essential that they are numbered and also clearly identified as inlet and exhaust caps.

The Triumph engine builder normally engraves the caps when the engine is built up and includes the engine build date on the front right cam cap.

Also ensure that the cam bolts and tubes are thoroughly cleaned before reuse. I use a small parts washer, but a plastic bowl and a stiff paintbrush and some paraffin will suffice.

Wet liners

All the engines are fitted with wet liners that can be taken out when the cylinder head is removed. The liners have a bevel at the bottom that mates with a bevel in the crankcases and is made watertight with special sealant. If the liners are not sealed correctly at the bottom, it can allow water to seep into the sump. Don't use just any old sealant – Triumph suggest Hoylomar in the workshop manual, but you can use something else that is specifically designed for this job, such as Wurth Super RTV silicone or Yamabond. The requirement is for something that seals and sets. If the engine requires turning over, make sure that the liners are held down.

It is important that the liner bottoms are sealed just before the cylinder head is replaced, as when the cylinder head is torqued down, it presses the liners down on their seats and allows the seal to harden. If the liners are pushed in with the sealant and the head is not immediately fitted, the liners can 'lift' and a good, watertight seal is not made.

Once the cylinder head has been removed but before taking out the liners, you will need to remove any sludge and sediment at the bottom of the crankcase – if this is left in when the liners are removed, it will drop into the sump.

Removing the liners can be challenging, but Gordon Smith has found a way of getting them out that uses a plumber's drain pipe bung (the metal disc part needs to be around approximately 73mm in diameter to fit in the 76mm bore) as follows:

1. Place a pad (Gordon uses a piece of carpet cut to shape) onto the top of the piston.
2. Insert the pipe bung and tighten the bung wing nut, which expands the rubber bung and grips the liner.
3. Turn the crankshaft on the 24mm nut (towards the front) and, as it approaches Top Dead Centre, it will lift the liner away from the crankcase. Always rotate the engine forward.
4. Remove the bung and pad and repeat for the other cylinders.

Once the seals are broken the liners lift out easily.

Liner removal tool.

Liner removal tool, a plumber's bung!

Padding (a piece of carpet cut to shape) on top of the piston before using the liner removal tool.

Liner removal tool in action.

Cylinder liners.

Liners removed, leaving pistons in situ.

Liners removed, as well as the pistons and crank.

Clean up the bottom of the liners and the surface in the top of the crankcase where the liners sit.

The liners also need to go back in with the correct orientation.

If these liner seals fail it can be catastrophic to the engine, depending how much water weeps into the sump. I had this happen to me and as a consequence the clutch plates corroded and glued themselves together due to the water in the oil. The bike was continually running hot and risked overheating the engine. The worst case scenario is that it ruins all the bearings and the engine is wrecked. The oil and oil filter were also contaminated with water.

Pistons

One of the few ways to reliably modify the 900 triple engines is to use pistons from the 750 Trident engines or from the 1200 4-cylinder engines. This will give a higher compression ratio, but the fuelling will need to be adjusted to suit. The only known issue with the pistons is that the gudgeon pins need changing on high-mileage engines as a safety measure. Fitting 750/1200 pistons is popular with T300 owners, however, so supply is scarce!

Valve Recession

The first indication of valve recession is when no amount of shimming will give you the required clearance.

Cylinder block with the liners removed.

This problem is a particular issue with the Super 3, as one of the engine modifications made by Triumph was to fit some high-lift cams and this can accelerate valve recession. As these camshafts were also fitted to the 1200 Daytona, similar issues may occur there.

The heads will need to be sent to a specialist for new valve seats to be fitted and new valves will be required.

Sump Service

The sump can be removed and the metal strainer can be cleaned out. In a bike without a service history, this is a worthwhile job. The strainer, part of the oil pickup, is designed to trap any metal particles and bits of gasket before the oil passes through the oil filter. Don't be to alarmed to see sundry bits in the strainer, that's what it was designed to do! The photos here show a typical engine. They also show how much oil is retained in the engine after the oil has been dropped, which explains why you can never get the standard amount of oil back into the bike.

If the strainer is absolutely full of metal swarf then it may indicate that all is not well with the engine.

Cylinder Head Gaskets

Triumph changed their supplier for cylinder head gaskets and there have been problems reported with premature failure with the new supplier. An American company can now offer an alternative, as can a French supplier.

Camshaft Oil Feed Pipes

The very early bike from 1991 had plain rubber (without internal braiding) camshaft oil feed pipes. These should be replaced by braided hoses as soon as possible to avoid failure and consequently engine failure. All subsequent bikes have the braided type and can easily be identified.

Exhaust Studs

Given that the bikes are over twenty years old, removing the exhaust studs can be a challenge. The standard technique is to run two nuts down the

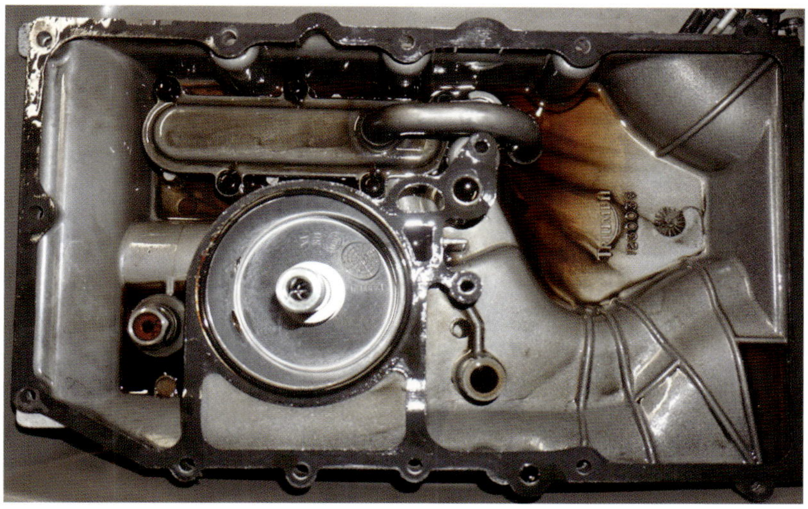

Interior of the sump; note how much oil is left, and the casting date to the right.

Sump strainer, showing how it traps any bits floating in the engine.

Changing exhaust studs.

Triumph exhaust studs; note the shoulder on the bolt.

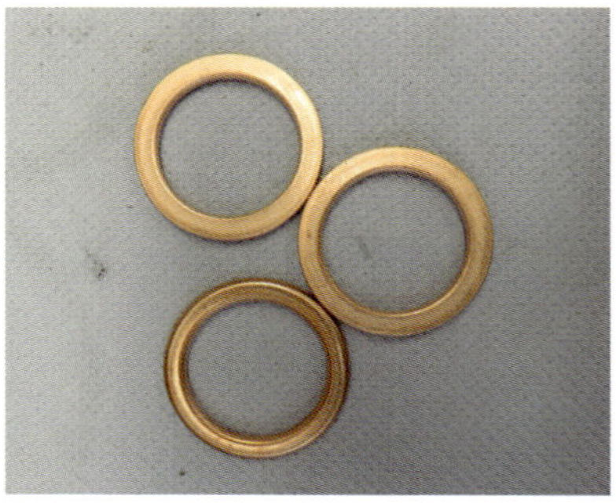

Exhaust gaskets. Always replace with new ones.

stud and use the friction between the nuts to turn the stud out. Heat may be required! If the stud snaps off flush with the cylinder head, then it will need careful drilling and the use of a stud extractor.

If removal has been successful, then the replacement studs should have a shoulder to prevent the stud from being over-tightened (if they are Triumph ones). The exhaust studs are 8mm. They are not expensive so I would not bother with any aftermarket ones.

Some people have suggested that copper slip should be used in the studs when inserting into the cylinder head; however, copper slip does not have a sufficiently high temperature range, so a high-temperature ceramic paste should be used instead. The exposed end of the stud should also be protected by ceramic paste and an 8mm domed nut otherwise it can corrode over time.

Spark Plugs

Triumph recommended NGK DPR 9EA -9 for most of the engines and suggested replacement every 20,000km (12,000 miles). Unless the engine has been tuned, don't be tempted to get different temperature-range plugs or go to the expense of iridium ones. There are no particular problems with the spark plugs, with two provisos.

First, ensure that the plugs are genuine NGK plugs; the market is now full of counterfeit NGK plugs so only buy from a recognized source and not off the internet. If in any doubt, check with NGK that the seller is an authorized agent. Counterfeit plugs can be catastrophic as they have been known to fall apart, damaging or wrecking the engine, they can break when removed (which would require the cylinder head to be removed to allow better access to the plug) and – worst of all – just fail with no warning. Some reports have had the plugs failing within 160km (100 miles); it's not worth the risk of saving a few pounds on fake plugs. The problem is so bad that the NGK website has a detailed description with photos showing how to spot the fake plugs. If you have bought fake plugs, please report back to NGK as they will chase up the counterfeiters.

Paul Messenger has now found a good alternative to the NGK plug – the Denso X24EPR-U9 4096 – as he is very suspicious of any NGK plug because of the level of counterfeiting in the marketplace.

Second, make sure you have an 18mm thin-walled plug spanner, as getting to the centre plug, which sits under the spine frame, can be difficult. The box spanner as supplied by Triumph can save the day, but these are hard to find. I bought a quality thin-walled spanner on eBay for around £10 and it came with a rubber insert inside to help grip the plug.

If you see reference to the plugs being 12mm, that is not the plug spanner size but the size of the threaded part of the plug – the socket size is 18mm.

Always check the grade of the plug, unless you have severely modified the engine, then go with the plug that Triumph recommended; they spent a lot of time and effort setting up the fuelling of the bikes.

Checking and Changing Valve Shims

Triumph has the camshaft working directly on shims (that sit on top of the valve buckets) that dictate the clearance. The specific reason for checking the shims at the recommended intervals and making sure the valve clearances are correct is to ensure that the valves fully close, as if they are partially open at some point in the 4-cylinder cycle then the valve face and seats will be burnt – affecting performance and potentially damaging the engine.

Triumph suggest that the shims be checked every 20,000km (12,000) miles; the Triumph service schedule states every 10,000km (6,000 miles) but after the first 20,000km the shims should need replacing less often, though they should still be checked regularly. The check can be done by a competent home mechanic as long as the correct tools are used and spare shims are to hand. If you don't have spare shims, you will need to order them from your Triumph dealer when

Triumph valve shim tool in the expert hands of Clive Wood.

you have identified all the ones that need replacing. Triumph had a specific tool (part no. T3880012) to facilitate the changing of shims without removing the cams, but none of these official service tools are now available; a similar-pattern part tool can be bought on the internet at a cost of around £60.

The most usual shims you will need are 2.5 and 2.6 but, as Gordon Smith has highlighted, you can also get half size (thickness) shims to get things really accurate (*see* below, Using a Valve Shim Tool).

There are two different methods for checking and changing them:

- Removing the camshafts
- Keeping the camshafts in place and using a valve shim tool to compress the buckets to allow the shims to be removed and checked

The first stage of the process is the same for both options, which is checking each shim; where the methods diverge is the point at which you have to change a shim (or shims).

Removing the Camshafts Method

The first method of removing the camshaft to replace shims is the 'old-fashioned' way (and where you don't have a valve shim tool). The following notes have been provided by Mark Gaylard.

Tools

- 24mm/19mm socket
- Micrometer/feeler gauges (metric)
- Crankcase cover gasket
- 3 new spark plugs
- RTV silicone sealant
- Oil can
- Telescopic magnetic tool
- Metal pick (small like a tooth pick)
- Zip tie
- Torque wrench
- Various Torx and Allen head sockets
- 12mm Allen socket and Triumph/aftermarket thin-walled spark plug removal tool
- Brake cleaner/rags/paper towel

The feeler gauges can be in a set, or do as Clive Wood does – separate feeler gauges, with the handles colour coded for size.

When taking out the camshafts, remember the camshaft caps holding the camshafts in were line bored when the head was manufactured, so they must go back in exactly the same place. Therefore it is essential that they are numbered and also clearly identified as inlet and exhaust caps. If you don't, you run the risk of damaging the camshaft.

Separate feeler gauges.

The bike must be completely cold, otherwise the readings will be out. Then the steps are as follows:

1. Read the Triumph workshop manual or the Haynes manual a couple of times to familiarize yourself with what you are doing.
2. First take the seat, bodywork and tank off and remove the negative lead of the battery. Zip tie the cables and tubes on the left of the main frame tube tightly up and out of the way of the cam.
3. Clean the top of the cam cover to remove any dirt, then pull the spark plug caps and rest them over the tank mounting bars.
4. Now remove the cam cover. The eight cam cover bolts need to be loosened in a criss-cross manner and removed. (When loosening items like this, start from the outside and work your way in, and when tightening, work from the centre outwards.) The cam cover is now only held in place with the silicone sealant at each end. Take a rubber mallet and a small piece of wood and gently tap the wood up against the underside edge of each end of the cam cover to loosen it.

A set of feeler gauges.

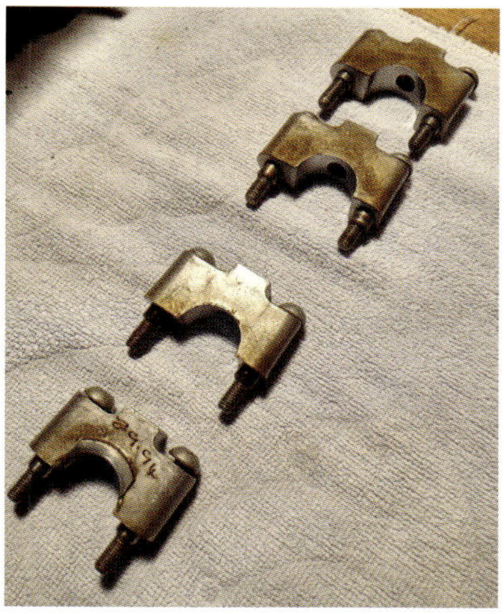
Cam caps, placed in order as they were line bored when the engine was manufactured.

Cam cover removed.

Feeler gauge in use.

5. Carefully lift the cover upwards. It needs to come out on the right-hand side of the bike. Twisting the cover towards the back of the bike as you do this allows the half-moon gasket end caps more room to come out between the cams, but whichever way you do it, it is a tight fit.
6. Next remove the crankshaft cover. Be ready for some oil loss at this point, but don't worry – it's only a dribble.
7. There are two options for rotating the engine. If the rear wheel is free (the bike is on a paddock or centre stand), select a high gear and move the rear wheel by hand – this will turn the engine over. Alternatively, remove the cover for the pickup coil and rotate by using a 24mm ring spanner or socket on a breaker bar (but not a ratchet, as you can't control the position of the timing marks or cam lobes as the pistons fall).

   Now you can gain access to the large nut on the end of the crankshaft to turn the engine over by hand, and so that you can see the timing marks necessary to put everything back together the right way, should you need pull the cams off the engine.

   At this stage it's best to make sure you are organized. You will need to draw a diagram of the valves so you can record any readings and work out and note down the necessary adjustments.
8. You will now need to loosen or remove the spark plugs so no compression happens as the pistons rise. I removed mine because I wanted to check the gaps and condition, replacing if necessary. The gaps should be 0.8–0.9mm. I then poked kitchen roll in the holes to stop any muck falling down there. It's much easier to get access to the plugs with the cam cover off as they are seated fairly deep into the top of the engine. The Triumph spark plug tool (or quality aftermarket thin-walled plug spanner) grips the plugs well and a 12mm Allen socket fits in the top a treat, allowing you to get deep enough and also to torque them down properly later.
9. Stop! Move the handlebars to the left; this will save you from regularly head-butting the bar end weight as you peer along the exhaust cam!
10. Time to check those clearances. They should be 0.15–0.20mm for the exhaust valves and 0.10–0.15mm for the inlet valves. Start with the valves on piston 1 (far left) and rotate the engine with the spanner clockwise until the top of the egg on the cam is opposite the shim beneath it. Take your feeler gauges and slide in a gauge until you find one that is a firm, smooth, sliding fit without forcing. Once you have the size of the gap measured,

Crank nut on the right to turn the engine over.

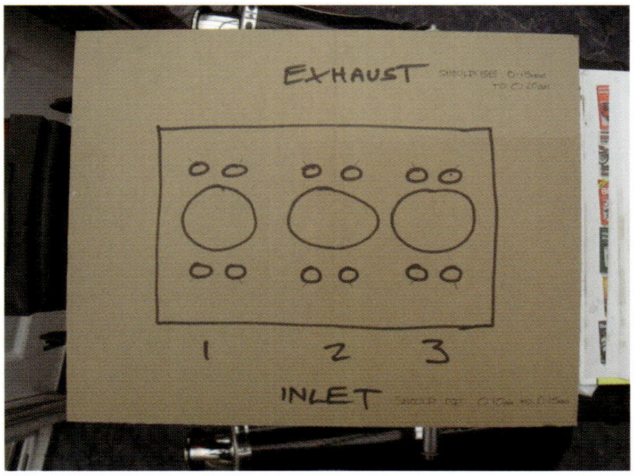

Chart for recording shim values.

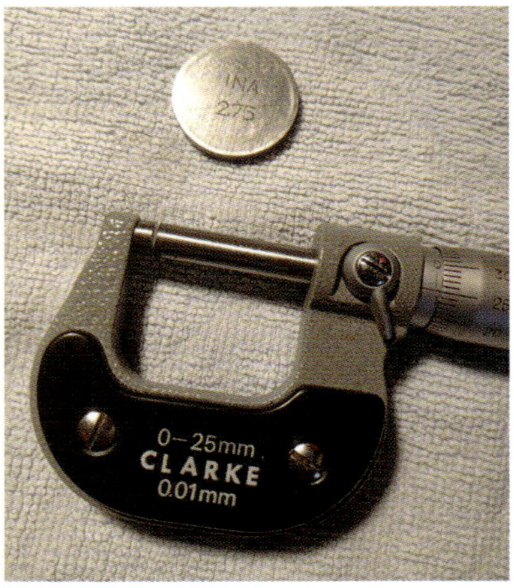

A shim and micrometer.

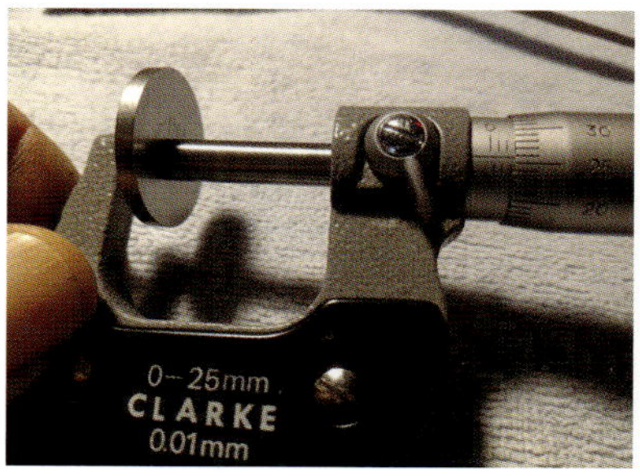

Measuring a shim.

Cam chain tensioner removed.

note it on your valve chart and move onto the next. Rotate the engine until the cam is pointing upwards and repeat.

The shims should be marked with the sizes but you may find shims with no markings, so always check with a micrometer.

When you have finished, note all the valves that are not within spec on your chart. On mine I had five that were not all right – two exhaust and three inlet valves, so in this instance both cams would have to come off.

11. To do this, rotate the engine to a set point so that everything comes out and goes back in the same place in the engine's cycle. Two points of reference are marked, one on the ignition rotor and one on the camshaft sprockets.

    As you can see the T1 mark has to line up with the centre of the pickup, then you have to have the two arrows on the camshaft sprockets pointing towards each other and level with the top of the engine.

12. Now remove the cam chain tensioner. First loosen the 19mm nut on the end, or remove it all together – but if you do, watch out for the spring within trying to make its escape. Remove the two mounting bolts and bring the tensioner out completely. Press the catch in – you'll find if you push the end of the plunger a little, the catch for the ratchet will be easier to press – and retract the plunger all the way back into the body of the tensioner ready to go back in later.
13. Remove the four Torx screws from the upper cam chain guide (it sits between the two cam chain sprockets) and lift it off. Now the cam chain is not being held in place and, if the cam chain guide has not released the tension on the chain (it may stick a bit), it may suddenly go with a bang and a clatter as the cam chain jumps off the sprockets and the guide leaps forwards in the cam chain tunnel.
14. With the tensioner off and top guide off, you can see the top run of the chain sagging, as it is no longer under tension. Now you can give the camshaft caps a little closer inspection. You'll see numbers scribed into the top of each of them and 'A B' on the top of the ones by the cam sprockets; make a note as to what goes where and which way round.
15. Now, working on the inlet cam, start to loosen the cap retaining bolts in a criss-cross pattern the same as before. Remove the caps and bolts, watching out for the dowels that sit inserted between the caps and the cylinder head; put them in a safe place. Remember the camshaft caps must go back in the same place, so it is essential that they are numbered and also clearly identified as inlet and exhaust caps.
16. Slip the cam chain off the cam sprocket and carefully remove the camshaft. Do the same for the exhaust cam, but be aware that you will need to have a piece of wood handy to rest under the chain, to stop it falling down the cam chain tunnel.

    The cams can be identified by a groove at the centre for the inlet cam.

16. You can now gain access to the shims that need changing, which you will need to measure in order

Timing marks, arrows on the gear wheels.

Block of wood under the cam chain after cam removal.

Cam cap removed, showing the camshaft ready for lifting out; the inlet cam is on the left, with the groove.

to ascertain what thickness has to go back in to give the correct gap. To get the shims out, I used a telescopic magnetic pickup tool and a metal toothpick. First I used the magnet to stick to the shim and tried to lever the shim away with the toothpick, but in the end I found it easier to lift the shim and the bucket it sits in out completely, which allowed me to get to work on it with more room.

There are two cutouts at the top of the bucket and this is where you can gain access to get the shim out. Be firm but careful. Only work on one shim at a time so you do not confuse where things came from. Now measure the offending shim with the micrometer; the one shown here measured 2.56mm.

17. Make a note of the thickness and pop the shim back into the bucket it came from (after oiling the bucket), and repeat this for all the out-of-spec shims. You will now have all the information you need to work out what thickness shim will need to be fitted to rectify the gap to within spec. The Triumph and the Haynes manual both have a table where you can look up measured gap against measured shim: where the two intersect is the thickness of the shim that should be fitted. Alternatively, you can work it out:

- For gaps that are too small, the difference in the measured gap to the gap required **minus** the measured shim thickness equals the shim required.
- For gaps that are too large (unlikely), the difference in the measured gap to the gap required **plus** the measured shim thickness equals the shim required.

At this point, I ended up having a bit of a run-around as my Triumph dealer gave me the wrong thickness shims (note to self: take micrometer and double-check everything before leaving the shop!). After a bit of internet research, I discovered the 25mm shims that are fitted to the early Triumph triples and fours also fit the Yamaha FJ1100/1200, XJ600 and V-Max, XT350 and so on, plus nearly all the early Honda CB Range – 750, 900, 1000. This opened up a way I could get some, and, after a call to my local bike shop, I could pop round with my micrometer and buy some shims to fit.

18. Fit the new shims, making sure they are seated flush, and give all the shims and bearing surfaces a good squirt of oil.
19. Check the T1 mark on the ignition rotor is still aligned with the pick-up and then slip the exhaust camshaft back in (you can tell it's the exhaust cam because it doesn't have a groove in the centre, whereas the inlet cam does).

Cylinder head showing shims and buckets.

Using a pick to get shims out (camshaft removed).

Cams removed.

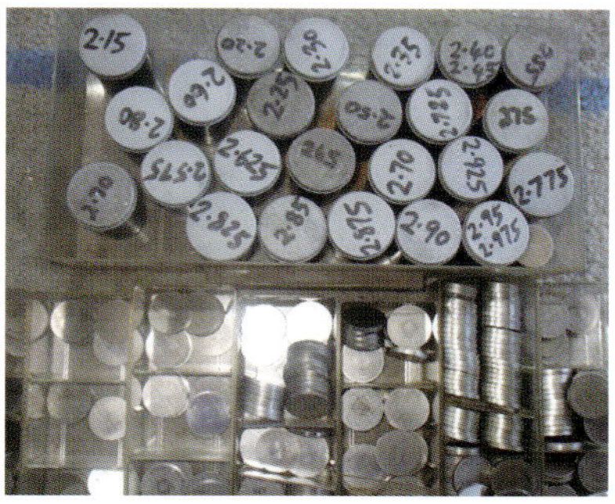

A set of shims all numbered up.

20. Hook the cam chain over the sprocket, losing the piece of wood at the same time. The chain needs to be taut between the crankshaft sprocket and the exhaust cam shaft sprocket, with the arrow on the sprocket facing inwards level with the head, as before. Place the inlet camshaft in and position it with the arrow facing inwards and the chain hooked on the sprocket with no slack.
21. Insert the cam chain tensioner back into the head and tighten up the two mounting bolts to 9Nm. Squirt a little more oil on the camshaft journals before the cam caps go back on, then put them on one shaft at a time in the right order, and tighten them in a criss-cross pattern as before, down to 10Nm. I couldn't fit the torque wrench on the closest bolt under the frame on the inlet cam cab bolt so I had to guess it.
22. Put the cam chain tensioner spring and bolt back into the tensioner body and wind the bolt in – you will hear the tensioner click into place – then tighten the bolt up to 23Nm. Place the cam chain upper guide back and tighten the four bolts down to 12Nm. Double-check everything as you go!

   This procedure took me a few attempts, as things moved, fell off and generally misbehaved, but perseverance won through in the end.
23. Once the cams are reinstalled, recheck your clearances just to be sure your calculations have given you the correct gap. Wind the engine over by hand a few times to see that everything is all right and you are happy with how it's all set. Double-check the timing marks are correct. Replace the crankshaft end cover back with a new gasket and tighten the bolts up to 9Nm.
24. Now is a good time to put your spark plugs back in; torque them up to 18Nm.
25. Clean the silicone sealant off the head, the cam cover and gasket. I scraped and picked and wiped it down with solvent until all trace had gone. Brake cleaner is good for the final clean-up, but spray it on a rag first.
26. You need to stick the rubber gasket back onto the cam cover. Use the sealant very sparingly, on the outside edge of all the surfaces to be stuck, then press it all home. It needs to go on the half-moon cut-outs and round to the corners on the head at each end; apply it to only half the width of the surface towards the outside edge. This stuff will get everywhere unless you are careful with it!
27. Slide the cover back into place, going in at an angle to help avoid the cams catching on the half-moon projections on the gasket – it is a tight fit. Torque down the cam cover bolts in a criss-cross fashion to 10Nm.
28. Fit the tank and bodywork back on and start the engine.

Using a Valve Shim Tool

The option of using the Triumph tool (or an aftermarket replacement) is as follows.

Gordon Smith kindly allowed me to use his notes and photographs for a shim check using a valve shim tool. The aftermarket tool was £58 from Square-deals (UK) when bought in 2011.

Always measure the valve clearance twice before deciding on what action to take. If you have done this operation many times, you must always record the clearances (results), together with the shim value (thickness) fitted and

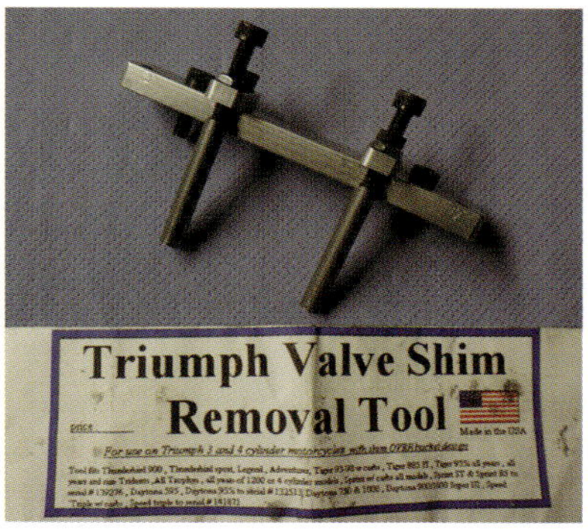

Aftermarket shim tool.

Using feeler gauges.

Using feeler gauges.

retain these records so you can refer back and see what has happened since the last time the shims were checked.

Be aware that if you use the Triumph tool (or a copy), a full 360-degree rotation of the engine and camshaft is not possible. The engine must be turned such that the camshaft lobes turn within the available space allowed by the tool. This means the camshaft lobe is approximately vertical. Severe tool and camshaft damage will result if the camshaft comes into contact with the tool.

Checking valve clearances against values recorded at 40,000 miles (64,000km), I found two inlet shims – on #2 cylinder, which just happen to be the most awkward to get at – just over the top limit of 0.15mm. Using the shim tool to depress the two buckets in turn, I removed the shims and they were 2.700mm. Previous records showed that I'd replaced these last time because the clearance on these two valves was just on the bottom limit of 0.10mm and I'd rather they were too wide than too narrow.

The steps for this operation are as follows:

1. Mount the valve compression tool across two convenient cam caps, being careful not to cross-thread the attachment Allen bolts and only doing them up finger-tight; I have an O-ring on each bolt on the underside of the bar to prevent them from being over-tightened.
2. With the bar in place, loosely attach one of the compression fingers (CFs) adjacent to the bucket you need to depress. Rotate the bucket until the 'notch' in the bucket is in plain view and will not be obscured by the CF.
3. Position the CF on the bucket lip (not on the shim) and carefully screw down the compression screw – a 5mm Allen key in this instance.

   The CFs are adjustable for length and locked in position by a thin 10mm nut. Once adjusted for length, the CFs can be left until such time as their tips become worn; then simply rotate them to give a better grip on the bucket rim.

   You should only tighten down the compression screw slowly. If you try to go too quickly, the CFs will slip off with a loud 'snap' as the bucket springs back upwards. I always hold the CFs in place with my other hand until the compression screw has completely depressed the bucket.
4. Once the bucket has been depressed about 4mm, insert a thin, flat watchmaker's screwdriver blade into the bucket notch to gently prise the shim upwards. When the shim is free, use a pair of tweezers or very slim needle-nose pliers to withdraw the shim carefully (inwards, normally).
5. Check the shim thickness using a metric micrometer; you can use a digital vernier but unless it is a really good one, the measurement obtained can be variable.
6. Source replacement shims. I make use of the full list of shims available from Triumph for the T300 Series. Both the Triumph service manual and the Haynes workshop manual #2162 only list twenty-five shims in 0.05mm steps. In actual fact, there are a further twenty-four shims in 0.025mm steps available from Triumph. Using only the 0.05mm shims, I find the valve clearance will invariably be too close to either the top or bottom limit. This is probably fine for most people but could lead to there being too big a difference in clearance between adjacent valves and/or cylinders. I prefer to use the 'half sizes' where I can so that all the clearances are nearer to the mid-point; using the 0.05mm shims, I can usually get the difference between adjacent valves/cylinders to be no more than 0.02mm across the head. I've done this with all my T300s and they run very well like this.

   In this case, I ordered a pair of the 'half-size' shims at 2.725mm from my local Triumph dealer.
7. Having selected the correct re-

Aftermarket shim tool in place.

Pressing down the bucket.

Pressing down to release the shim.

Pulling out the shim with tweezers.

Lifting up a shim with a small screwdriver.

Levering up the shim.

placement, shim fitting is the reverse of removal, although you have to wipe the shim with some fresh engine oil and gently lever it down into the bucket until it lies flat – it takes practice to get this right – but if it isn't flat there will be another 'snap' as you gently undo the compression screw, or when you turn the crankshaft forwards and the cam lobe presses on to the shim you've just replaced and pushes it fully home.

8. Repeat the clearance check. If all is good, then move on the next shim to be replaced. The CFs must be removed before turning the crankshaft but the CT bar can be left in place temporarily (definitely remove it before refitting).
9. The rest is a repeat of the previous section.

If you don't feel confident checking the shims, then have a look at the half-hour YouTube video by Terry Cox, which shows you how he did the job. The video is called 'Using the Hinckley Triumph Valve Shim Tool', and he uses it on a Daytona 1200.

Lifting out the shim with tweezers.

Shim levered up.

BRAKE AND CLUTCH CYLINDERS

Brake Master Cylinder Overhaul

The brake master cylinder is no longer available from Triumph as a complete assembly so an overhaul kit will be required.

It will be easier to overhaul the master cylinder by removing it from the bike, which will also avoid brake fluid finding its way onto the bike. The brake fluid will therefore need to be drained off. The next steps are as below:

1. Once the master cylinder is on the bench, the first issue is removing the circlip holding the piston assembly into the body. Before attempting to remove it, spray in some penetrating fluid (not WD40) and then ensure that the circlip is free by using a scriber or pick to move it round before trying to remove it. I found that, as well as the circlip pliers, I needed a separate small screwdriver to help lever out the circlip. Take the pressure off the circlip by pressing on the piston.
2. Once the spring and piston assembly has been removed, clean out the body using tissues and then wash out with water (brake fluid is hygroscopic) and dry out. If there is some surface corrosion around where the lever pivots, use a Dremel or other small drill and a small brass wire brush (brass is less aggressive than steel) to clean off the corrosion and polish up the aluminium. If you are going to repaint the master cylinder now is the time to do it.
3. Check the assembly of the parts that have been removed and check the packet of the overhaul kit.
4. When reassembly commences, use some red rubber grease on the seals before refitting. Don't forget to check the small vent hole at the bottom of the master cylinder – if this is blocked, it can affect the performance of the brakes. Use a piece of brass wire to ensure that is clear. Also clean the groove in the underside of the reservoir cover.
5. Before refitting the master cylin-

A pick being used to help get the old circlip out of the brake master cylinder.

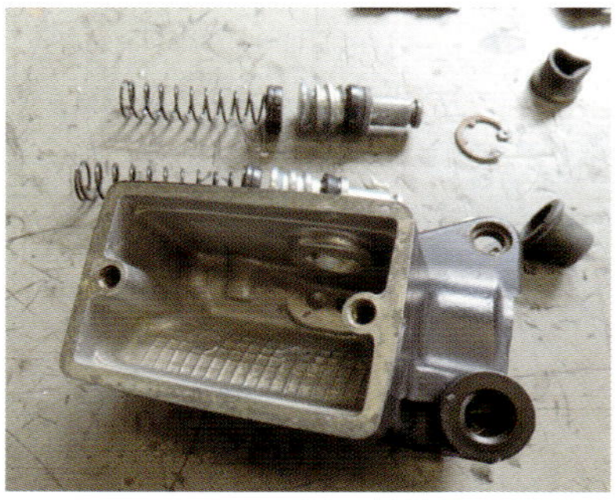

Brake master cylinder.

Brake master cylinder cleaned out.

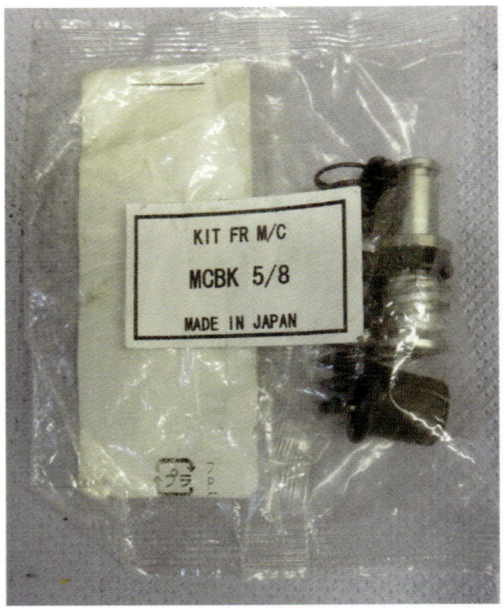

Nissin overhaul kit for the brake master cylinder.

Brake master cylinder pistons, old (top) and new (bottom).

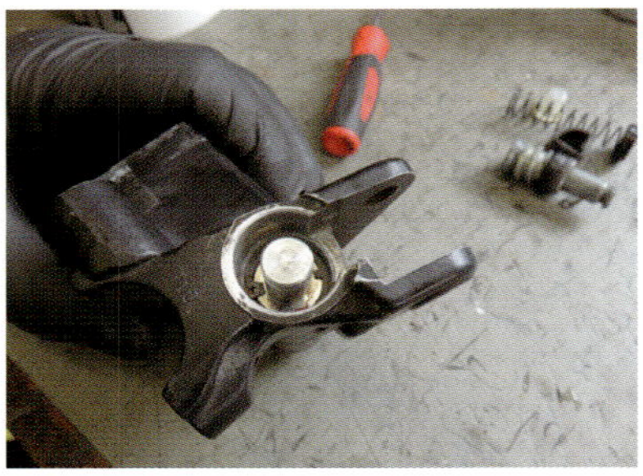

Brake master cylinder with new piston and circlip installed.

Brake master cylinder showing the small vent hole at middle left – this must be cleaned out.

Brake master cylinder overhaul completed.

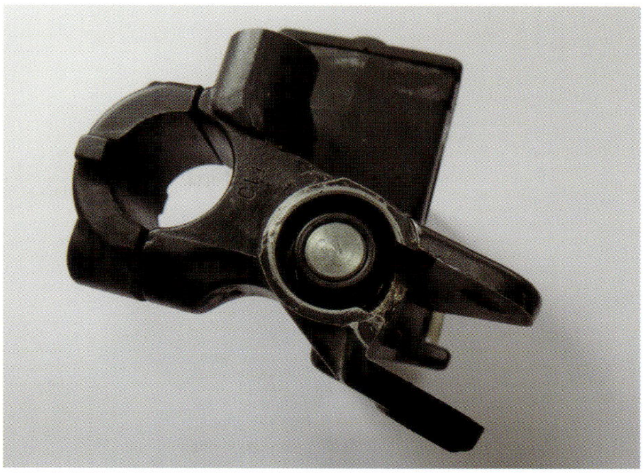

Inserting a new circlip in the brake master cylinder.

der, check the brake hose splitter that sits on the front of the forks by removing it, as this can be full of brake fluid crud, reducing brake performance.

6. Fitting the overhaul kit is the reverse of disassembly, but getting the circlip back in can be a challenge. Check that the circlip has seated properly before proceeding any further and reinstalling the master cylinder.

Clutch master cylinder before cleaning.

Clutch Master Cylinder Overhaul

The clutch master cylinder is no longer available so, as with the brake master cylinder, an overhaul kit will have to be used. Again, open up the overhaul kit and check the parts. The picture overleaf shows all the parts you'll need to rebuild the master cylinder. As with the brake master cylinder, it is best to remove the clutch master cylinder from the bike.

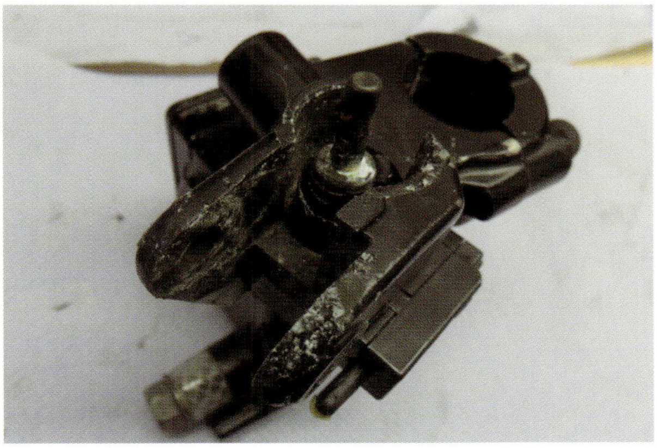

Clutch master cylinder before overhaul.

1. First things first: drain out the fluid so you can pull the master cylinder apart. Put a short section of silicone tubing on the bleed nipple on the slave cylinder, crack the bleed screw and let the fluid start to drain out of the system. I open up the top of the master cylinder so I can watch the fluid drain out and make sure it is empty before removing it.
2. Once the clutch lever is out of the way, remove the dust boot. When I did this, I noticed another problem. The dust boot is supposed to be attached to the clutch pushrod and it was torn – not a major problem, but it did underscore that the master cylinder probably did need a rebuild.
3. Once the master cylinder is removed from the handlebars, you can tackle the circlip removal, which can be a pain! I would always start with some penetrating fluid

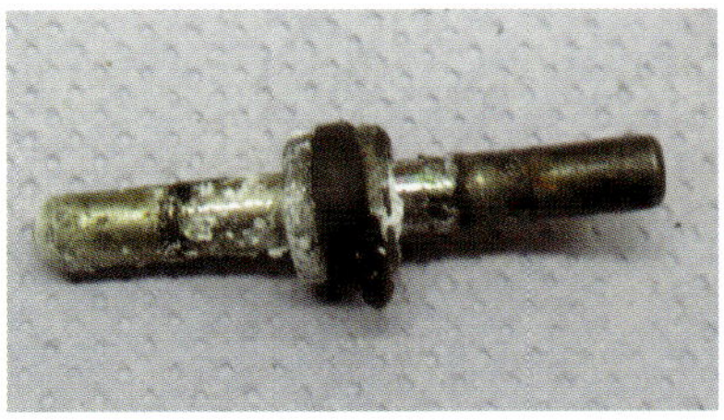

Clutch master cylinder plunger.

Pulling out old piston on the clutch master cylinder.

Clutch master cylinder: old piston and seals (top) and new (bottom).

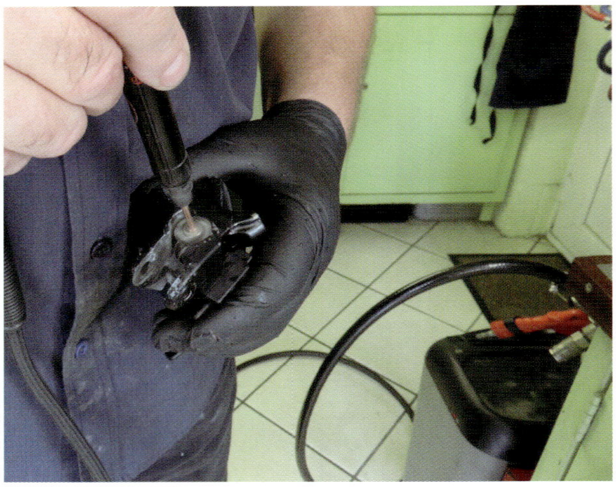

Cleaning corrosion off the clutch master cylinder using a small wire brush in a drill.

and use a small pick to ensure that the circlip can move before trying to remove it. It's a bit fiddly, but it's easier to remove the circlip if you take a small screwdriver and press inward on the piston, which releases pressure on the circlip.

4. Once the circlip is out, the guts of the master cylinder come out easily. The only parts inside behind the circlip are the washer, piston with integral seal and spring with seal. Next out of the master cylinder is the spring and rear seal.
5. With everything out, it's time to clean out the bore of the cylinder. Spray everything down with brake cleaner and blow it dry with compressed air, or wash out with warm water and then dry out. The master cylinder is now clean and ready to accept the new parts.
6. First thing in is the rear spring and seal (lubricated with fresh DOT 4 or red rubber grease), followed by the piston with front seal (lubricated as well).
7. Then comes the fiddly part of the washer, circlip and compressing the piston in to seat the circlip in its groove. You should manage to seat the clip after a few minutes' effort. You might want to use a pointed object, such as a pick, to see if you can rotate the circlip once it's installed. This will confirm that the circlip is properly seated.
8. Next, install the master cylinder pushrod and dust boot. Lubricate the dust boot first with silicone grease to help keep it supple. Then apply some molybdenum paste to the end of the pushrod where it will fit into the piston cup to combat friction through its lifetime; since it's on the dry side of the piston, there are no issues with contamination.
9. Once everything's fitted, simply remount the master cylinder to the handlebars and reinstall the banjo bolts.

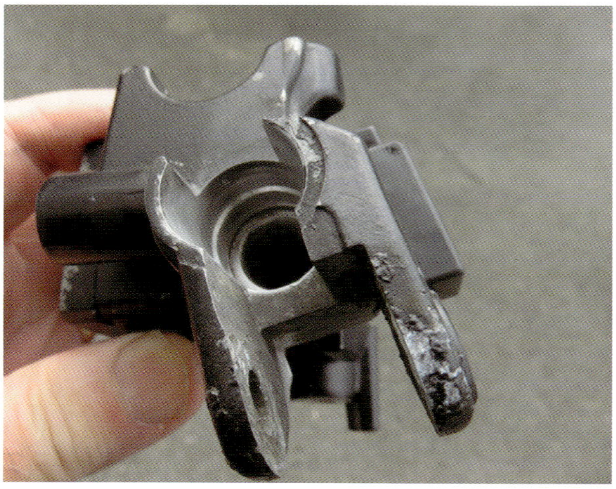

Clutch master cylinder after cleaning.

The clutch master cylinder circlip goes in.

The factory service manual recommends you replace the crush washers on the banjo bolts every time to guarantee you will have a leak-free seal. If you look at the crush washer you can see why: it's hard and inflexible and often appears crushed.

However, if you want to reuse it, you can try this remedy. With a propane torch, heat the washer to red hot. This will soften the copper and return it to its flexible state, which is exactly what you need to have for a proper seal. If you have grooves on the washer, you should file these flat with a sharp mill file. In the picture here, you can see the

Don't forget the washer when rebuilding the clutch master cylinder.

Ready for the plunger.

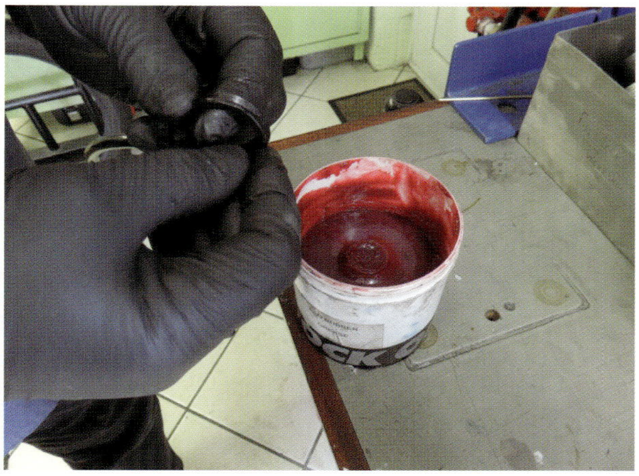

Use some red rubber grease for lubrication.

Clutch lever and brass nipple; this also needs a little grease.

circular area that is slightly raised, and this is the area that needs to be filed flat.

After the heat treatment, let the washer cool and scuff it lightly with a Scotch-Brite pad and you're good to go. You can do this heat treatment and filing several times before the washer finally becomes too thin to reuse.

If you find severe wear of the brass bushing in the clutch lever handle, it will be because lack of maintenance inspections and lack of lubrication have caused the master cylinder push-rod to eat through the bushing and into the clutch lever. Of course, regular inspection and lubrication would prevent this, but molybdenum paste will help tide things over between extended service intervals.

The finished clutch master cylinder.

Clutch Slave Cylinder

If the master cylinder was in dire need of rebuilding, the slave cylinder is also likely to require attention; the choice is then between a replacement slave cylinder (at around £60) or a new seal kit at around £40. The service kit is the same as for the 2012–18 Triumph Trophy if you have problems getting hold of one.

The slave cylinder comes off easily by removing the banjo bolt and the three bolts that secure the slave to the engine. Keep in mind that the bolt facing the rear of the bike on the slave is the short bolt and needs to go back in the same place once you're done.

There's nothing fancy going on with the rebuild kit, as you can see in the picture showing the old and new parts.

When I removed the slave cylinder piston, I found a large amount of jelly-like contamination in the cylinder bore behind the piston.

This is not to be confused with the regular grease on the face of the piston that lubricates the clutch pushrod. It is noteworthy that before I tackled

Clutch slave cylinder.

Clutch slave cylinder removal. Note the different-length bolts; ensure the short one goes towards the rear of the bike.

Clutch slave cylinder before cleaning.

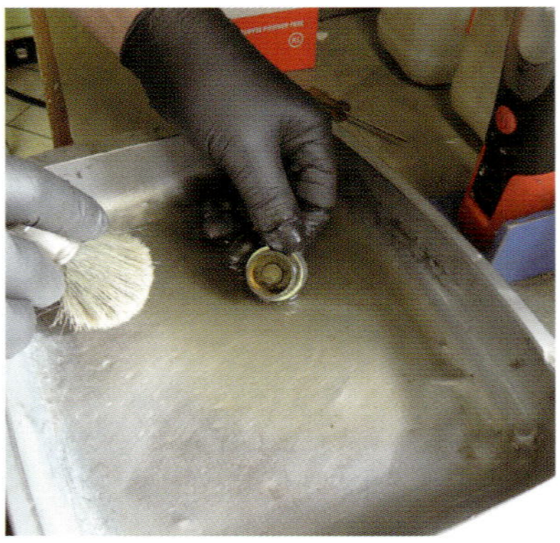

Cleaning out the slave cylinder.

Cleaned out and ready for new parts.

Old piston and spring.

New parts ready for installation.

Ready for installation. Note the new washers, banjo bolt, bleed screw and rubber cover.

this rebuild, I had completely flushed the system thoroughly until the fluid was clean. This apparently was not sufficient to remove the jelly-like contamination inside the slave cylinder. What did the trick, however, was cleaning with brake cleaner or hot water.

Again, clean up any surface corrosion with a Dremel and a small wire brush and repaint if necessary.

Rebuilding the slave is about as easy as it gets. Lubricate up the piston and seal with DOT 4 or red rubber grease and install the spring on the rear of the piston. Insert the piston into the bore and compress, confirming smooth action through the piston.

Finish off the slave rebuild with molybdenum paste applied to the face of the piston to lubricate the clutch pushrod.

Once everything is completed, reinstall the slave on the engine, remembering to put the short bolt on the rear of the slave. I didn't forget to anneal the crush washers, so time to tighten the banjo bolt.

Refill the master cylinder with DOT 4 and bleed the system.

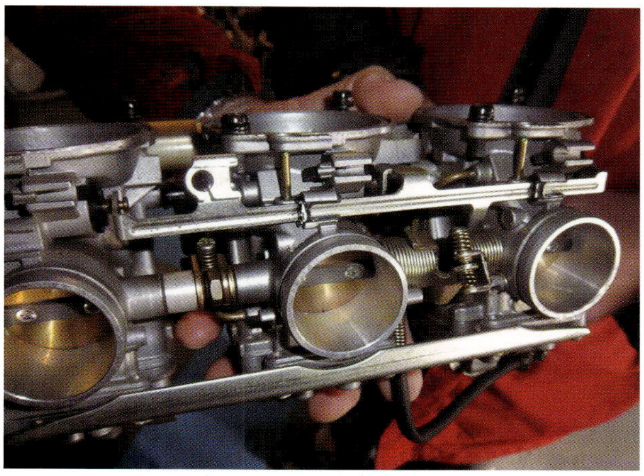

A set of three carburettors.

A float bowl removed from a carburettor.

The insides of a carburettor, full of muck and residue. I have seen much worse!

CARBURETTORS

The carburettors are now over twenty years old. They may have been subject to standing unused for extended periods, and the addition of ethanol to the petrol will have done them no favours either. If the bike's running and fuelling is problematic then the only recourse is to take the carburettors off the bike and give them a good overhaul. Check for wear and, if in doubt, replace parts such as the diaphragms (including springs), floats, O-rings, seals and float valves. The parts that wear include the needle jets (having grooves), slide guides and pilot jets stuck in the carburettor body. The most important thing is to clean out the pilot and needle jets thoroughly – just cleaning ultrasonically will not suffice here.

Some parts now are also resistant to ethanol so that is a worthwhile modification to make. Buy parts from a specialized carburettor company, such as Allens Performance. Rebuild with Viton seals to help resist modern fuel problems (ethanol). Float needles are normally Viton-tipped.

If you are going to strip the carburettors down then replace everything from a service kit, it's a false economy to do only part of the job. Lots of owners have reported that the bike does not run properly after a carburettor 'overhaul' because they did not do a thorough-enough job and ensured pilot jets and running jets were cleaned out. Low-speed running is dependent on the pilot jets, so they must be clean.

Popular opinion is that Keihin carburettors may be more economical but Mikunis are better for performance. This may be linked to more restrictive exhaust regulation being introduced as the T300 progressed.

Restricted inlet rubbers, presumably to give more bottom end, were used on the Thunderbird 900 for Mikuni carburettor models only (and can be changed to unrestricted versions fitted to other models). Keihin inlet rubbers were not restricted and remained the same on all models, even the carburettor Bonneville range. Inlet rubbers and airbox rubbers do not interchange between Mikuni and Keihin, so if you fit Keihins to a bike formally fitted with Mikunis then you will also need to fit the appropriate inlet and airbox rubbers.

Having taken the carburettors off the bike, dismantle them, keeping parts for each carburettor together. Remember that you will need JIS screwdrivers for this job.

The carburettor bodies can then be put into a ultrasonic cleaner; if you don't have one, find a local company who does and can do the job for you. The holes in the jets, particularly the ones in the pilot jet, will need cleaning out using a piece of copper wire, which is soft enough not to score or damage the brass jet (which could happen if you use steel wire). If the carburettors are only ultrasonically cleaned (and the jets left alone) and then put back on the bike, the running may be impaired.

As a general tip, if the new gaskets appear not to fit, let the carburettor bodies warm up!

The sequence below showing how to overhaul a dismantled Mikuni carburettor was provided by Gordon Smith.

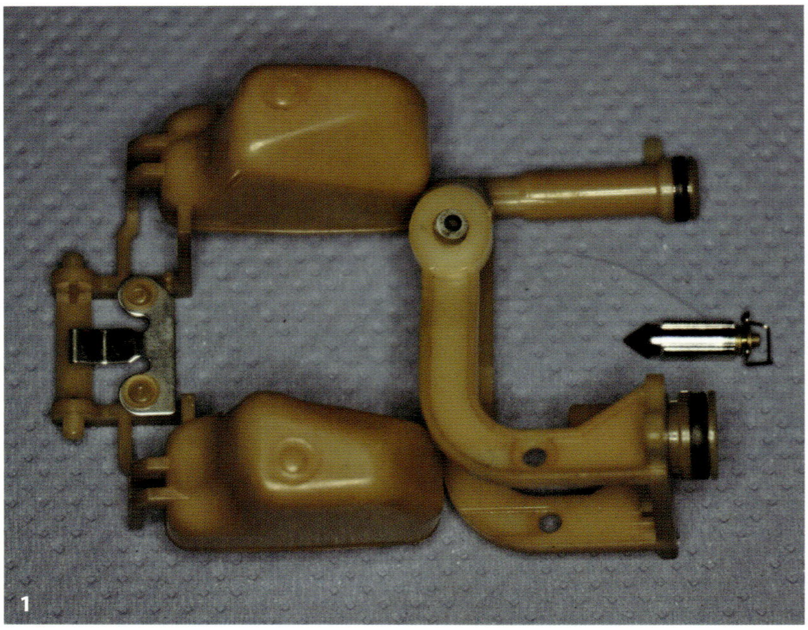

1

This shows a typical Mikuni float assembly. New ones are lovely and white, but with time and immersion in fuel they darken – some are almost walnut colour.

On the left is the metal tang that is used to adjust the float level. The O-rings often need replacing to ensure a snug fit, otherwise over-fuelling will result. The float needle on the right is a new one; the tips are Viton rubber, which is very good at resisting the ethanol in the fuel. Over time, the original float needle tips become worn or 'ridged', which can best be seen using a watchmaker's eyeglass. Note also the longitudinal vanes on the aluminium body. Like the rubber tips, these wear down and get 'stuck', leaving the float valve open. This is what can cause the air filter box and/or crankcase to fill with fuel. Hopefully the owner will smell the fuel or spot the puddle on the floor before starting the engine.

Near the centre is the fuel enrichment jet – these are press-fit into the plastic and can become blocked by contamination/debris. They can get blown out by over-enthusiastic use of a high-pressure air line and really mess with starting on choke.

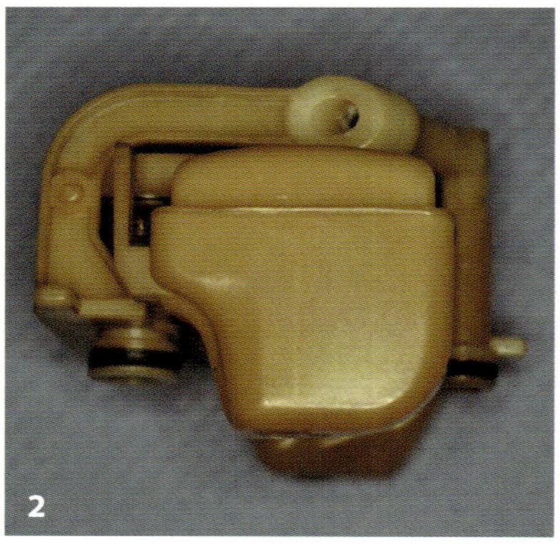

2

Float assembly correctly assembled.

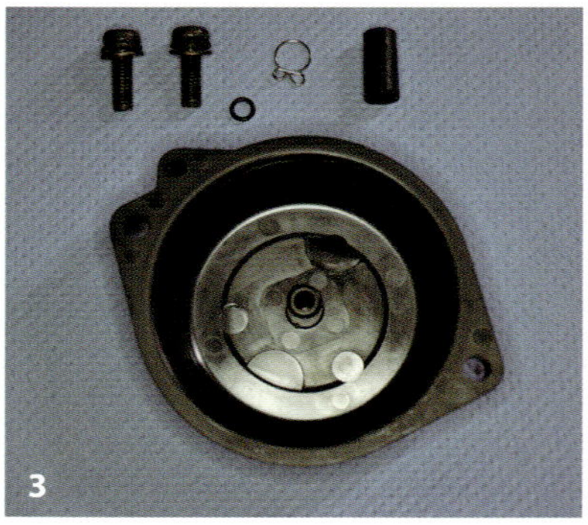

3

Mikuni carburettor top cover. Keihins have four screws securing them to the carburettor body. Shown from left to right here: two (original) JIS screws with spring and plain washers, vacuum spigot O-ring (important for sealing – it goes between the cover and the carburettor body), vacuum spigot cap spring clip and vacuum spigot cap – these can pop off at times or get dislodged, which will result in poor running at idle and small throttle openings.

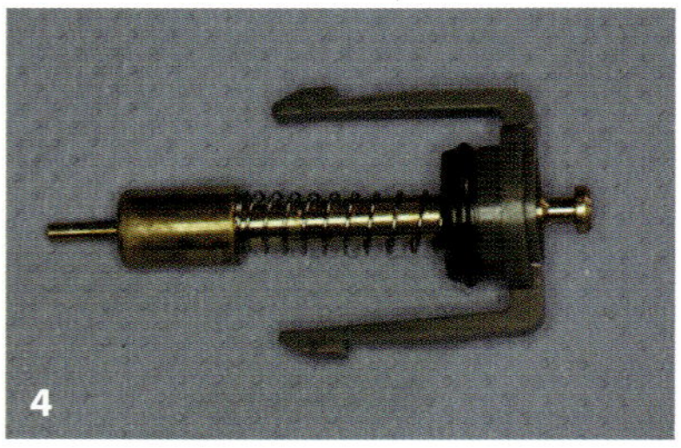

4

The choke plunger rarely gives trouble, though sometimes the actuator (sliding) bar can get bent or distorted and become disconnected from one or more plungers.

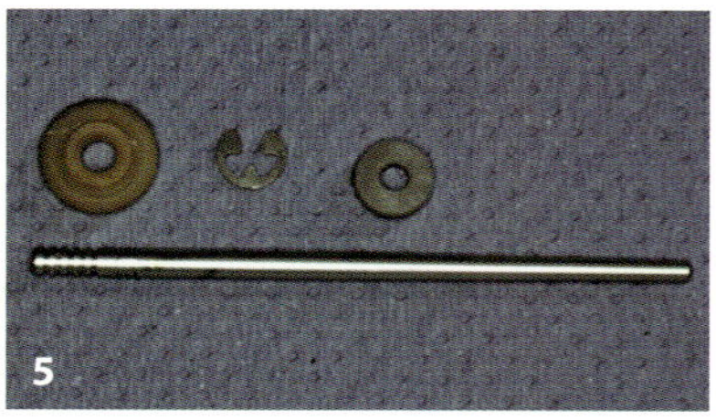

5

Typical needle assembly components: spring spacer, E clip – generally inserted in the middle slot – and needle spacer.

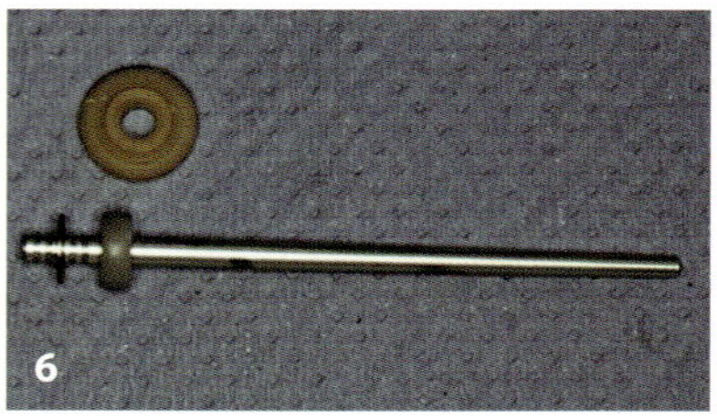

6

Put the needle spacer on first – it's a tight fit – then E clip in the middle slot and pressed home so that all three E Clip tangs are engaged correctly in the chosen slot.

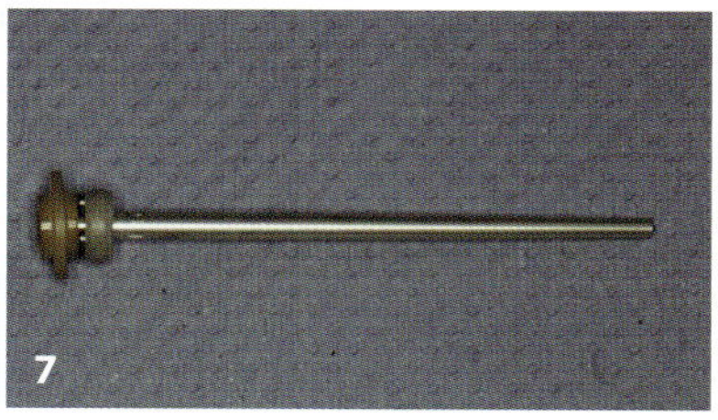

The needle spacer is pushed back to the E clip, and the spring spacer goes on top. It's often easier to leave the spring spacer off until the needle is correctly inserted into the piston.

This bottom view of the Mikuni piston highlights the two most common examples. On the left is the Trophy type, with the two large vent holes, and on the right is the Speed Triple/Daytona type with one tiny vent hole. Pistons with the larger vent holes give a much smoother throttle response; the smaller vent hole piston is slower to respond.

I recently sorted two sets of carburettor, one from a Daytona 1200 where the owner complained of a flat spot then surging around 4,000rpm, and one from a Speed Triple. I used the ST set on my 900 and found the throttle response to be truly awful (certainly not what I'm used to), but by retro-fitting a complete set of carburettor tops (pistons, diaphragms, needles and so on) from my 'Trodent' to the ST 'bodies', I found it transformed the throttle response. So, with the permission of the owner, I drilled his ST slides. Both the ST and Daytona owners were extremely happy with the results.

BELOW 9 AND 10: Mikuni diaphragm and piston. Diaphragms are very robust and, when new, extremely flexible. Worn or old ones are not very uniform or circular. Always replace it if it's torn, holed or distorted. A new one is easy to install with a light spray of silicone; slip it into the groove at the top of the piston and centralize.

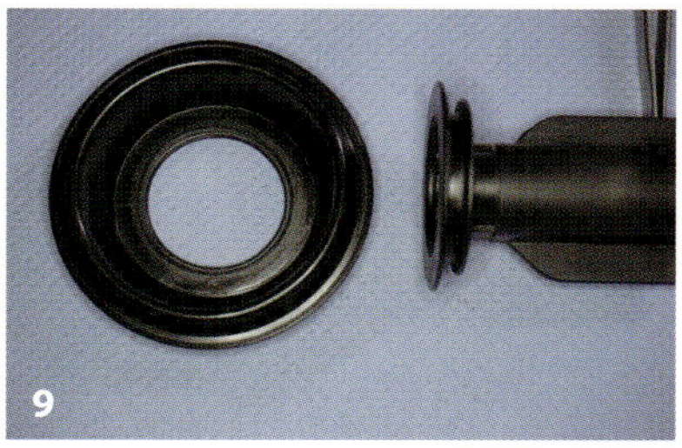

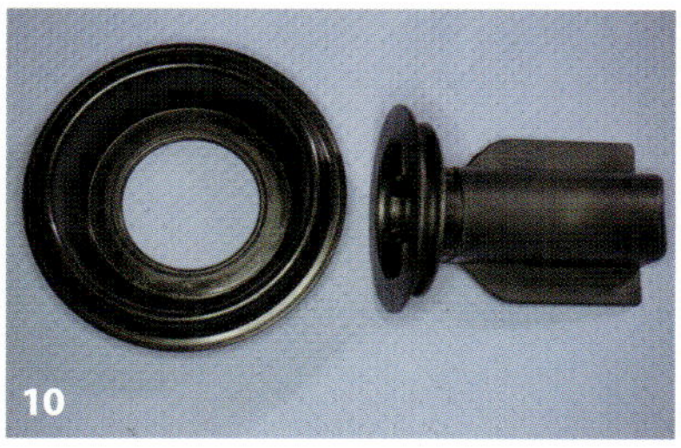

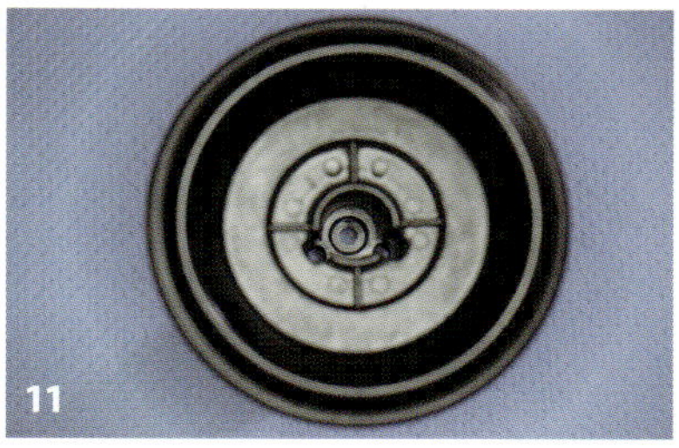

View of the Mikuni piston with the diaphragm correctly fitted. The central needle hole and the two vent holes are lower left and right.

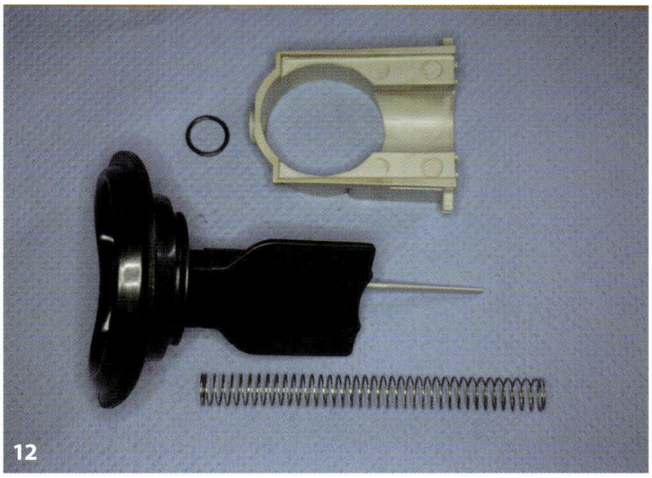

Piston guide O-ring (always replace if the guide is removed) and piston guide. Diaphragm fitted to piston with needle in place. Piston spring.

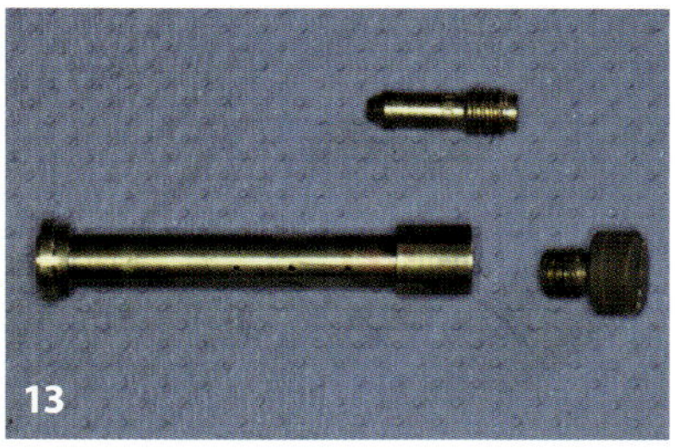

Pilot jet (top), needle jet, also known as the emulsifier tube (left) and main jet (right).

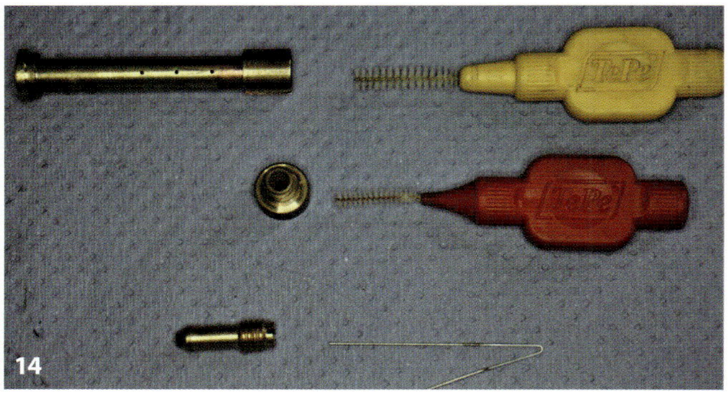

Here are the three important jets and my chosen cleaning tools (TePe dental brushes). The thin wire used for the pilot and other small jets and orifices is your standard DIY store wire brush (only use copper or brass, as steel is too harsh and will score a hole in the jet. The TePe brushes are used for main jets). With a new one I just pluck out one tuft of bristles to keep for cleaning/probing purposes. The ends are not always square cut, so check carefully; try to use only bristles with clean, square ends and very gently, in conjunction with carburettor cleaner and close visual examination (eyeglass or similar).

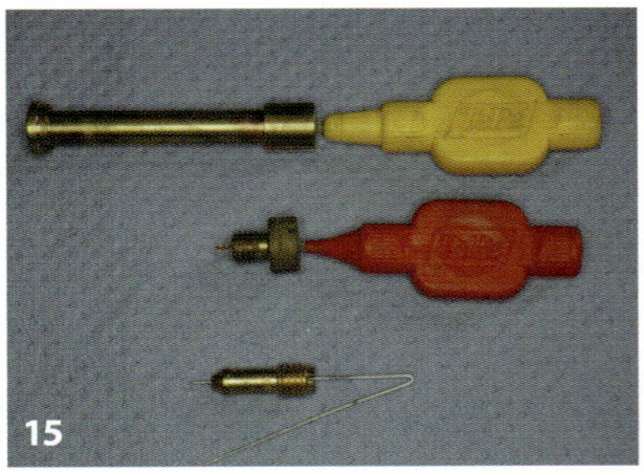

15

This shows the TePe dental brushes inserted into the jets. The brushes are normally used to clean the gaps between teeth and can be bought from any chemist or big supermarkets.

16

Bottom view of the Mikuni carburettor body. The main jet goes in the larger central hole (into the bottom end of the needle jet), and the pilot jet into the hole just to the right and up slightly from the main jet. The pilot/air screw goes into the middle (of three) threaded hole on the right (engine) side.

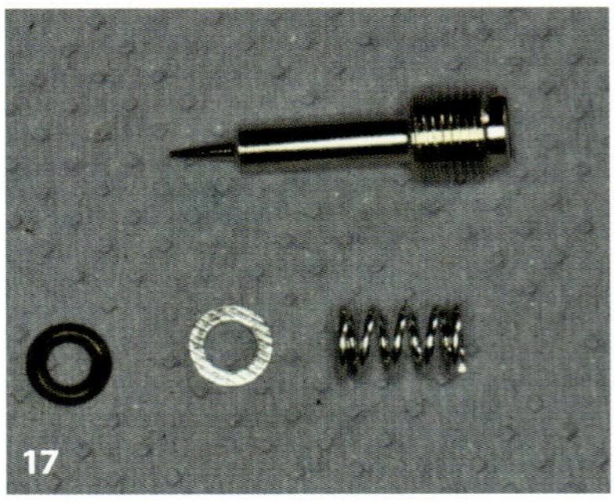

17

Mikuni pilot/air screw (new replacement). Screw slots are often worn and tips bent. The rubber O-ring should be flat and hard. Always replace it when cleaning out the carburettor – it gives a much better 'soft stop' when fully screwed in and a more accurate 'turns out' setting.

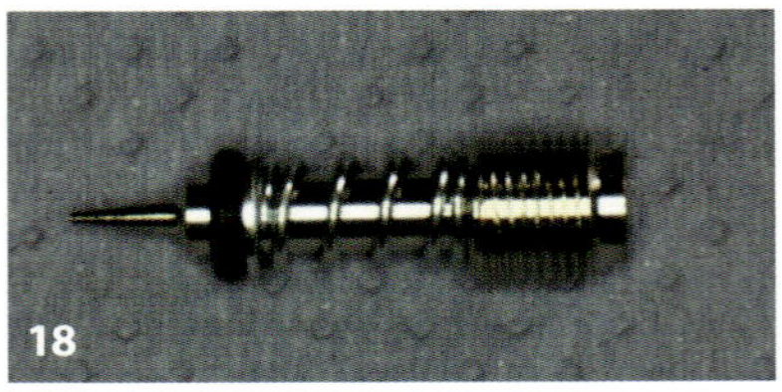

18

Pilot/air screw correctly assembled prior to fitting.

19

Pilot/air screw backed in squarely to the carburettor body to ensure correct thread engagement. Backing any screw/bolt into a thread should ensure correct engagement and so prevent a cross-threaded scenario.

20

Pilot/air screw screwed all the way down to a 'soft stop', so that the (fully compressed) spring can be felt to compress the new O-ring.

21

Pilot/air screw unscrewed two and a quarter turns out from the 'soft stop' – this is my preferred starting point, rather than the one and a half turns out mentioned in the Haynes and Triumph service manuals. It gives me the correct amount of throttle (rpm) decay with the minimum of hang-up. I have used this method for setting the carburettors on T300s for the last ten years and, together with my setting of the throttle (butterfly) valves by eye (using a bright light shone through the Venturi), means that the final carburettor synchronization requires only the smallest of adjustments using a set of Davida vacuum gauges.

Pilot jet backed in to engage the thread.

Thin wire probe inserted through the pilot jet (in situ).

Thin wire probe inserted into the cold start jet.

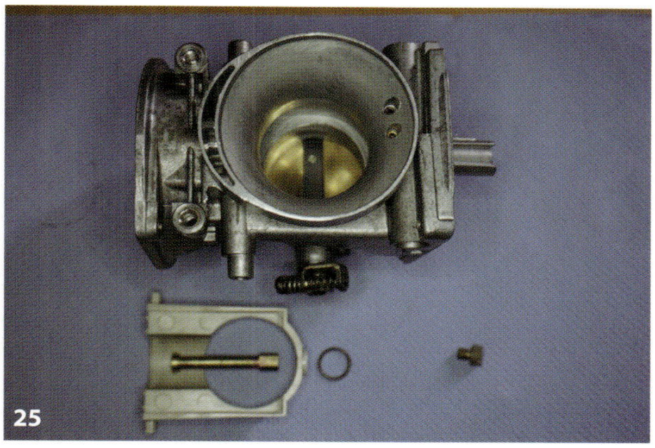

Mikuni carburettor body before fitting of the piston guide and O-ring, needle valve and main jet. On the right-hand side of the carburettor bell mouth the lower (central) orifice contains the main air jet; the offset one above is the pilot air jet.

The 'flat' on the bottom end of the needle jet. This locates with the small brass peg (just visible) inside the main jet orifice, locking the needle jet in position as the main jet is screwed home.

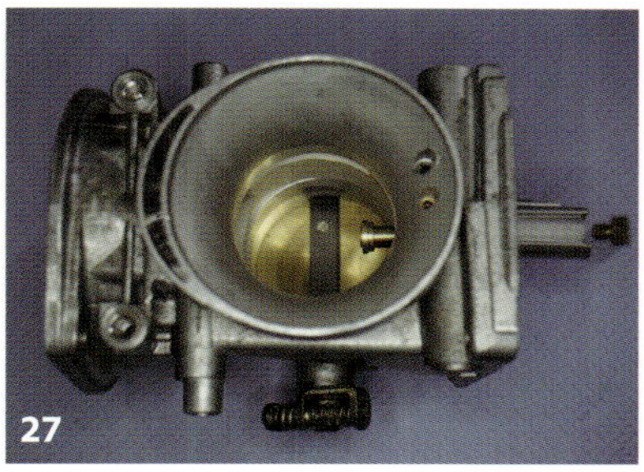

Here the piston guide and O-ring are pressed down and the needle jet is partially inserted. The main jet screws into the bottom of the needle jet once it is correctly located. I usually use a #7 knitting needle into the top of the needle jet to rotate and press it home before inserting the main jet.

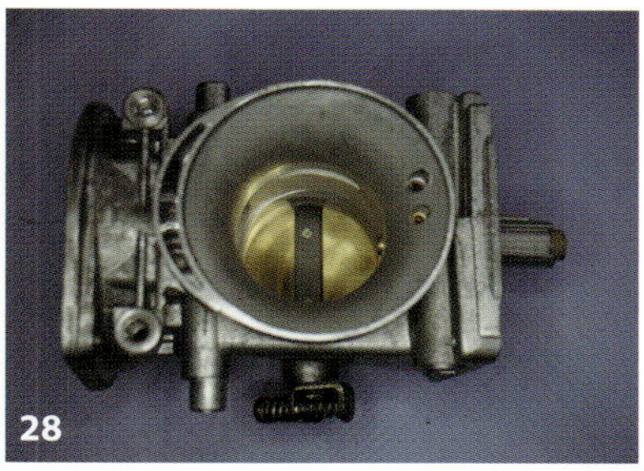

Piston guide, needle jet and main jet fitted. The guide sits flush with the Venturi, while the top of the needle jet sits slightly proud.

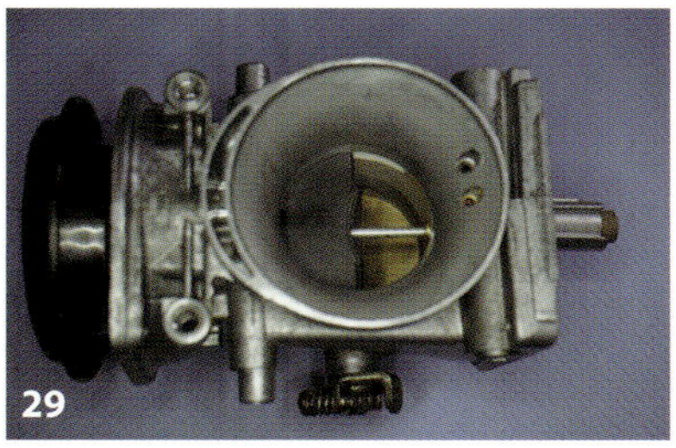

Diaphragm, piston and needle partially inserted; the needle goes into the needle jet.

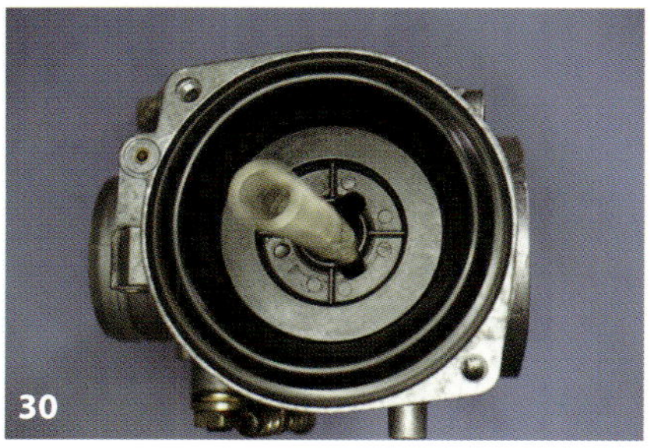

Top view of the Mikuni with the diaphragm outer rim correctly located in the groove in the carburettor body. The piston spring has been fitted but not the vacuum spigot O-ring (in 10 o'clock position).

31

This is the same view but with the vacuum spigot O-ring fitted (top left).

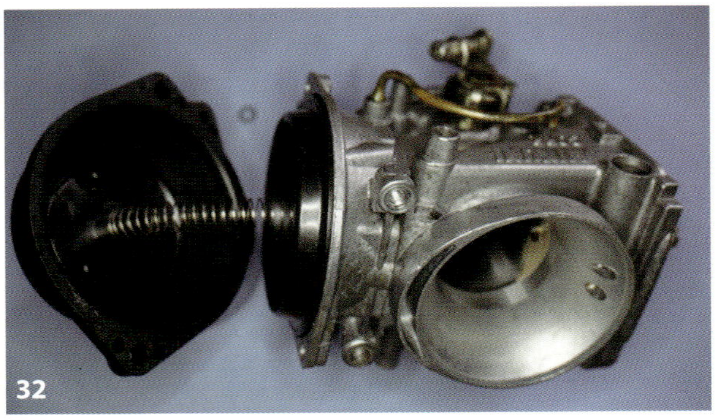
32

The piston spring located on to the underside of the carburettor top cover.

33

The Mikuni top cover fitted. Note the vacuum spigot cap and spring clip on the left. The cross-head screws on both Mikuni and Keihin carburettors (covers, float bowls and mounting strips) are JIS screws, so use JIS screwdrivers to avoid messing up the heads. I replace all JIS screws (apart from those for the top cover) with readily available stainless Allen-headed screws.

34

Mikuni float assembly fitted; with new O-rings it will be a press fit.

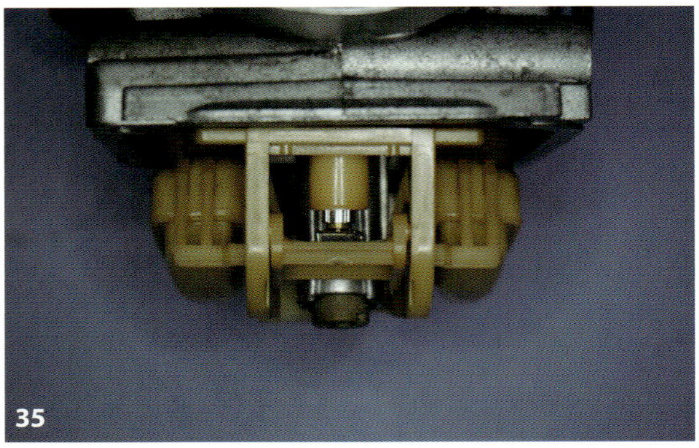
35

View of the Mikuni float assembly float valve; note the right-hand side of the float assembly is not yet properly home because I had no new O-rings available.

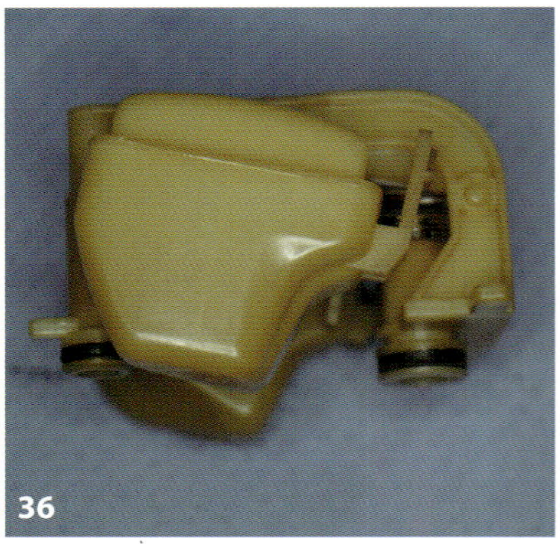
36

This shows the 'float level set too low' position.

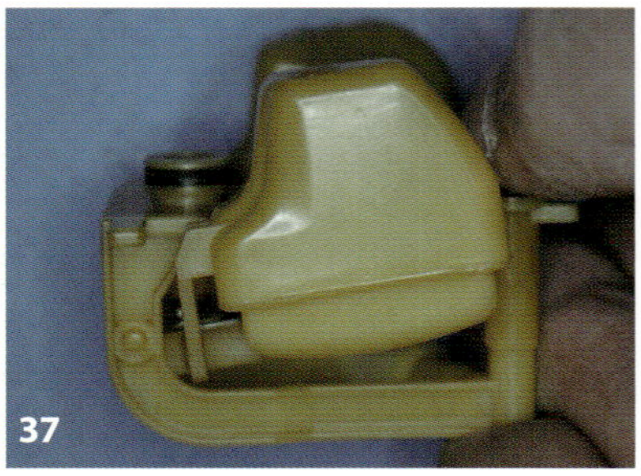
37

The 'float level too high' position.

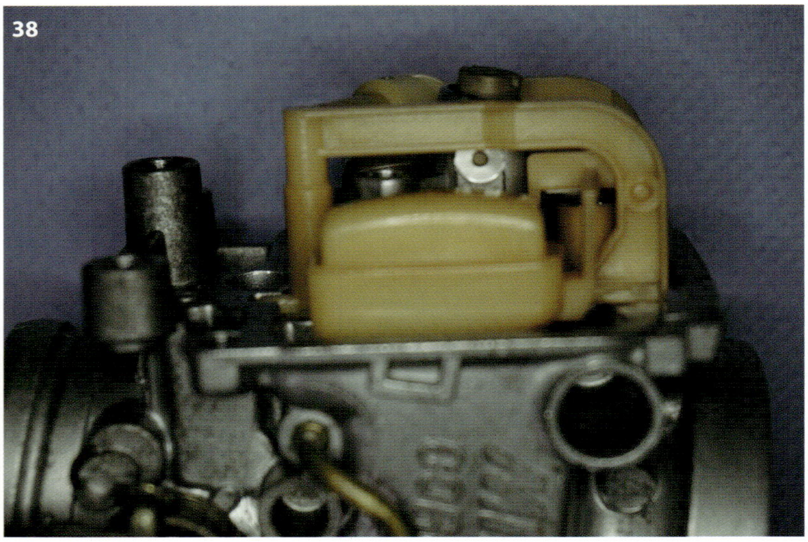
38

The correct float level position. The float 'seam' should be parallel to the float bowl/carburettor body gasket line – far easier than measuring 14.5mm across three or four carburettors held at 15 degrees.

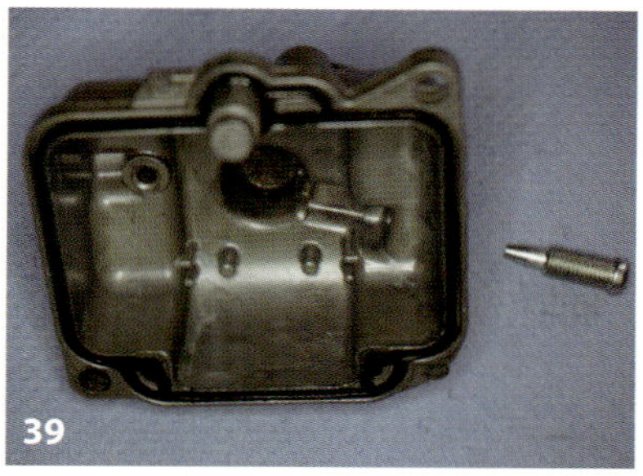

Mikuni float bowl, gasket and drain screw. I replace about 50 per cent of the float bowl gaskets I see, either because of cracking or severe indentation from the float assembly tabs.

One complete Mikuni carburettor.

Mikuni float bowl view; note the Allen-headed S/S screws to the float bowl replacing the JIS-headed screws.

Engine-side view of the Mikuni carburettor (choke plunger not fitted).

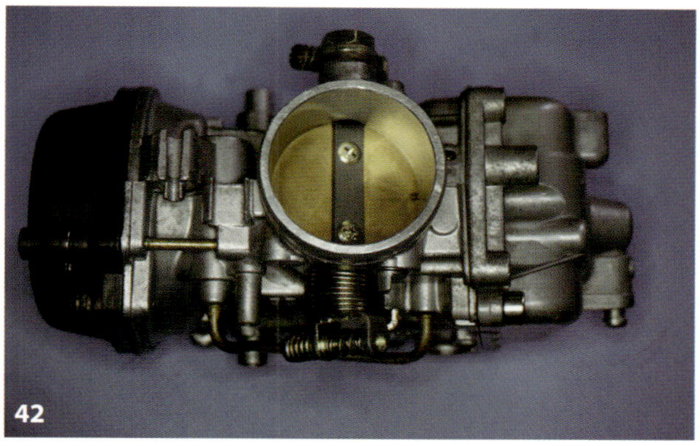

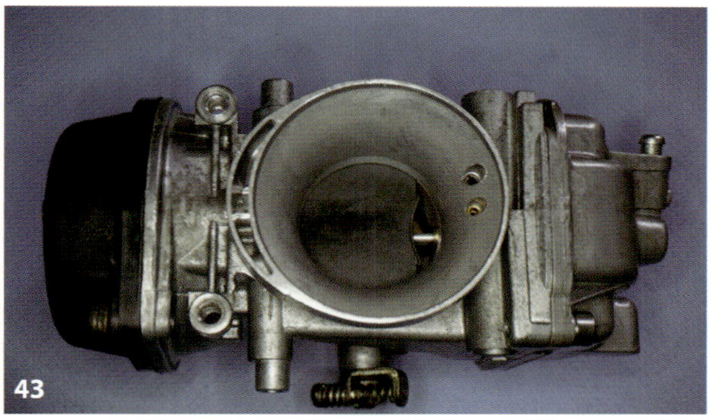

Air filter (intake)-side view of the Mikuni carburettor; the choke plunger has still not been fitted.

The choke plunger almost fitted.

BELOW: A completed and overhauled carburettor!

The choke plunger pressed home: two plastic prongs engage with the slots in the carburettor body.

Inlet rubber showing the small 'pip' at the top. The pip goes at the front towards the engine.

Carburettor to airbox rubbers.

Before putting the carburettors back onto the bike, check the condition of the rubbers connecting the carburettors to the cylinder head as these can crack and split with age, letting air into the mixture and resulting in poor running.

There are also rubbers that go between the airbox and carburettors, and these will also need checking for cracking.

After reinstalling the carburettors, make sure that the throttle cable has a smooth, uninterrupted run – do not be tempted to cable tie it to something else for neatness. If you have a separate mini fuel tank, you can check the running and throttle with that before putting on the tank.

The air filter as supplied by Triumph is sold as a complete airbox with a new filter inside. If the carburettors have been taken off and serviced then I would replace the air filter at the same time. There have been suggestions that other brands of replacement filter, such as K&N, have not been successful, but a Pipercross filter element seems to work.

If fitting an aftermarket exhaust, it will be worth putting the bike on a dynamometer to maximize power and torque. As an example, the suggested jetting for the Sebring system is as follows:

Pilot	40
Main	127 (could be 130)
Needle raise	20 thou (1 clip position)

You can buy rejetting kits from Dynojet, but in my experience putting the bike on a dynamometer is the only way to successfully rejet your carburettors. The Dynojet kits reputedly work well and improve throttle response, but when I took my Sprint Sports to John Wilcox (who helped Triumph develop the engines, as he had engine dynamometers just across the road from Triumph), he re-jetted the bike and handed me back the Dynojet kit unopened in its box! The throttle response was fabulous.

What not to do – Keihin carburettors

I have no personal experience of Keihin carburettors as the majority of models were fitted with Mikunis, but Paul Barnett (of Triumph Motorbike Spares, who rebuilds carburettors) recently had a set of Keihin carburettors in for overhaul. They had been 'meddled' with and had been fitted with Mikuni main jets, the pilot jets were damaged, the diaphragms were damaged, the needle and spring seats melted, the choke plunger seized and sealant used instead of the proper gaskets. The cost of replacing all the damaged parts and an overhaul kit was in the region of £200 (plus the £100 charge for a strip-down and overhaul) so the owner of the carburettors decided it was cheaper to replace with another set.

Paul took some photos of the strip-down to give an indication of the damage inside. The carburettors had been fitted with pod filters, and whoever rebuilt them 'guessed' at the main jet size and fitted 152.5 on all three, when the standard set up on a Keihin is 120 on cylinders 1 and 3 and 115 on cylinder 2. Even allowing for the pod filters, these were oversized to say the least.

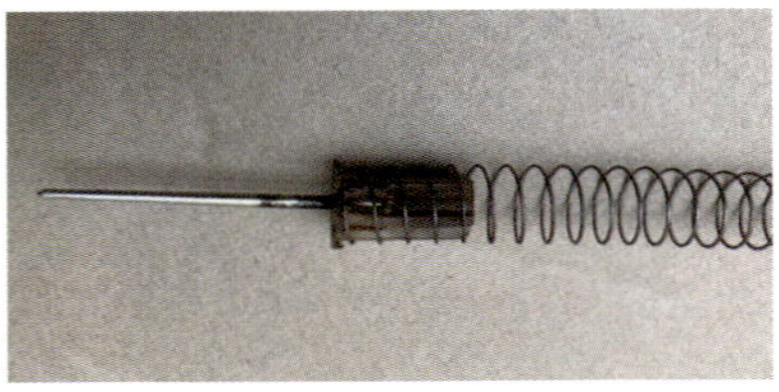

Keihin needle, needle seat and spring melted by excessive heat.

Mikuni main jet fitted to a Keihin carburettor.

Diaphragm incorrectly seated and pinched.

The photos here show the true horror of what can be done if you don't know what you are doing and use the wrong parts.

Keihin stamp in the carburettor body, showing the Keihin star.

LEFT: Diaphragm squeezed out of the cap after being incorrectly seated.

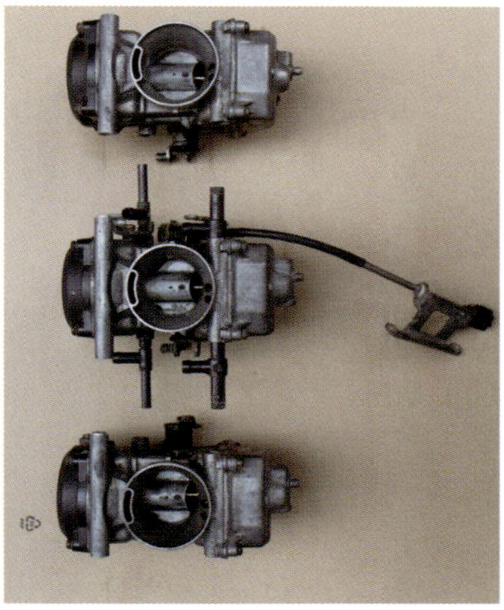

Keihin carburettors, as removed from the rail.

Sticking choke plunger.

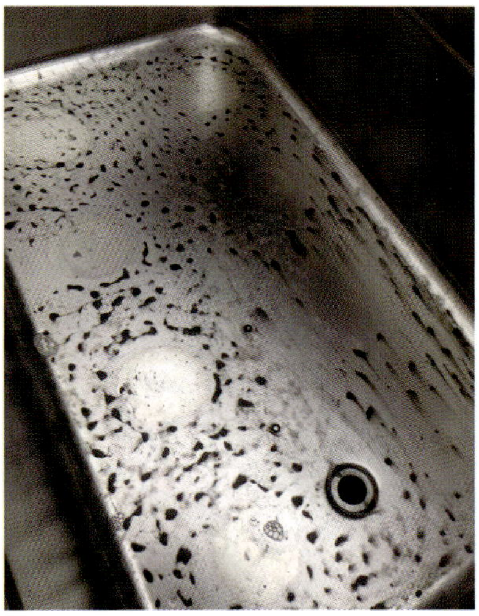

Debris in the ultrasonic cleaner tank following cleaning.

Damaged pilot jet in situ.

Float seals fitted with sealant.

Damaged float needle seat caused by aggressive cleaning.

An undamaged float needle seat.

Force used to remove a float needle seat.

Choke, main jet, pilot jet and float needle seating point.

Float bowls sealed with sealant, not a proper gasket.

WHEEL BEARINGS

The play in the bearings can be checked and, if necessary, they can be changed. You will also need to remove the bearings and spacer if the wheels are to be powder coated.

If replacing the wheel bearings, do not replace with cheap Chinese copies of branded bearings bought on the internet. As with spark plugs, there are lots of counterfeit branded bearings around, so beware. A front wheel bearing collapsing on a bike can have very serious consequences, including death! Saving a few pence on bearings is not worth it, so either buy them from Triumph or from a reputable bearing factor. The bearings have a set of numbers on the cage that identifies the type, dimensions, running accuracy and internal clearance. If you take the bearings that have been removed from the bike with you to a bearing factor then they can supply the appropriate bearings.

Always replace bearings as a pair, never singularly.

Tools

- Allen head sockets, including a 12mm one
- T55 Torx socket
- Hammer (a nice heavy one)
- Torque wrench, 10–60Nm
- Flat-bladed and Phillips screwdriver
- Pair of internal circlip pliers
- Metal punch or drift
- 34mm impact socket
- Some way of raising the front of the bike (to remove the front wheel), for example a trolley jack and an Abba stand
- Couple of bungee straps
- Tub of general-purpose grease
- Kitchen roll
- Blocks of wood
- Lump of scaffold pole (optional)
- Wheel bearings (in this example, code on the box says Koyo 60052RSC3FGGSR, and on the bearing says 600SRS).

As you dismantle everything, clean it up along the way with some kitchen roll or rag. You can then apply fresh grease on reassembly and also properly inspect things as you go along.

1. Before you do anything, pop the new bearings in the freezer (it makes them a lot easier to fit as they shrink)
2. Loosen the axle nut. I use a breaker bar connected to the 12mm Allen socket and a length of scaffold tube to add a bit of leverage; this makes light work of it.
3. Loosen the axle clamp bolts with a 6mm Allen key. Later bikes have 14mm hex bolts.
4. Remove the brake calipers and support them with a bungee. You will need the T55 Torx socket for this.
5. Remove the speedometer cable from the drive at the wheel.
6. You are now ready to lift the bike so that you can remove the front wheel. I use an Abba superbike stand to stabilize the bike, and lift the front with a trolley jack with a lump of wood under the front of the engine.
7. Undo the axle nut completely, slide out the axle and remove the front wheel. Once you've got the front wheel off, remove the spacer from the left-hand side and the speedometer drive from the right, which will allow you to prise out the seals with a flat-bladed screwdriver.
8. Lift out the speedometer drive flange and remove the circlip from the other side with your internal circlip pliers.

Removing the bearing seal.

Circlip exposed.

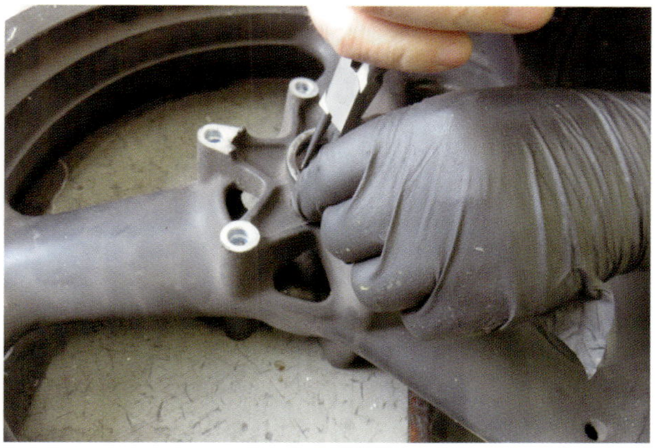

Circlip removal.

Circlip ready to come out.

Bearing exposed.

9. The wheel is now ready for you to attack. In order to put the wheel on its side and hammer out the old bearings, you will need to be able to support it off the ground so that the brake discs are protected, and for this purpose I made a frame out of 10 × 5cm (4 × 2in) timber. I cut four lengths of 43cm (17in) and screwed the ends together.
10. With some old rag over the wheel, you can lay it down safely and get to work with the hammer and punch/drift. If you look through the axle hole, you will see a couple of small cutouts in the internal spacer that will allow you to locate the drift on the inside race of the opposite bearing and tap it out.

    Tap the bearing out by hitting it evenly through the two cutouts in the spacer. When the bearing is free, it will fall away and the spacer will go with it. Retrieve and clean these, then flip the wheel over and knock out the other bearing; you will now have plenty of access to the inner race of this one.

A wheel resting on a frame of wood to allow the brake disc to sit above the ground when removing the bearing.

Ready to knock out the bearing.

Indent in the spacer visible.

Spacer, bearings and seal.

11. Once they are both out, you are ready to put the new bearings back in. Clean the areas on the wheel to take the new ones and apply a smear of grease. Take your bearings out of the freezer and remove one from the box, smear a small amount of grease over it and locate it in the wheel, then use your 34mm impact socket to gently tap it home until it is flush. Flip the wheel over and insert the spacer in – don't forget this!
12. You are now on the home straight. With the bearings in, reassemble the rest of the wheel. Grease everything, put the circlip back in the left-hand side, then the drive flange for the speedometer, which has the contact lips facing outwards. Tap home the seals on both sides. Fit the speedometer drive, noting that the drive plate has to match up with flange contact lips, spacer to the left-hand side.
13. Refit the wheel back into the bike and refit the speedometer cable and brake calipers, and do all the nuts and bolts up finger tight.
14. Lower the bike then tighten everything up. Note the speedometer drive has a stop that needs to butt up against the stop on the fork leg.

Torque settings

Brake caliper bolts	40Nm
Axle nut	60Nm
Axle pinch bolts	35Nm (do not over tighten!)

The rear wheel follows the same principle but also has a bearing in the sprocket carrier. They are different sizes from the front, too, so you'll need different-sized impact sockets to drive them home.

OIL CHANGES

In the handbook, Triumph recommended Shell Gemini 10/40 oil for most models, with Shell Ultra Helix 5/40 for the Daytona Super 3 and Daytona 1200. Capacity is given as 3.75ltr (0.82gal), except the Daytona 1200, which is 3.5ltr (0.77gal). However, after draining the oil, there will be some residual oil in the sump so you don't need to put all 3.75ltr back in. I would put just over 3ltr (0.66gal) in, let it settle and then check with the dipstick. I sit on the bike with a piece of tissue in hand and then check the dipstick and if necessary top up; you don't want to overfill.

When checking the oil level you have to screw the dipstick right down and in, not just rest it on the top face.

I would always go for a recognized brand of semi-synthetic oil for motorcycles. Never be tempted to put car oil into a motorcycle, as this may cause the clutch to slip. Triumph recommended an oil change every 10,000km (6,000 miles) or yearly, whichever came first, with the filter changed at the same time.

Oil Filter

Triumph used old-style filter elements that fit inside the filter housing rather than the more modern spin-off cartridge filters. Don't lose the two washers, one either side of the filter! When taking out the old filter, the washer that sits on the top of the filter sticks to it, which is then thrown away and lost.

Also remember that the oil filter bolt is only torqued up to 18Nm, and if you over-tighten then you risk damaging the bottom crankcase, which will then need to be replaced. This has effectively wrecked the engine so be careful!

If you struggle to get hold of a Triumph oil filter, a Kawasaki 106099 003 will also fit and has the advantage of being slightly cheaper. The oil filter supplied by Triumph is now a bit smaller than it was with more 'folds' in the paper element to make up for the slight reduction in height, but it works just fine.

SUMP PLUG

Be aware that there are two different sizes of sump plug. Most of the bikes are fitted with an M22 thread plug, which uses a 12mm Allen key, but late in the life of the range this was changed to an M14 thread using a 13mm hex socket. Don't over-tighten; always use a torque wrench, as there is a possibility of damaging the sump. The torque setting for the sump plug is 48Nm for the 22mm plug and 28Nm for the 14mm one. You should change the washer at the same time, but if a new one is not to hand then heat up the old one and quench as this will make it more malleable (this is called re-annealing).

CAM CHAIN AND TENSIONER

As with all motorcycles and cars, the cam chain tensioner and cam chain should be changed at high mileage. I took the opportunity to change both the chain and tensioner at 72,000km (45,000 miles) on my Speed Triple as a precaution rather than wait for a problem. A cam chain failure usually results in a wrecked engine.

Triumph have a test for the cam chain but it requires removal of the chain and is very laborious and time-consuming, so it's easier just to replace it.

The cam chain tensioner spring can also be changed. The service limit is 73.7mm.

To remove the spring, undo the 19mm bolt carefully and gently remove the plunger and spring and then measure the length – if it's anything less than 73.7mm, the spring must be changed. Triumph don't sell a replacement spring (just a complete spring and blade assembly) but Sprint Manufacturing have one.

If you need to check the tensioner itself then it is essential that you set the timing disc to the T1 position –

this is on the disc on the pickup sensor – and also (after removing the cam cover) align the two arrows on the end of the camshaft timing wheels and lock the cam chain tensioner by placing a suitable wedge between the tensioner blade and the crankcase (to hold the chain taut during the removal of the tensioner). Otherwise, the cam chain will jump a tooth or two and then the valve timing will be out!

If you are checking the tensioner blade, lock the blade and cam chain before removing the spring.

Triumph note in their workshop manual that there are three different cam chain tensioners fitted so it is essential that the VIN number be quoted to get the correct part.

REAR SUSPENSION, LINKAGE AND REAR SHOCK ABSORBER

The rear shock absorbers from either Showa or Kayaba cannot be rebuilt, so a new one will have to be fitted. Some companies advertise that they can rebuild but in most cases all they do is repaint the shock and spring. There is no way to re-pressurize the shock. New rear shocks are no longer available from Triumph but there are a number of aftermarket ones.

Replacing the rear shock absorber can be a right pain if it has not been disturbed for twenty years (never mind the layers of filth!). I would always start with a good clean down, finishing with a rag soaked in paraffin, so everything is clean before stripping down commences.

The major problem is removing the spindle that goes through the suspension linkage and the bottom of the shock absorber, as this can seize up and prove difficult to press out. If the spindle refuses to come out then remove the whole linkage and shock absorber assembly so you can get better access to the spindle. If you know someone with a hydraulic press then that will make it easy, otherwise you need to get creative with a hammer! The spindle is threaded internally at each end for the cap bolt (which also has the grease nipple in) and this has a thread of 18mm with a 1.5 pitch, so if you can find something with the same thread and pitch, screw it into the spindle and knock out with a hammer. The

Suspension linkage after removing the old swing arm.

Triumph tool for inserting into the swing arm shaft to ease entry through all the holes.

spindle can then be cleaned up with 1500 grit wet and dry. Be careful not to damage the end of the spindle.

When putting in the new shock absorber, it is helpful to wrap it in some thin foam to prevent damage to the paintwork on the spring. The biggest problem Triumph have when assembling bikes in the factory is scratches on components being fitted, so be careful!

SWING ARM

The swing arm can be removed by taking off the caps on the outside of the frame, followed by the circlips that stop it moving.

The shaft that goes across the bike between the frame, engine supports and swing arm can then be knocked out with a suitable drift. Having re-greased the swing arm bearings, the swing arm can be replaced, although it can be a bit of a squeeze. The problem will be lining up the engine plate holes, the suspension linkage and the holes in the swing arm. The solution is to use the special service tool from Triumph that fits into the end of the shaft that goes through the components. This guides the shaft through all the holes.

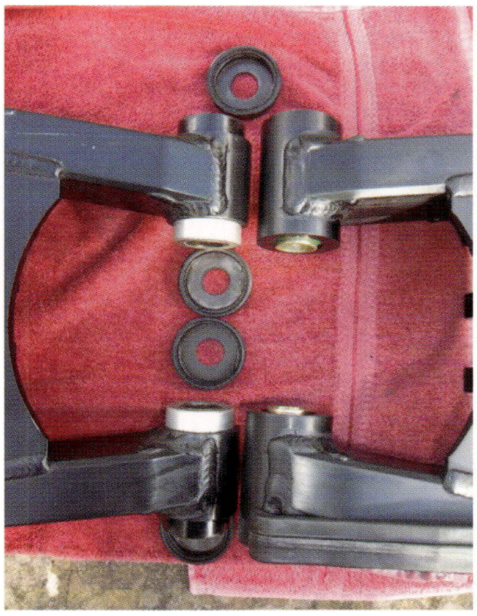

Old and new swing arms.

The engine plates showing where the swing arm shaft goes across the bike.

To help with realignment, especially on a bike with a centre stand, slacken off the rear engine mounting bolts.

The early swing arms have shims at either side of the swing arm so don't lose these, and note which side they

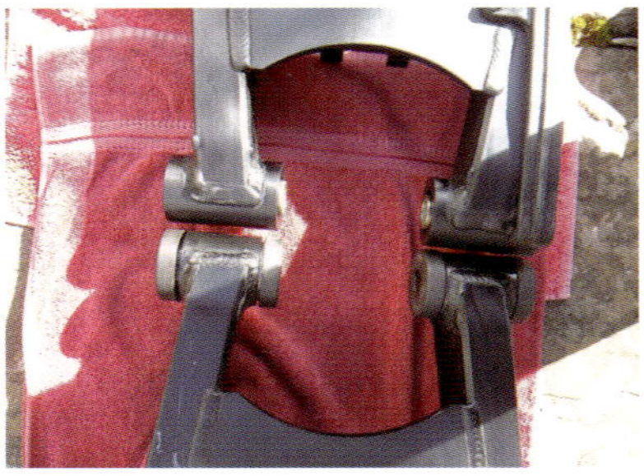

Old-style swing arm (bottom) compared to new style (top).

Worn chain rubbing block on the swing arm.

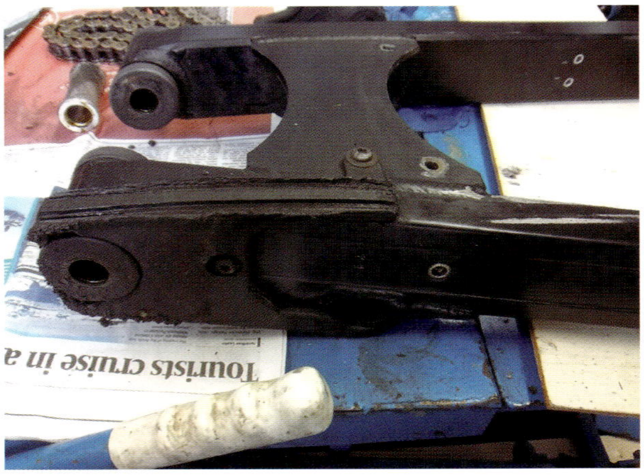

came from. Later bikes had different end caps to the swing arm and therefore do not have shims.

Chain Rubbing Block

The swing arm has a rubber rubbing block, which is bolted to the top of the swing arm and is classified as a service item; this should be changed on a regular basis as, if left, and with a slack chain, then the chain can cut into the swing arm. I have seen swing arms reduced to scrap as the chain has cut into the top. This was a common problem with the Speed Triple Challenge bikes, which had the back of the bike raised (by a different rear shock absorber to give quicker steering), dropping the forks through the yoke by an amount much larger than the Triumph-recommended 28mm and giving the bike a nose-down stance that did not help the chain run.

It was not unknown for race teams to change swing arms every five or six races.

If the standard sprocket ratios are changed then it is possible that this will accelerate the wear of the rubbing block, so if contemplating sprocket size changes, do consider the chain run.

Normally, to change the rubbing block, the swing arm needs to be removed, which also requires the shock absorber linkage to be separated from the swing arm. The chain rubbing strip is no longer available from Triumph, but Sprint Manufacturing can now supply this part and they have taken the opportunity to upgrade it to give a longer life.

It is just possible to change the rubbing strip without taking out the swing arm off. This involves removing the rear suspension links to the swing arm (the ones fitted with grease nipples) – this should give just enough clearance to get at the side fixing for the rubbing block, enabling you to remove it.

I would always take the swing arm out, however, as this gives an opportunity to inspect and clean the swing arm bearings, suspension linkage and shock absorber. Using the correct swing arm tool to aid putting the swing arm back does make life easier.

New chain rubbing block.

Chain rubbing strip, old and new.

LEFT: Ex-race bike with a swing arm damaged by the chain.

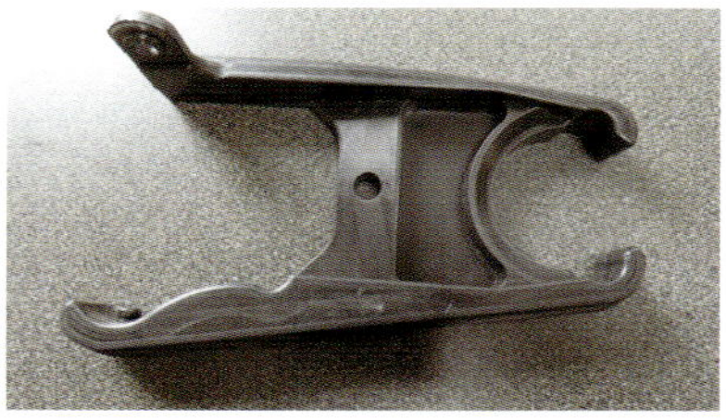

RIGHT: The reverse side of a new chain rubbing block.

CHAINS AND SPROCKETS

Chains

Triumph fitted all bikes with a Regina 136 ORT chain (530 ORT). Most of the models are fitted with 110-link chains, except the Trident 900 and Sprint 900, which have 112-link chains, and the Trident 750, which has a 114-link chain. Always buy your chain from a recognized supplier and be wary of unbranded chains; I have been told of chainsaw chain being sold for motorcycles, with no mention of its provenance. Not only will it wear quickly but is dangerous – a snapped chain can not only lead to a broken crankcase but could cause an accident. Stick to quality branded chains, but be aware that counterfeits are now very common.

I am not a fan of the sliding link method of connecting a chain, preferring a riveted link. In the past I have had a sliding link fall off (despite checking it was facing the right direction), although fortunately I spotted it before the link fell apart. This is another case of saving a few pence where a consequent repair would cost a lot more.

When adjusting the chain, the maximum movement vertically should not exceed 35–40mm.

Remember that to adjust the chain you only need to slacken off the swing arm adjuster clamp bolts; you don't need to slacken off the axle bolt.

When re-clamping the swing arm adjuster clamp bolts after adjusting the chain, don't exceed the torque setting of 36Nm; if more force is applied then you run the risk of cracking the clamp, which is not repairable and would reduce your swing arm to scrap! Many owners have made this mistake, so be warned.

Front Sprocket

This is a bit of a pain because, when removing the sprocket cover, the oil needs to be drained from the sump. In an emergency, you can lean the bike against a wall and this should enable the oil to be retained, but I would not recommend this as the bike is not properly secured and you run the risk of it falling over.

The sprocket is held on with a 36mm nut. To remove it, it's best to use an air-powered or electric impact driver. Failing that, you can us a scaffold pole to loosen the nut (which is torqued down to 132Nm and needs a 36mm socket). Rather than putting the bike in gear (and therefore putting a strain on the gears), place a substantial piece of wood between the spokes of the rear wheel (and some padding to prevent marking the wheel and swing arm) and then undo the sprocket retaining nut – this is where a long scaffold pole comes in to help if you don't have a powered impact driver. Don't forget to fold the tabs back on the retaining washer before you start. Use a cold chisel and a hammer for this. Do not use the old sprocket retainer, but always fit a new one and ensure that it securely holds the sprocket nut before replacing the cover.

Front sprocket with original-style retaining washer.

When removing the front sprocket, take the opportunity to change the various seals behind the cover (such as the clutch shaft seal) and the seal behind the sprocket.

Triumph have changed the retainer for the front sprocket so make sure you buy a Triumph part and ensure that you have bent it over to fully prevent the sprocket nut from moving.

Rear Sprocket

The rear sprocket should be changed when the chain is changed and, again, don't scrimp on quality – buy a quality brand chain from a recognized supplier. I usually buy a matching chain and sprocket, unless you want to save a bit of weight and buy an alloy one. I also like to spend a bit more and have some nice stainless steel nuts to retain the sprockets, just because they look good.

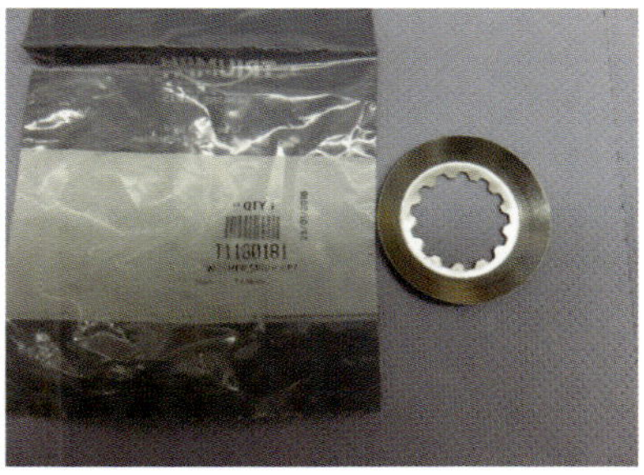

Revised sprocket retaining washer.

Gear/Sprocket Combinations

Always check the final drive ratio code letter in the VIN number (see Chapter 1), as the ratios can change between models and the country the bike is built for. The following list shows the letter codes for the standard sprocket combinations for the UK market:

A	17/52 (17 front, 52 rear)
B	17/50
C	17/48
D	17/46
E	17/44
F	18/45
G	18/43
H	19/43
J	19/42
K	18/48
M	17/43
R	18/44

Triumph models have the following codes:

Tiger	K	18/48
Speed Triple/Daytona	M	17/43
Trident/Sprint 900	D	17/46
Trident 750	C	17/48
Daytona 1200		18/42
Daytona 900	M	17/43
Thunderbird Sport (six-speed)	G	18/43
Thunderbird/ Adventurer (five-speed, up to VIN 29155)	M	17/43
Trophy 1200	R	18/44
Later Mk 2 Trophy	S	19/40
Trophy 900	M	17/43
Early Mk 1 Trophy	D	17/46

As with all bikes, the standard sprocket pairings can be changed, but it is important to remember that there is a chain rubbing strip mounted on the front sprocket end of the swing arm (*see* above), and reducing the size of the rear sprocket can have consequences in that the chain can then start to cut through the chain rubbing strip and into the swing arm.

If you want to change the gear ratio by changing sprocket sizes, seek out the website www.gearingcommander.com, which shows the effect on speed and acceleration for different sprockets.

Given the age of the bikes and the massive torque delivered by the engines, I don't personally think sprocket changes achieve very much and, as stated above, you run the risk of altering the chain run to such an extent that damage to the swing arm will occur.

It is important that the chain and sprockets are lubricated regularly to stop premature wear of the chain rubbing strip. People have their favourite lubricants, but I use the oil supplied by Scottoil for their automatic chain lubrication systems, applied manually every 320km (200 miles).

For touring, I have used Scottoiler systems in the past and found them very effective. When I was using my Sprint Sports to commute to work every day with a round trip of over 160km (100 miles), it was an absolute godsend.

Gear Linkage

The linkage between the gear lever and the gearbox input varies between the models – some are straight and some have a bend in them.

The rose joints are generally reliable but can be replaced if worn. Replacements can be found on the internet.

WHEELS AND TYRES

There only two types of wheel – a six-spoke version (17in front and 18in rear), fitted to early Tridents, and a later three-spoke wheel (17in front and rear), fitted to the Speed Triples, Daytonas, Sprints, Sprint Sports and so on. Finding tyres for the 18in wheels is not impossible but is more of a challenge: but most motorbike manufacturers fit 17in wheels so there is a wider range of tyres available in this size.

Do not be tempted to fit tyre sizes outside those recommended by Triumph. At one point I had three Speed Triples and one of them exhibited some very strange handling quirks. Upon investigation, I found that the rear tyre was undersized (compared to the specification for the bike), giving a different radius to the tyre and hence strange handling.

You can fit a Daytona 17in wheel to the rear of a Trident (which normally has an 18in wheel), but there is then a 10mm difference in the rear shock length (the Trident one being shorter). As rear shock absorbers cannot be rebuilt, a Daytona replacement should be used. The difference in ride height is minimal and is equivalent to the difference between a new and worn rear tyre.

There may also be some difficulties with the centre stand as, when lifted, the rear tyre will still be in contact with the ground!

Triumph made small changes to models as wheels changed and power increased. The tyre sizes listed in Appendix VI are from Triumph documentation and specifications for each model.

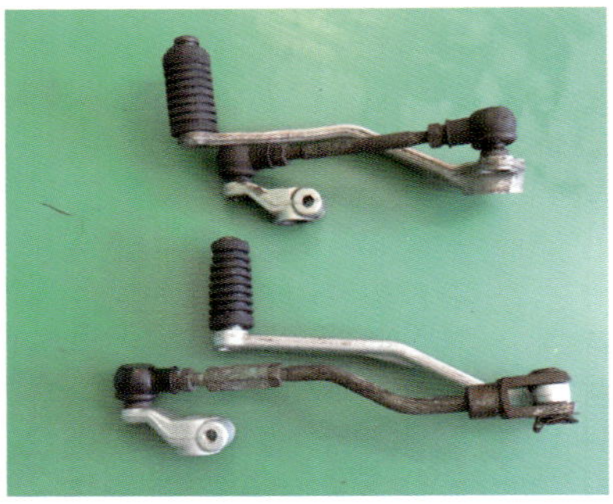

Straight and kinked gear linkages.

Radiator with cover from a Daytona.

COOLING SYSTEM

The radiators exhibit small differences (particularly the outer covers) but are now more than twenty-five years old,

Radiator fan switch under its cover.

Fan switch with the cover removed.

so check for bent fins and weeping. The core can be of course replaced.

The radiator fan is mounted on the back of the radiator and is triggered by a switch mounted on the side of the radiator (on the near side, facing forward).

To check the operation of the fan, short out the two wires that go into the switch (with the ignition turned on) and the fan should kick in. The sender units turn on the fan at 99°C (210°F).

Cooling on the naked bikes has never been a problem, but the faired bikes can get hot and that is why some of them have a temperature gauge rather than a warning light. This is also the reason the faired bikes have an oil cooler. Some Speed Triple Challenge bikes were fitted with oil coolers as the bikes were being thrashed, but these are not necessary on a road bike. If taking a faired bike touring in very hot countries, it may be worth considering fitting a fan override switch to bring on the fan before the sender would start. This can be a simple single-pole switch wired directly across the fan switch terminals using 'piggy-back' spade terminals. Another option is to fit a sender unit that initiates the fan at a lower temperature.

The sender unit (a thermistor) is the same across the T300 range, but there is an impedance matching unit in the instrument wiring loom to drive either a moving coil temperature gauge or switch on a warning light as required. The head temperature sensor can be checked for resistance – 255–310 ohms at 65°C (149°F). Often the spade terminal and the surrounding epoxy become loose in the brass body, and a flickering temperature warning light may need nothing more that wiping away the accumulated damp/oily muck surrounding it.

EXHAUSTS

The standard exhaust manifolds from Triumph were manufactured in house at Hinckley and were of black-chromed stainless steel. The silencers were made by Motad in the West Midlands. For the 3-cylinder bikes these were arranged 3-2 on each side, and on 4-cylinders 4-2.

The manifolds are long-lasting but can look scruffy if not cleaned regularly. One way of cleaning them is to use Harpic cleaner and a scrubbing pad (Scotch-Brite). Once cleaned, they can be painted with black barbeque paint, which is cheap yet gives a good finish. However, if the back chrome has come away, it is not possible to get them re-chromed; first, the chroming companies do not want to put some dirty manifold into their chroming tanks (full of expensive clean fluids), and second, the use of black chroming is now severely restricted due to the chemicals used.

The standard silencers and link pipes are now suffering from corrosion, which is difficult to repair, and replacements are no longer available from Triumph.

There are three (four for the 4-cylinder engines) 10mm bolt heads visible in the down pipes and these can be removed to measure the CO of each cylinder.

Be careful when removing these bolt heads as the down pipes are quite thin and, if the bolts are seized in the holes, you can crease the manifold. To be on the safe side, apply some releasing fluid to the bolts and leave overnight. Remember that WD40 is not a penetrating fluid!

Bolts for the CO_2 sensors in exhaust manifold.

Sebring silencer but branded 'Triumph'.

Sebring 3-1 manifold.

Non-adjustable fork top.

Adjustable fork top.

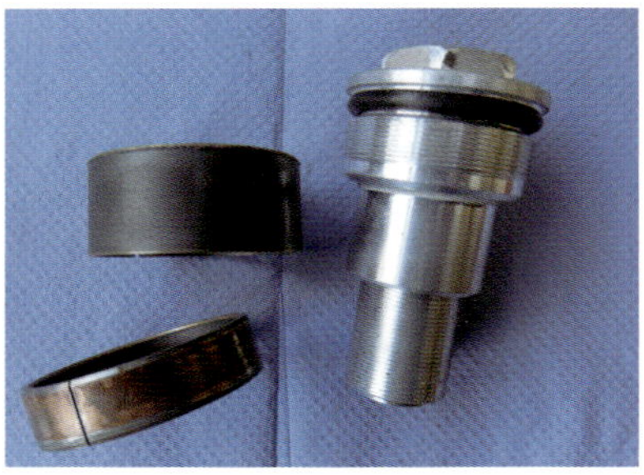

Adjustable fork top removed from the forks, along with the fork bushes.

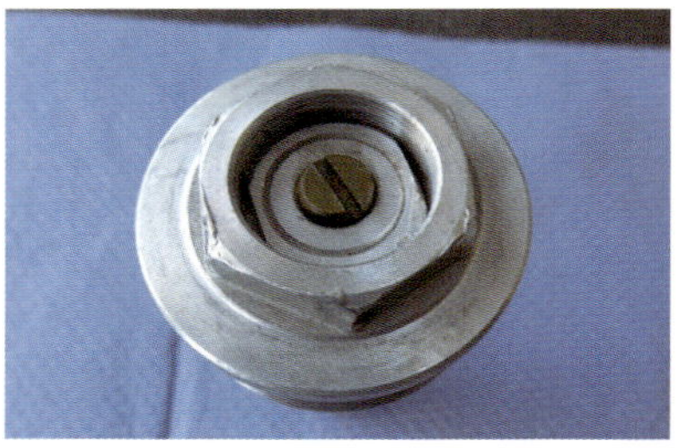

Adjustable fork top showing damage to the corners.

Compression damping emulators – an aftermarket one on top and a standard one underneath.

Triumph did offer a 3-1 manifold and silencer made for them by the Austrian company Sebring, and these were available from Triumph dealers.

They were developed for the Speed Triple Challenge series and gave a little power increase at the top end of the revs, but were considered to be inferior to the TTS/Yoshimura systems (3-4-3-2-1), also developed for the Speed Triple Challenge. The TTS/Yoshimura system gave a better midrange but it had the disadvantage that the main pipe went under the sump, requiring the whole exhaust system to be removed to change the oil filter. There were only around ninety sets of genuine TTS manifolds made, but a number of copies were produced by other manufacturers.

A number of companies have made replacement or performance silencers for the T300 range and these are covered in Chapter 7.

DRAINAGE PIPE FOR FUEL TANK

The internal vent/overflow tube for the fuel tank can get blocked; if it does, it can be cleared by using a length of bicycle brake cable inner. The sharp ends of the wire strands do a great job of cutting through any crud inside the pipe so keep turning the wire as you proceed. You can also soften the crud by spraying down some WD40.

INSTRUMENTS

There are a number of different instrument panels across the different models – for example, some have a clock and others do not. The revised Trophy has a temperature gauge. Some of the models have specific instruments, so, for instance, the speedometer and rev-counter on the Speed Triple is unique to that model. Some variations are small – for example, the colour on the Speed Triple clocks is different.

The mounting brackets for the Speed Triple clocks and the Thunderbird Sport look the same but they are not, as the distance between the two holes to bolt to the headstock are different.

The Speed Triple had a subtle change in the colour of the numbers on the instruments, so the 1994–5 bikes had brown numerals and the 1996 models had blue.

The rev-counter takes its feed from the coil for #1 cylinder, so if the bike coughs and splutters and the rev-counter bounces, it could signify that the #1 coil is breaking down.

FRONT FORKS

Do not use a screwdriver to lever out the dust seals; use a plastic chisel (these are usually used to remove wheel balance weights without marking the paint).

The fork damper holding tool for non-adjustable forks is a 30mm hexagonal nut welded to a long tube. Adjustable forks need a 20mm-long piece of square tubing (some people have used a 20mm square sourced from a metal kitchen chair).

One of the most common problems is removing the compression damping screw (at the bottom of the fork leg), which usually seizes solid. First, remove the forks from the bike and then place the fork leg in a soft-jawed vice and apply some heat from a heat gun (not a blow lamp, as this is too hot). Then use a screwdriver – which should be a good fit into the screw head – lean down on it and turn. Alternatively, put the screwdriver in the vice and press the fork leg bottom down onto the screwdriver and turn the fork leg.

The fork tops for the adjustable suspension are no longer available from Triumph and usually exhibit signs of the wrong-sized spanner having been used.

You can replace the fork compression valve either by talking to a suspension specialist or finding a flow control valve KYB 1.55mm (expect to pay around £75 each).

Surprisingly, Triumph recommend quite a few different quantities of fork oil; this could just be because it came from two different manufacturers and some forks were adjustable and some not.

The fork oil quantities and grades are given in the table below. Please note that the air gap above the oil means the max value can be lower than the standard.

BRAKES

Cleaning the Calipers

The following text has been extracted from Mark Gaylard's excellent Motley-biker website.

A regular general clean-up of the calipers will help keep them clean and hopefully reduce the need to strip them completely and pull out stuck pistons and leaking seals.

Tools

- Old toothbrush
- Soapy water
- Rags/paper towels
- Copper grease
- Renolit red rubber grease (optional)
- Zip ties
- Bungees or rope
- Brake/carburettor cleaner

Model	Oil grade	Oil level (std)	Oil level (max)
Trophy 1200, to VIN 4901	SAE 10	103mm	103mm
Trophy 900, to VIN 4901	SAE 10	84mm	84mm
Trophy 900 and 1200, VIN 4902 to 9082	SAE 10	117mm	102mm
Trophy 900 and 1200, VIN 9083 to 29155	SAE 15	117mm	102mm
Trophy 900 and 1200, VIN 29156 to 42274	SAE 10	105mm	105mm
Trophy 900 and 1200, from VIN 42275	SAE 10W–20	133mm	133mm
Daytona 750 (all)	SAE 10	139mm	139mm
Daytona 1200, 1000, 900, to VIN 9082	SAE 5	132mm	132mm
Daytona 1200, 900, Super 3, VIN 9083 to 29155	SAE 5	139mm	132mm
Daytona 1200, 900, Super 3, VIN 29156 to 33785	SAE 5	128mm	128mm
Daytona 1200, 900, Super 3, VIN 33786 to 36445	SAE 5	139mm	132mm
Daytona 1200, 900, Super 3, from VIN 36446	SAE 5	128mm	128mm
Sprint 900, to VIN 7491	SAE 10	109mm	97mm
Sprint 900, VIN 7492 to 11541	SAE 10	117mm	102mm
Sprint 900, from VIN 11542	SAE 15	117mm	102mm
Trident 900 and 750, to VIN 4901	SAE 10	94mm	94mm
Trident 900 and 750, VIN 4902 to VIN 44301	SAE 10	109mm	97mm
Trident 900 and 750, from VIN 44302	SAE 10W–20	141mm	141mm
Tiger 900, to VIN 43523	SAE 10	130mm	130mm
Tiger 900, from VIN 43524	SAE 10W–20	144mm	144mm
Speed Triple 900, to VIN 29155	SAE 10	141mm	141mm
Speed Triple 900, from VIN 29156	SAE 10	130mm	130mm
Speed Triple 750	SAE 10	141mm	141mm
Thunderbird and Adventurer, to VIN 43509	SAE 15	109mm	109mm
Thunderbird and Adventurer, from VIN 43510	SAE 10W–20	126mm	126mm
Thunderbird Sport	SAE 5	145mm	145mm
Sprint Executive	SAE 10	117mm	117mm
Sprint Sports	SAE 5	139mm	139mm
Legend TT	SAE 10–20	126mm	126mm

Before you start, a word of caution. Brake dust is unhealthy stuff; using the brake cleaner suppresses it, but brake cleaner is a strong solvent and will stain any bodywork it comes into contact with. Take care!

Working on one caliper at a time, loosen the pad pins, then unbolt the caliper from the fork leg (assuming it's the front brakes you're working on, of course!). Fully remove the pad pin and the pads and attach a support rope or bungee strap to the caliper to prevent over-stressing of the brake line. Give the caliper a general clean with a bucket of soapy water and a brush.

Once the caliper is dried off, the aim is to be able to pump out one piston at a time in order to clean it before pressing it back home and moving onto the next. Use plastic or wood to press the pistons back into the caliper so they don't get damaged. When the pistons you are not working on are pressed home, zip tie them in place so that when you use the brake lever to pump out the piston to be cleaned, they can't move too far; you can also hold them back with a block of wood or something – whatever you have to hand to keep all but the piston you want to work on coming out.

Don't pump the piston out too far: it needs to be out far enough so that all the dirt is accessible but not so far that you may be in danger of pumping it out all together!

Spray brake cleaner on the dirty piston and scrub it all around with your small brush; for stubborn deposits, spray some onto a rag and rub. Sometimes it can be difficult to get at the top of a piston because there is very little room between it and the end of the caliper. I have found spraying some cleaner onto a cloth, feeding the cloth through the caliper and then running the cloth over the piston and pulling to and fro in a sort of flossing action works quite well in this situation, though it is fiddly.

When you have cleaned the piston you are working on, press it back into the caliper body, zip tie it in and move onto the next. Occasionally I will lube the piston with a little Renolit red rubber grease before pushing it home, then wipe off any excess. When overhauling the calipers, never use copper slip on the pins and sliding pins as this will cause the rubber seals to swell. Always use red rubber grease.

Carry on until you have done them all, then clean the backs of the pads. Apply a smear of copper slip grease to them and pop them in, clean and grease the pad pins in the same manner and refit, put the caliper back onto the bike and do the other side.

Seized Pistons

Seized pistons may require a little more effort. The rear caliper is the worst culprit, as it's underslung and catches all the road dirt. After a good clean-up, I pumped the pistons out. The caliper was still connected to the bike, so pumping the brake lever made the pistons move; I had to hold one back to let the other catch up till they were both as far out as I could get them before one of them would start to leak brake fluid, at which point I would no longer be able to pump the other piston completely out. I was lucky this time, as I was able to pull the remaining piston clear by using some cloth and a pair of pliers.

A useful tool at this stage is a metal toothpick, which you can use to lift out the rubber seals and to scrape any corrosion out of the seal grooves. A quick tip is to pop the caliper in a low oven for a while beforehand; when you then start to scrape the corrosion out, it should powder away quite nicely.

The piston will need at least a clean-up and, if there are any stubborn marks or minor damage, you can use some 1500 grade wet and dry sandpaper to sort them out. A quick rub-over will normally do; any pitting that remains after this may mean new pistons. Have a good look and see if they are smooth and able to create the necessary seal to make the brakes work without leaking. Lube the new seals with brake fluid or rubber grease and press home the pistons.

Brake splitter under the headstock.

Bleeding the Brakes

I like to bleed the brakes roughly every three months. Sooner or later the travel on the front lever can get a bit too much. A temporary quick fix is to zip tie the lever back overnight, allowing any trapped air in the system to rise into the master cylinder.

I use a Mityvac to bleed the brakes; this is a vacuum pump that sucks the fluid through as opposed to the manual method of cracking the bleed nipple and pumping the lever. I find this works well even if the system is dry from replacing calipers or hoses.

If you are draining and replacing the brake fluid, it is a good idea to remove and clean out the brake splitter under the headstock before replacing the fluid. This can get full of gloppy fluid that won't be removed by simply flushing.

Draining as much fluid out as possible in situ and loosening the caliper body bolts a touch while still on the bike makes things a whole lot easier. Once it's off, split the calipers and remove all the pistons. I have just the tools to pop those pistons out without the compressed air/mauling with pliers that used to happen previously: most of the time, I can insert the expanding collet and twist them out.

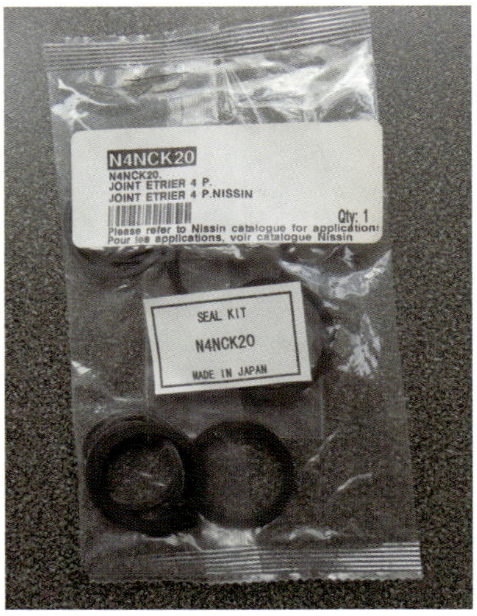

Nissin seal kit for the front brake pistons.

Front Calipers

The first bikes were fitted with two-piston sliding caliper brakes and these

LEFT: Front brake ready for reassembly.

RIGHT: Front brake caliper reassembled.

Triumph-branded calipers.

were superseded by four-piston calipers. The two-piston types are similar to the ones fitted at the rear and are prone to the same problems as the rear calipers, so a complete strip down and clean is required.

When refitting the calipers, don't over-tighten the mounting bolts, as this can strip the threads in the caliper body; they should be no more than 40Nm.

Brake Pads

As far as brake pads are concerned, I always try to use Triumph pads as they have been designed to match the discs. There are lots of quality branded brake pads out there but some of them can be very abrasive and accelerate wear on the discs. Given that brake discs are so expensive (and no longer available from Triumph), using these can be a costly mistake.

Brake Discs

Triumph fitted both fixed and floating discs to the front of T300 range. Some of the later discs (fitted to the Daytona 1200 SE and possibly others) have an alloy centre, offering a considerable weight saving of 0.8kg (2lb) per pair of discs. The gold colour is also slightly different to the usual gold on the Daytona and Speed Triples. I have checked with a magnet on my 1996 Daytona and they also have alloy centres.

Some of the later discs from Triumph have 'Sunstar' stamped on them, the OE manufacturer.

The discs are no longer available from Triumph so a secondary sup-

Alloy centred front disc from a 1200 SE.

plier will have to be found, but beware cheap discs from China, as these can be a false economy with a tendency to warp very easily. Failing Triumph discs, I would go for a reputable manufacture such as EBC.

I have fitted pattern parts as the rear disc, also marked 'Sunstar'.

Always check the brake thickness with a micrometer, not a vernier caliper, as there is usually a small ridge at the edge of the disc and using calipers will give a false reading.

If you have a dial gauge, check for run-out as well. This should not exceed 0.3mm, with the recommended figure being 0.1mm.

The minimum front disc thickness should be 4.5mm.

On the floating discs, the bobbins can get filled with brake dust, making the disc go solid. The bobbins can be cleaned out using brake cleaner if the bike does high mileage, especially if it's ridden over the winter months.

Problems with the rear brake caliper can result in warped rear discs as the caliper can stick and overheat the disc.

Brake Master Cylinder

There are two different sizes in the T300 range:

14mm These were fitted to the early bikes with the two-piston sliding calipers and continued with the Trident when the majority of the range moved to four-piston calipers.

$^{5}/_{8}$in These were fitted to the Speed Triple, Daytona, Trophy and so on

Floating brake disc.

Brake master cylinder showing the $^{5}/_{8}$ in marking.

when the four-piston calipers were introduced.

Rear Calipers

The rear calipers sit in a position where they are regularly covered in road muck and water (particularly the ones slung under the swing arm) and work on a sliding pin arrangement and, unless they are regularly dismantled and cleaned, can seize up, sometimes when they are partially on. I had the rear caliper on one of my Speed Triples do this and by the time I got home the rear disc was so hot I burnt my finger when I foolishly touched it! The only solution is to take the rear caliper off and dismantle completely, clean and reassemble (*see* above).

Points that need particular attention and cleaning on the rear caliper are the mounting bracket caliper slide pins and the pad pins. The pad pins can be a bit of a pain to remove as the standard Allen key that fits is fractionally undersize – why the pins have a non-standard hole in the top is a compete mys-

Rear brake caliper in need of rebuilding.

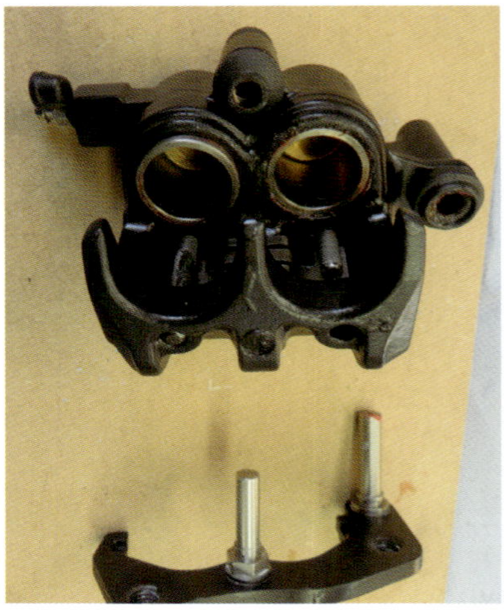

Rear brake caliper after rebuild, fitted with stainless pins.

Rear brake caliper with replacement stainless parts from Sprint Manufacturing.

Rear brake caliper after rebuild. Note the red rubber grease.

tery! – so if the pad pins are seized the Allen key will turn the internal edges of the pad pins and then they won't come out. The next step would be to hammer in a Torx bit and then try and turn. As a final resort, you may need to drill the pins out.

On a bike that does few miles per year, it is worth doing a clean down and remove the pad pins and re-grease the sliding pins on a yearly basis to avoid the grief of having to drill out the pins or have the caliper partially seize and have to replace the rear disc as well.

The reassembly process should not involve copper slip on the sliding pin or on any part of the caliper, as this causes the seals to swell and become less effective. Red rubber grease is the only thing to use on the caliper. As the sliding pin is steel, this can be severely corroded so requires a good cleaning with wet and dry; or you can buy new stainless steel pins from Sprint Manufacturing.

After popping the rear caliper free of the back wheel and torque arm, just ease the carrier plate out of the caliper.

Place the caliper into a vice and, with an Allen key (socket head), wind the brake pad rest off. This will come apart in two pieces. Use a spanner or long socket to remove the other pin.

Then simply wind in the new stainless pins. The one that attaches with the brake pad rest has a flat side to it, which stops it rotating as you tighten it. Lube with red rubber grease.

The caliper rubber boots from Triumph seem to be very expensive, but these calipers are made by Nissin and are also used by a number of other Japanese bikes. Honda, for example, can supply the same part at much reduced cost. The part numbers are 43109-MA3-006 for the small boot and 43132-166-016 for the boot.

THE IGNITION BARREL

Triumph used the same key for the ignition lock and the lock for the fuel tank (and seat lock), so if you change the ignition lock you will either have to have two keys or get the matching lock for the fuel tank. As an alternative, you can fit a non-locking fuel cap. If you need to remove the ignition barrel, you must remember that there are security features to deter thieves, so you will have to drill out the security bolts.

SPARK IGNITERS

The T300 series is fitted with a transistorized inductive digital electronic igniter. This is not like a modern ECU (which monitors and controls fuelling as well as the ignition system) on a car or bike, as it only controls the ignition system and is driven by the crank sensor on the end of the crank, which is located behind a cover on the offside of the bike. The igniter also controls the rev limit, depending on which model it is fitted to, so the 750 engines have a higher rev limit than the 900s. (This is why this was a 'cheat' on the Speed Triple Challenge bikes to get more power at the top end!).

The spark plug igniters all look similar but there are some differences between them. Some are in yellow, black or red. The igniters were supplied by either PVL or Gill, and the Gill

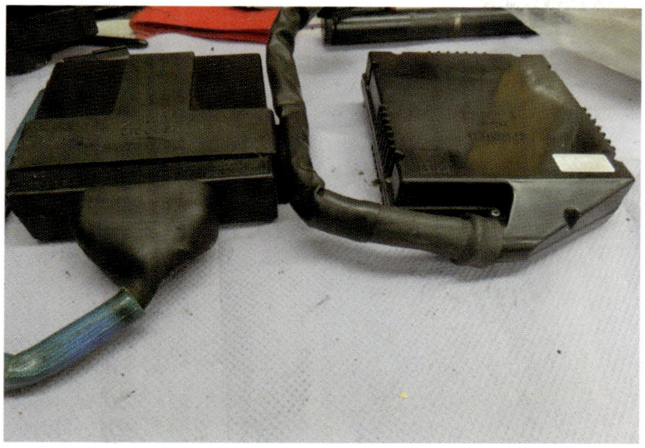

PVL igniter on the left and Gill on the right.

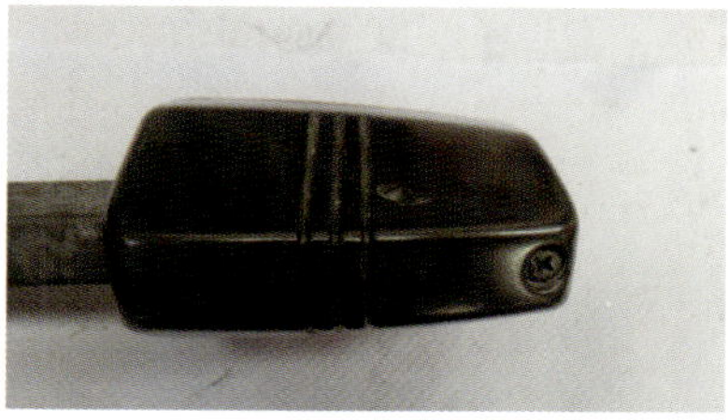

Rear of the indicator, showing screw for the lens cover.

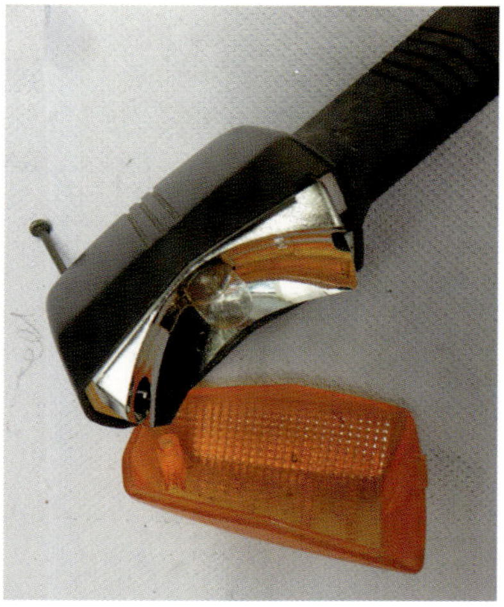

Indicator with lens cover removed.

Screws holding the lamp holder to the indicator stalk.

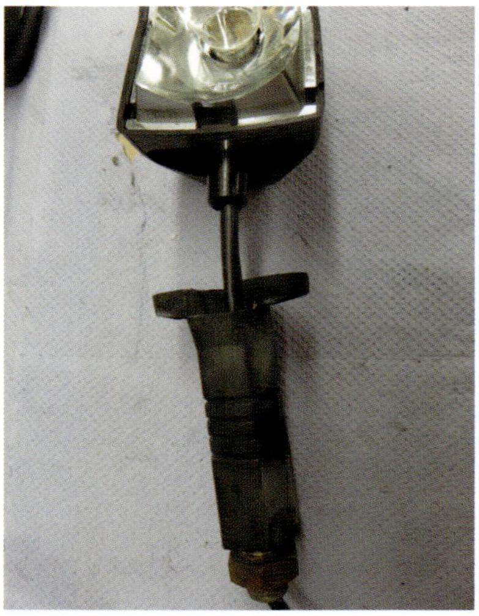

Stalk separated from the lamp holder.

has a softer advance curve and allows the engine to turn over twice before firing. This helps resolve any potential sprag clutch issues and is a worthwhile upgrade if you can find one. The PVL igniters have a wiring harness with a removable plug, but the wiring harness is built in on the Gill examples.

When the sprag clutch was revised, Triumph recommended that the igniters be changed as per the attached list.

The table below shows some of the part numbers for various igniters.

The Super 3 T12900331 is likely to be a PVL as it was replaced by a GILL.

There are also differences between the 1200 igniters. the T312 Trophy is a high torque and the Daytona 1200 is high power, and they have different advance curves, with the Daytona 1200 being 26 degrees fully advanced and the Trophy 1200 29 degrees. If you swap them round, the bikes will run but be are a bit rougher picking up from low revs.

INDICATORS

As mentioned earlier, the indicator stalks are prone to failure; also, if the bike falls over or is knocked, the orange indicator can be damaged. If the rest of the indicator is fine then the orange cover can be changed. There is a screw in the back of the indicator, and this can be undone and the lens lifted out and replaced.

Model	Part number
Trophy 1200 to VIN 4901 (not French market; Australia and Germany to VIN 9082)	T1290071
Trophy 1200 from VIN 4902 (all VINs for French market; Australia and Germany from VIN 9083)	T1290071
Trophy 900	T1290060
Trophy 900	T1290004 PVL
Mk 1 Trophy 1200 (underseat fitting, high torque)	T1290070 Gill
Mk 2 Trophy 1200 (behind nose section fitting)	T1290072 Gill
Sprint 900	T1290060
Daytona 1200 (except French market)	T1290071
Daytona 1200 (for French market, all VINs)	T1290070
Daytona 900	T1290060
Daytona Super 3	T1290062
Daytona 750	T1290080
Daytona 1000	T1290105
Trident 900	T1290060
Trident 750	T1290080
Tiger	T1290061
Speed Triple 900	T1290060
Speed Triple 900	T1290070 Gill
Thunderbird	T1290063

6 restoration

This section covers anything from doing up a 'barn find', where a bike has been standing for many years, right through to a rolling restoration, where the bike remains on the road and parts are restored while the bike is being used.

Bikes which have not run for many years need to be treated with great care; don't attempt to start the bike without first undertaking some basic checks and servicing – it could prove to be expensive. It is tempting to simply put in some fresh fuel and connect a battery, but being patient and doing some basic work first will really pay dividends later.

Battery If the bike has been standing for a few years, the battery will be next to useless so a new one needs to be connected into the system before trying to start the bike. Remember that the sprag clutch will not take kindly to a weak battery and you run the risk of causing some expensive damage.

Fuel Modern fuels have many volatile additives, which vaporize off over time, making the fuel next to useless, so replacing the fuel is a must.

Oil If the bike has been out of use for some time, the oil will have attracted moisture out of the air so needs to be changed. The first check is to see how much oil is in the sump and that it has not been contaminated with coolant or fuel. If coolant is visible on top of the oil on the dipstick then more investigation will be required before starting the bike. If fuel is present, that would point to problems with the float needles in the carburettor.

Carburettors If fuel has been sitting in the carburettors, they will be full of a slimy green residue that will almost certainly block the pilot jets. The only recourse is to take the carburettors off and get them ultrasonically cleaned, and the pilot jets checked and cleaned out. The carburettor inlet rubbers will also need checking for cracking and, if necessary, replacing. If the inlet rubbers are in a really bad way then air will be drawn into the carburettors and weaken the mixture, causing erratic running.

Fuel tap If there is fuel around the fuel tap then this should be removed and preferably replaced. It is possible to buy an overhaul kit, but this seems a bit hit and miss in curing the problem.

Coolant and antifreeze This should be changed every two years irrespective of mileage, so if a bike has been standing for some time, it's better to drain and refill. If the bike has been out of action for some time then the system will not only need draining but also flushing out, not forgetting the overflow expansion tank; this can be removed from the bike and sediment cleaned out by putting in some small bolts, shaking and then flushing out.

Chain and sprockets The chain should be cleaned, oiled and checked for wear, as should the sprockets. Because of the need to remove the front sprocket cover and drain the oil to check the front sprocket, it tends to get left until it has no teeth left. If you are doing an oil change, remove the front sprocket cover while you're at it and check, and if in doubt change the front sprocket. On the Daytona 900 I bought to convert into a CRK Café Racer, which had 53,000km (33,000 miles) on the clock, I found the front sprocket had virtually no teeth on it when I removed the sprocket cover; how an earth the chain was not slipping was beyond me.

Brakes The fluid will need to be changed as it will absorb moisture over time. Once the bike is fit to ride then you can decide if the calipers and master cylinder requires overhaul. Also change the clutch fluid.

Tyres Check for any cracking and, if in doubt, change. Every tyre, irrespective of manufacturer, has a date code showing which month and year it was manufactured. This is a four-digit code where the first two digits are the week number and the second two are the year, so 2812 would be week 28 of 2012.

The tyres should really be changed once they get to about eight years old, but this will be dictated by how much sunlight the tyre has been exposed to and how many heat cycles the tyre has been put through. As the tyre ages, many of the volatile compounds in the rubber (there is actually very little 'real' rubber in modern tyres, the bulk of the materials used are now manmade) are gradually released to the air and the tyre becomes harder and gives less grip. This may not be noticeable in the dry, but when braking in damp and wet conditions the tyre may lose its hold and, with no ABS on these bikes, you may find yourself sliding down the tarmac.

Tyre date code: the first two characters are the week number and the last two are the year.

Suspension settings If adjustable front forks are fitted, check that the preload, compression damping and rebound damping adjusters all work, as if they are seized then there is additional work to be carried out and this could prove expensive.

Engine cover bolts The coating on the bolts used by Triumph is excellent but if they are corroded and you want to replace them, there are two choices. You can replace with stainless steel bolts, which is expensive and, if you want to maintain originality, will look wrong (they usually come as cap head bolts). Also stainless bolts will react with the aluminium casings so will need to be covered in something like copper slip or a ceramic paste.

A better and cheaper solution is to get the bolts replated, which does keep the authentic look. You can also, of course, replace with new bolts from Triumph, but these are not cheap and may no longer be available, so check first with your local Triumph dealer.

The cam cover bolts can also be replated; in my case, however, I got a set of stainless bolts from Stuart Crump.

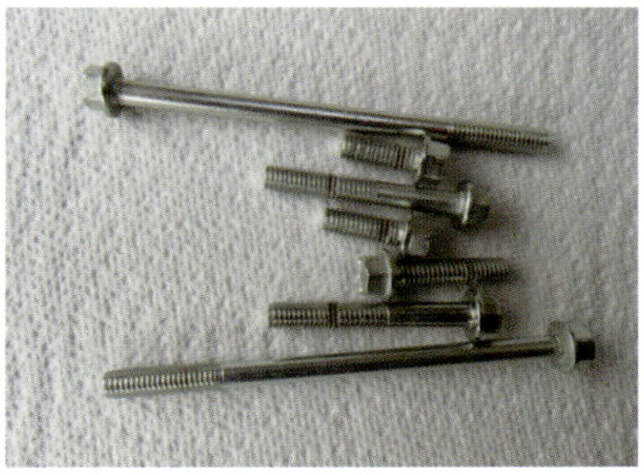

Original engine bolts replated.

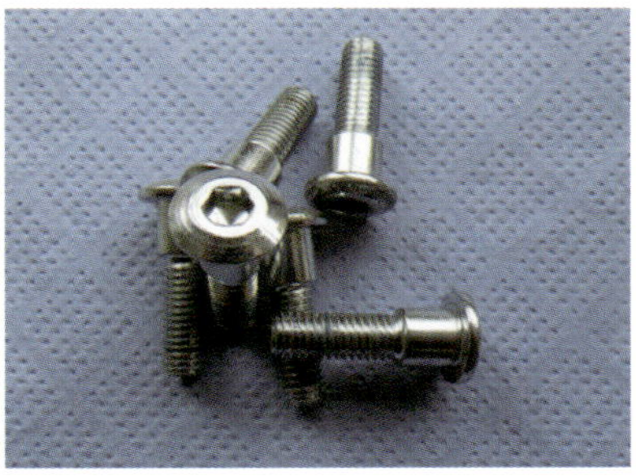

Replated cam cover bolts.

Engine covers Triumph powder coated the crankcases and engine covers and the machining was done afterwards, and, in the case of the engine covers, applied a 'crackle' finish for the black engines. Unfortunately, most powder-coating companies seem to struggle to match this crackle finish.

Stainless cam cover bolts.

My suggestion is to take an engine cover with you and ask them if they can replicate the finish.

The rubber-type inserts on the back of the covers are there for sound deadening purposes and can be removed if you wish.

Bodywork and decals Body panels and bodywork are no longer available from Triumph, so if panels are damaged or scuffed they will need to be repaired and repainted.

Decals on a Racing Yellow Daytona 900.

Similarly most of the decals are no longer available, but there are a number of third-party suppliers, such as Image Works in Ilkeston, who have been making motorcycle decals for many years.

The paint applied to the T300 series was really thick and then had a clear coat applied over the top. If there are marks in the paint you will find the clear coat very hard, so to start polishing out scratches use a 2000 grit wet

Adventurer in Amber and Copper.

1991 Daytona 1000 – 4.

and dry and then a polishing machine with some Menzerna 400 cutting/polishing compound.

Swing arm The swing arms are made of aluminium and are then anodized, which is microns thick. If the swing arm is in a scruffy state it is not possible to get it re-anodized as the original anodized coating will have to be removed first. A better solution is to strip the swing arm of all the bearings, blank off where the bearings fit and get it shot blasted and powder coated.

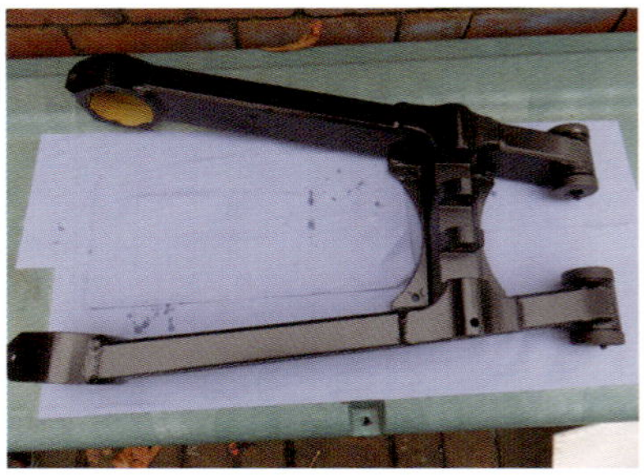

A powder-coated swing arm (top).

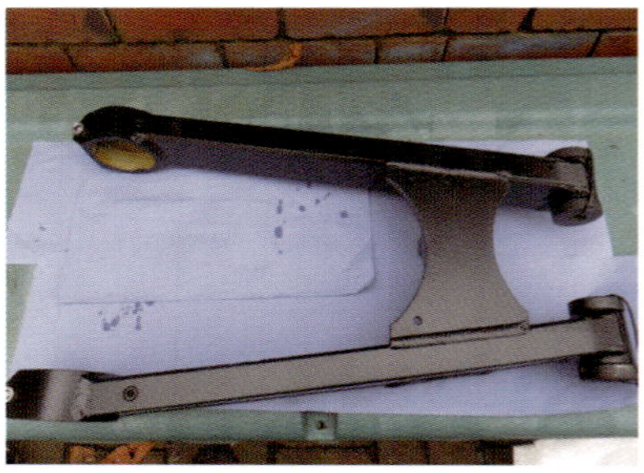

A powder-coated swing arm (underneath).

A new set of bearings can then be placed in and a new chain rubbing strip fitted before it's refitted to the bike. Using the Triumph tool that fits into the end of the long bar that goes through the engine mounts and swing arm makes refitting the swing arm a relatively easy job.

Seats As with many parts, seats are no longer available from Triumph. They tend to wear through on the front edge closest to the fuel tank. There are a number of companies who can recover your seat in whatever material you wish. Be aware that there are a number of variations to the seats so, for instance, the Trophy seats have fold-out lugs for luggage attachment and will not fit a Speed Triple (I tried!) as the fold-out attachments foul the bodywork.

Fold-out luggage hooks on the seat.

The Daytona and Speed Triples have captive bobbins in the seat to allow for the fitment of the pillion passenger seat hump. The seat for the Tiger also has a different shape at the front to meet the tank.

An American company, Corbin, have made seats for the T300 range and very comfortable they are, if expensive. If you are intending to travel long distances, however, they are worth considering.

Earthing Many owners consider that the earthing straps are marginal on all the bikes in the T300 range, particularly given the need to give the engine a fat spark and to spin it over quickly. It is easy to get a local motor factor or electrical/battery company to make up a set of leads with the correct terminals. Get leads rated at 250 amps. Also check any earthing contacts on the frame and clean them up. Gordon Smith reports that he has resolved more than one non-starter by cleaning up the earth terminals to the frame and alternator using a brass wire brush to remove the surface patina and oxidization to make them bright and shiny, then treating with contact cleaner.

Don't forget the battery to harness in-line connectors under the left-hand side panels behind the plenum chamber (by the battery box). Check for continuity (0 ohms) between the battery, negative frame and alternator earths.

Wheels The wheels are powder coated, but after twenty-plus years of use they can look shabby. The solution is to strip out the wheel bearings and spacer, blank off the centre of the wheel and get them shot blasted and re-powder coated. It is important to use a company for this work that is used to working on motorcycle wheels so they know how to blank off the machined

Second earthing point to frame.

Earthing point.

surface where the brake discs locate. If the wheel comes back to you with this machined surface also powder coated, it will take hours of work to scrape it all off – which you have to do, otherwise the brake discs will not fit. The bolts for the brake discs are M8 × 1.25, so if you want to blank off the area underneath the bolts, use a washer to ensure that it keeps the surface clear.

PAINTWORK

Appendix 3 lists all the paint colours used by Triumph on the various models, and Appendix 4 gives the paint name, the manufacturer and the manufacturer's code. If you give the manufacturer and code to a good spray shop, they should be able to mix up the correct paint. However, at time of writing it now appears that these paint codes are difficult to replicate as most paint suppliers don't have these Dupont or IVC schemes anymore. Some suppliers also have a scanner, so if you present a panel or tank to them they can scan it and get a paint match that way to mix you the paint.

Daytona petrol tank.

As far as I am aware, the touch-up paints supplied by Triumph for the T300 range are no longer available, although there are some independent suppliers for this. However, paints fade over time, particularly in strong sunlight, so even if the touch-up paint is the correct colour it won't necessarily match!

Another factor to consider is that Triumph used cellulose paints and lacquers, and some elements and compounds of the paint are no longer allowed for health and safety reasons or available because of supply issues. For example, there is a component (Chrome) within Racing Yellow that can no longer be used so it is impossible to get an exact match by mixing the current set of compounds. This I know from personal experience. Triumph actually listed three different Racing Yellows – one from Dupont, one from IVC and a second one from Dupont but a 2K version.

Some (if not most) of the paints used by Triumph originated in the car industry but were renamed for marketing purposes. The only colour I definitely know was a carry-over from a car manufacturer was Aluminium Silver (used on Legends, I believe), which was originally Honda Titan Silver. So if you want some touch-up paint, it may be useful to have a look at some car paint swatches and see how close a match you can get.

Be aware that Triumph listed five different Blacks applicable to the T300 range (Assam Black, Cherry Black, Diablo Black, Jet Black and Obsidian Black) and they all have different manufacturer's code even where they're from the same manufacturer, so don't assume they are all the same colour. The marketing department's imagination in coming up with so many different names for black is certainly impressive!

There are also bikes out there that have non-standard paint colours, some because a Triumph employee buying a bike could have it painted any colour they wanted, and some because the owner simply wanted a different colour. All Super 3s were painted Racing Yellow; the one I bought (becoming its fourth owner) had sat in the dealer's showroom for some time as a new bike, until a customer decided he liked the bike but not the colour, so the dealer painted it black to make the sale. The bike was then subsequently repainted back to Racing Yellow. Of course, if you are building a CRK then none of the original tank or body panels will be carried over, so you can paint it any colour you like.

Some colours proved unpopular so were only listed for a short time, usually for one model year; as an example, Sandstone Gold was a colour option in 1993 for the Tiger but was not continued or the following year and was not seen again.

Decals

Depending on the colour and the age of the bike, the Triumph decal on the tanks and body panels can vary.

For a black tank, the interior of the 'Triumph' lettering should be black; however some decals have a dark grey interior. I have included some photos of various tanks to show the different colours used. (*See* Chapter 1 for more examples.)

When Triumph painted the bikes, the decals were covered by the final coat of lacquer (to make them petrol resistant) and this should be the case if the bikes are repainted.

Beware of small changes – for instance, the first Sprints had 'Trident 900' on the side panel but this was deleted for later versions of the Sprint.

The supply of decals from Triumph is a little patchy but they can be sourced from third-party suppliers; some stock the more popular models and all will be able to make one up if a photo and

Speed Triple in Racing Yellow, with matching helmet.

dimensions are supplied. Don't be surprised, however, at the cost of some of these decals, particularly the 'Tiger' decals for the fuel tank – it's very big!

Painting Smaller Parts

Parts such as the fork bottoms (which get a real blasting from road detritus), brake and clutch master cylinders can start to look a little shabby, as the bikes are now over twenty years old. With all painting, the key is spending time on the preparation. As far as fork bottoms go, start by taking them off the bike. I use paint stripper to get rid of the old paint, then rub down with a fine-grade wet and dry (1500 grit). Once I am happy with the surface finish, I spray with an etched primer and leave to dry for a few days. I am fortunate that I have an airbrush and use that to spray the etched primer on; it is a two-part paint, and I add some cellulose thinners to ensure the paint is thin enough to spray. To finish, I use Black Hammerite Smooth out of an aerosol can (I put the can into hot water after shaking as this helps to mix the paint properly and spray better) and leave to dry for a few more days. It takes a long time for this paint to dry, and you have to leave it alone or you will get fingerprints on it.

Other people in the T300 community, such as Mick Perry, have had good results using Halfords Satin Black, but again preparation is the key, with an etch primer being used. Mick has also used the same paint for the crankcases and block – with the engine removed – and he has also used this paint on the wheels. It is allegedly resistant to brake fluid. The most effective paint would be epoxy caliper paint if you can get it.

Daytona 1200 in Diablo Black.

If you repaint the silver surround to the petrol filler and the black centre (with a rattle can), ensure you finish with a petrol-resistant lacquer, or the first time there is a petrol spillage the paint will blister.

Hammerite Satin Black paint.

Petrol-resistant lacquer.

7

upgrades and using non-Triumph parts

Triumph continually improves their bikes so components are reviewed and, if necessary, changed. Feedback from dealers and warranty claims all aid this process and Triumph in turn issue technical changes to the dealers.

Battery As mentioned many times, a good-quality, fully charged battery is essential to the health of the sprag clutch. The first upgrade that any owner should consider is upgrading the battery to at least an AGM one, such as Yuasa YTX14AHL-BS.

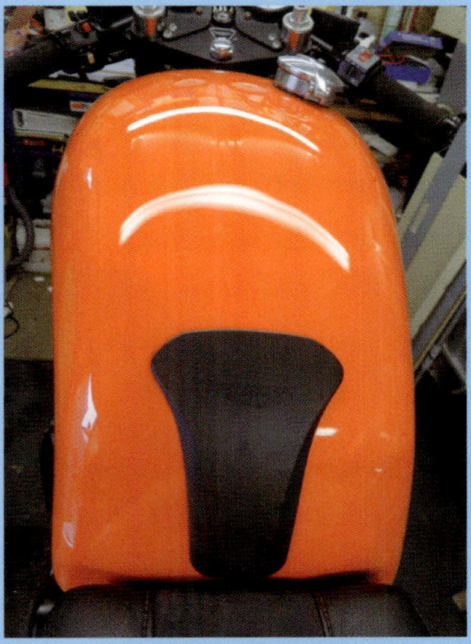

A modern Triumph tank pad on a CRK.

A Triumph tank pad from the 1990s.

Triumph tank pads The original tank pads were an aftermarket accessory and have not been available for many years. There were two versions, the later one, I think, being for the Thunderbird Sport and smaller than the original. They fetch good money second-hand – expect to pay around £50. Some people have even resorted to buying a tank just to get the tank pad. The latest tank protectors from Triumph can of course be used but these are much smaller; I have fitted one to my CRK as the one on my Speed Triple is far too large for the CRK tank.

Wing mirrors The mirrors fitted to the early Trophies (and Daytonas) were circular and quite small and can be swapped for the larger rectangular ones from the 1993–5 Trophy. These are similar to the mirrors on the Sprint and Sprint Sports. The original mirrors for the Speed Triple are no longer available from Triumph, but Sprint Manufacturing do a very close aftermarket part.

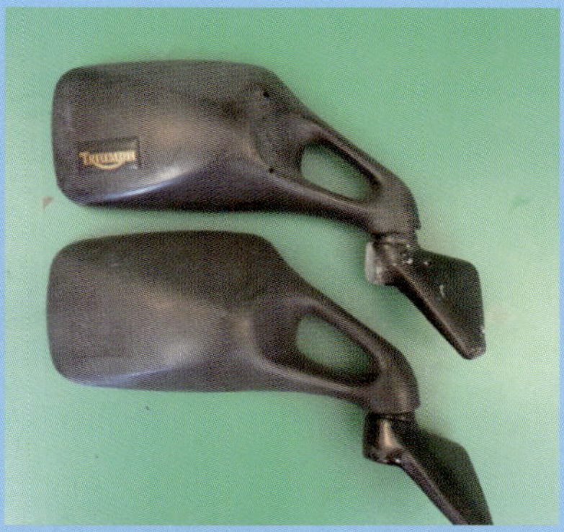

Trophy mirrors from 1993–5 were an upgrade on the earlier small, circular mirrors.

Bar end mirrors For me, the Speed Triple and the CRK conversions always look better with bar end mirrors. Most of those available in the aftermarket parts arena require the bar end weights (which are designed to dampen out vibrations from the engine) to be removed, but I was not happy with that so I had a set of Triumph bar end weights machined so that the bar end mirror clamp went around the machined part of the Triumph weight.

Modern Speed Triple mirror fixed to a Mk 1 Speed Triple.

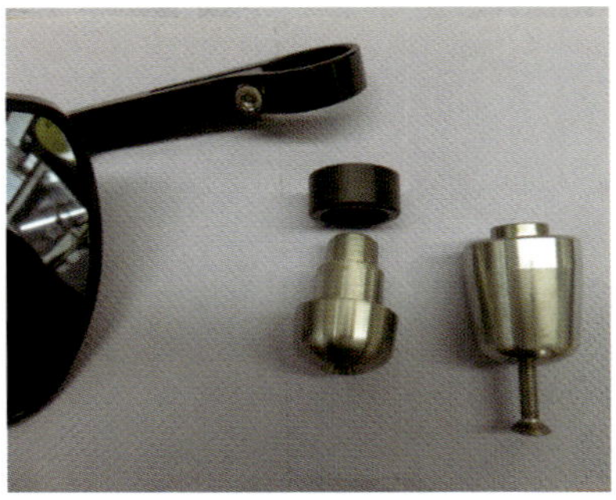

Bar end mirror with modified bar end weights compared to the standard bar ends.

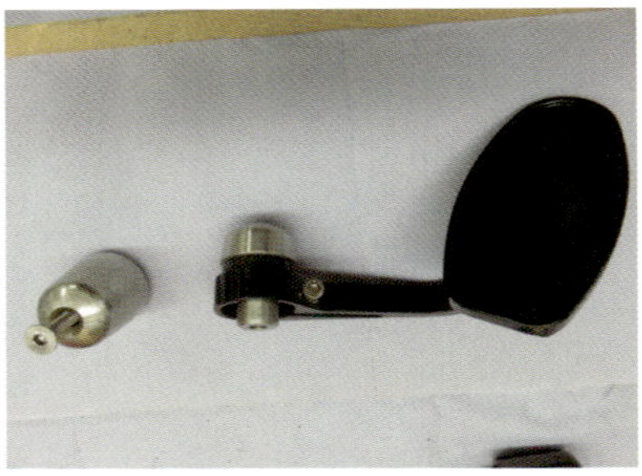

Bar end mirror.

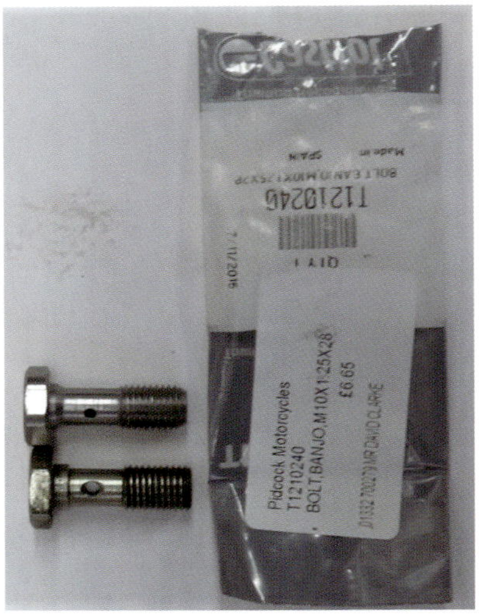

Modified oil feed union.

Bar end mirrors and modified bar end weights on a Speed Triple.

This retained some of the mass of the bar end weight. I also changed the screws that hold the bar end weights to the handlebar for stainless ones.

Igniters When Triumph modified the sprag clutch (by changing the speed at which the engine turns over), they also modified the igniter to spin the engine over twice before firing and changed the advance curve to give the sprag clutch an easier time. The revised igniter is a Gill one and is a worthwhile upgrade if you can find one (they don't seem to appear very often on the second-hand market). Combined with a decent battery and a conversion to stick coils, this should eliminate any sprag issues and improve running. I have now upgraded to a Gill igniter on my 1994 Speed Triple (along with stick coils).

Oil feed banjo While the T300 was still in production, Triumph modified the banjo bolt that fits at the rear of the cylinder head and feeds oil into the cylinder head from the crank. The original banjo bolt had a larger bore hole down the centre and a large hole on the side near the end. The replacement bolt has a smaller bore hole down the middle and a smaller hole in the side. The reasoning behind this change was to increase the oil pressure at the crank without compromising the flow of oil to the cylinder head. The part number for the revised item is the same as for the original part, which is a common practice by Triumph.

BELOW: Oil feed union (top) and cam chain tensioner (bottom).

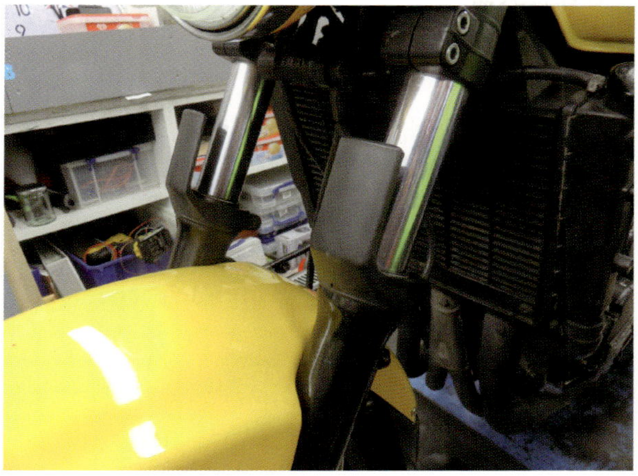

Fork protectors stop insects splattering on the fork legs, hardening and ruining the fork seals.

Centre stand.

Fork protectors These are a Triumph accessory and have been fitted to all my T300 bikes as a means of stopping dead bugs from drying on the fork legs and ripping the fork seals to bits. If you do lots of riding in hot countries or in Scotland in the midge season, these are essential and not expensive.

Mudguard extender The front mudguard on some of the models is quite short and can therefore throw up lots of road debris over the exhaust manifold and the front of the engine cases. Therefore I have fitted a mudguard extender to most of my bikes. These are an aftermarket item.

Mudguard extender; this will stop road muck landing on the downpipes and engine front.

Replacement dipstick The standard engine oil dipstick is made of plastic and can sometimes cross-thread itself when being screwed in and out. Sprint Manufacturing can sell you a

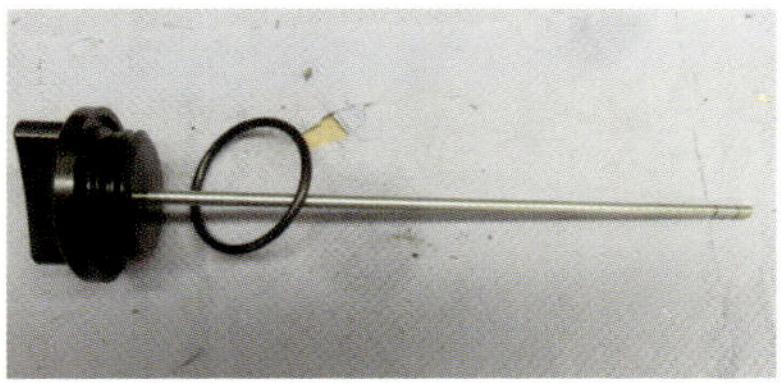

Replacement dipstick from Sprint Manufacturing.

quality dipstick CNC machined out of aluminium at a cost of around £30; I have one on my CRK.

Centre stand Triumph usually offered this as an accessory but it can be retro-fitted. However, there were different part numbers depending on the model, so buying on the second-hand market can be chancy. I know of at least four different centre stands, the main difference being the length of the lever part that goes under the foot when operating the stand.

If buying second-hand, be sure also to buy the handle that bolts to the subframe (on the near side) and allows the right hand to lift the bike onto the centre stand. You also need to check that the centre stand does not hit the silencers in the up position. Triumph sold a rubber stop, but if this is not available, a rubber door stop and a clamp can be improvised. The pivots on the centre

Rear engine plates. The centre stand goes into the half round at the bottom of the plate, and the spring goes into the small hole.

stand can also wear; the way to check is twist the centre stand with someone else holding the bike, and you should be able to feel any wear. The centre stand springs (two of these, one for each side engine plate) go into a small hole on one of the engine plates at the rear of the engine.

Longer side stand Triumph produced a modified side stand bracket, as the earlier type could bend (particularly on the 1200 bikes), and there was also a longer side stand fitted to the later Trophies, which was available as an accessory for a short time. Fitting the later side stand bracket is a worthwhile upgrade and the longer side stand if you can find one.

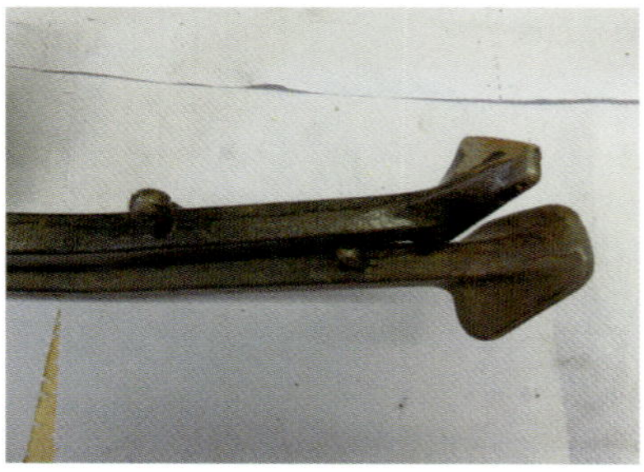

Side stands: original version (top) and revised (bottom). The increase in length is noticeable.

Original side stand bracket (top) and revised version (bottom).

Higher-compression pistons The engines in the range are modular so even if the crankcases remain the same, fitting a different crank and pistons would give different capacities, as the bore was always the same.

So pistons from the 750, 1000 and 1200, if fitted to a 900, will give a higher compression ratio and therefore more power. In fact, these were fitted to the Daytona Super 3 (along with high-lift and duration camshafts). These should give around a 10bhp increase. The only problem with this change is the availability of 750 or 1200 pistons – everybody wants them, so they are hard to find!

Super 3 cams The Super 3 is fitted with higher-compression pistons and some high-lift cams, which boosts power at the top end; the downside is the high-lift cams can cause accelerated valve seat recession. One solution is to fit Speed Triple cams and a standard 900 igniter. This will improve the mid-range and reduce the probability of valve recession. The Super 3 cams have the same profile as the cams fitted to the Daytona 1200.

Airbox modifications Triumph supplies the air filter complete with its airbox as a sealed unit, which should be changed every 40,000km (24,000 miles) or four years, whichever comes sooner. With all the bikes I have worked on, the air filter airbox was usually full of rubbish.

To change the air filter, you first need to remove the carburettors and inlet rubbers to gain access to the air cleaner. One possible modification is to cut the rear cover of the airbox down the middle so that, once the screws are removed, the two separate sections of the airbox can be taken out and the filter removed without removing the airbox from the bike. The four stainless steel screws go into brass inserts in the plastic housing and can be difficult to remove; sometimes the plastic boss breaks away. The solution is to drill the heads of the screws and do without. If you manage to get the screws out, lubricate with copper slip. Only one half of the modified rear cover needs to be removed.

An aftermarket air filter from K&N or Pipercross can be fitted, and this can be cleaned on a regular basis. If the standard Triumph air filter is in good condition it can also be cleaned, but in my experience they usually fall apart by the time they need changing!

It is tempting to fit three cone filters (such as K&N or similar), but the carburettors and induction system are designed around the standard Triumph snorkels and airbox so the fuelling may be affected. A session on a dynamometer will ensure the fuelling is spot on.

When building a CRK, the standard airbox and snorkels look horrible (as there is no bodywork to hide behind), so it is tempting to go down the route of fitting cone filters; however, the standard airbox can be fitted if the extensions at the back of the airbox are shortened and some aluminium mesh is placed inside to prevent larger stones from being sucked in. This will also give a neat appearance. Cavan Holden has made an excellent job of modifying the airbox on his CRK and there is more detail in the CRK section in Chapter 8.

Airbox and snorkels.

Rear of the Triumph airbox cut in half.

First half of the airbox cover screwed back on.

Both halves of the airbox cover back on.

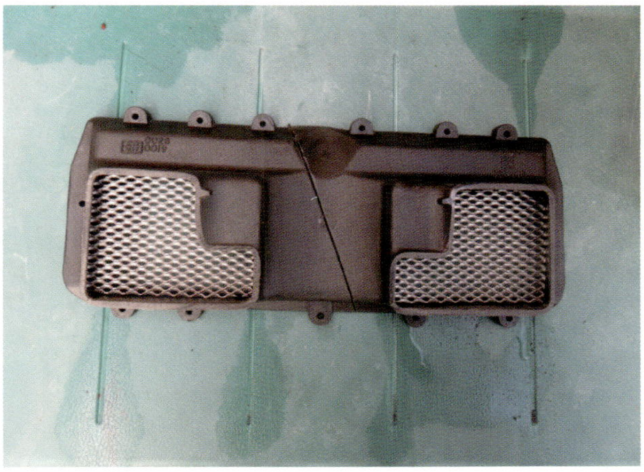

Cutting the back off the Triumph airbox.

A modified Triumph airbox on a Café Racer kit.

Front calipers and brake discs As mentioned elsewhere, Triumph can no longer supply new brake discs so aftermarket ones are the only ones available. Do not be tempted to buy cheap Chinese discs as they can warp very quickly and need changing again, so don't actually offer much cost saving. Given how safety-critical the brake discs are, don't skimp, buy quality discs and buy from recognized suppliers (such as EBC), not some unknown website, and, where possible, buy matching pads. There are some very nasty brake discs out there and I would not fit them to a push bike never mind a motorcycle. Triumph can still supply brake pads and I use these on the basis that they are designed to match the discs.

Bikes fitted with the early fixed discs and two-piston calipers can be upgraded to the floating discs from the later bikes along with the four-piston calipers. Under no circumstances should the four-piston calipers be fitted to the fixed discs (296mm) – you must use the larger-diameter floating discs (310mm). When upgrading to the four-piston calipers, you will find that the caliper mounting bolts are too long (there is a spacer on the two-piston ones), so you will need a new set of bolts specifically for them.

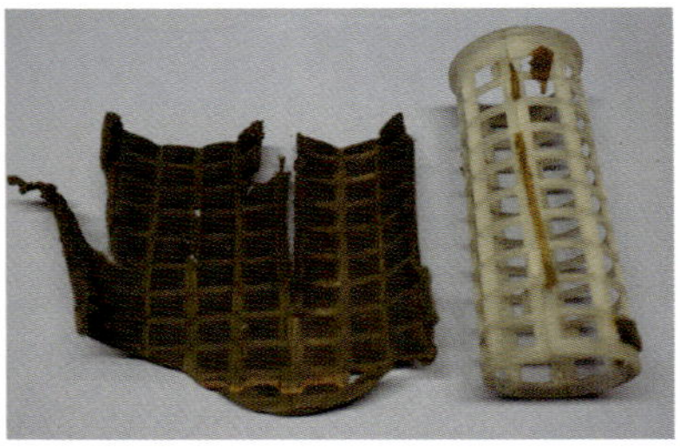

Degraded inserts to the snorkel; the foam was for sound-deadening purposes only.

Airbox trumpets.

Sebring manifold.

Air trumpets The airbox is connected at the rear with two snorkel tubes (one each side), which feed air into the airbox, and these tubes have inserts that are designed to reduce intake roar. The inserts have foam rubber, which disintegrates, but these inserts can be removed to increase power. If they are removed, then you can go up one size on the main jets in the carburettor. When John Wilcox tuned my Sprint Sports on a rolling road, these intake silencers were removed and, with rejetting, gave a 3bhp increase at 5,000rpm.

However, don't be tempted to remove the whole snorkel tube entirely. Mark Ambroz did some dynamometer tests many years ago where he found that doing this resulted in a drop in horsepower of between 3 and 5bhp. He then experimented with increasing the length of the snorkel tubes by fitting 30cm (1ft) of tubing (Toyota water hoses) over the ends, and found a 5bhp increase in power, as the extra tubes effectively increased the airbox volume.

Sound-deadening inserts into snorkels.

Exhausts Triumph can no longer supply any standard silencers of any type. These were made by Motad, who unfortunately are no longer in business. The ones used on the Daytona, Sprint Sports and Speed Triple models were in black chrome with a vinyl-type finish on the silencer body. There are small differences between the various models but they are all similar. With age, they rust through the junction of the silencer body and the link pipe, and are therefore difficult to repair.

As an aside, these original Daytona and Speed Triple silencers were extremely heavy, weighing in at a hefty 5.5kg (12lb) each. This compares with a set of Scorpion silencers and link pipes at 2.48kg (5.5lb), which thus give a significant weight saving of 3kg (6.5lb). I have a set of Scorpions on my Speed Triple and they also make a nice noise (when the removable baffles are taken out!). I also had a set of Yoshimura twin silencers, but they weighed in at 4.2kg (9lb) each, so not much lighter than the standard ones, and were also very quiet. Laser silencers are around

Sebring silencer fitted to a Speed Triple.

Another view of a Sebring exhaust, showing the clamp and Triumph badge.

2kg (4.5lb) each, so again offer a significant weight saving.

As an aftermarket system, Triumph offered a 3-1 system manufactured by Austrian company Sebring (but with a Triumph badge on the silencer), and this offered a little more power at the top end and some weight saving. Some of the teams in the Speed Triple Challenge used this system as an alternative to the TTS/Yoshimura system.

The Sebring system cost £599 when new but can be bought for around £350 on the second-hand market, although it is hard to find, and the silencer may need to be reskinned.

The jetting needs to be changed to get the best out of the Sebring system:

Pilot	40
Main jets	127 (possibly130)
Needle raised by	20 thou (1 clip position)
Air screws	3ppm CO

Fuel consumption will drop from 41mpg (6.9ltr/100km) to 37mpg (7.6ltr/100km).

The ultimate performance system to fit to the T300 range is the system allowed in the Speed Triple Challenge race series. The manifold was made by TTS (in Silverstone) and was a 3-4-3-2-1 configuration usually fitted with a Yoshimura silencer – hence the fact that it was usually referred to as a Yoshimura system.

Approximately seventy sets of the TTS manifolds were made so they are hard to find, but I am aware that some

TTS manifold 3-4-3-2-1.

Yoshimura silencer fitted to a Sprint.

Twin Yoshimura silencers fitted to a Speed Triple.

Mark Gaylard's Speed Triple when it was fitted with Scorpion exhaust silencers.

Delvic silencer.

copies were made. This system gives a better mid-range as well as at the top of the rev range; I can vouch for that as my restored Speed Triple Challenge bike had one fitted. The major disadvantage of the system is that it covers the oil filter, so for an oil change the system has to be dismantled. The TTS system is sometimes mated to a Sebring silencer as these are cheaper than a Yoshimura one, as the race teams found out! The TTS manifolds are very hard to find in the UK and, if found, are expensive.

A number of manufacturers made replacement and performance silencers for the T300 range, but most of these are no longer available, although they do turn up on Triumph forums or eBay:

- Mark Gaylard had a set of reverse cone megaphones from a company in America, Cone Engineering.
- Micron made a 3-1 system, and this saved about 11kg (24lb) over the standard system.
- Delvic.
- German company Remus made a 3-1 system with a distinct bulge just in front of the silencer.
- Scorpion made very nice carbon-style silencers of excellent quality, which are significantly lighter than the standard Triumph silencers. I have a set on my Speed Triple and, with the removable baffles taken out, they make a really nice, fruity noise. Expect to pay around £250-plus for a good set second-hand. Scorpion also made a 3-1 system with a single silencer.
- SP Engineering are still manufacturing silencers, which are excellent quality, but they no longer do the correct style end caps, having moved to a Moto GP-style end cap.
- ART silencers are no longer available and reports are that they were not of the highest build quality.
- Laser.

The performance gains of fitting aftermarket exhausts are limited without putting on a dynamometer, but they usually save a significant amount of weight over standard.

The exhaust manifold, being stainless steel, can of course be polished, which is what I have done with my CRK;

Remus silencer.

These 8mm domed brass nuts cover the cylinder head studs; don't forget to apply ceramic paste on the studs before screwing on.

Remus exhaust, as fitted to a Speed Triple.

Domed nuts fitted to the engine.

A polished exhaust manifold, showing the stainless steel construction on a CRK.

you just have to remember to clean this regularly.

To protect the ends of the exhaust studs, I fitted some 8mm brass domed nuts over the studs and used some ceramic paste before screwing on the nuts.

Wheels Upgrading from the earlier six-spoke 18in wheels to the later three-spoke 17in ones is possible but this will lower the bike, so a replacement longer rear shock absorber will be required to maintain the handling. The 18in wheels are now limited with regard to what tyre sizes are available as most bikes now run 17in wheels, although Avon have recently announced the Spirit ST tyres in 160/60 ZR18.

The three-spoke wheels are relatively heavy but are fine for general road use. Mark Gaylard, who hill climbs and does track days on his Mk 1 Speed Triple, has however fitted a set of Dymag forged alloy wheels to save weight and improve the handling. Dymag have in the past been the main suppliers of lightweight wheels for T300 series in the UK, and supplied the three-spoke magnesium race wheels used back in

Dymag forged alloy wheels.

Dymag forged alloy front wheel.

the day. They now make a retro copy of these wheels but in forged aluminium. Other options are carbon, or their UP7X forged aluminium wheel, which is the lightest forged wheel they do and is used at the TT and other races.

The three-spokes weren't available when Mark wanted to order some, so the UP7X it was to be. Dymag carries all the spacer gaps and mounting info to make these wheels for T300s, but this was probably a first fit for this type of wheel onto his Speed Triple, and a few minor things were thrown up as a result. Given a choice of 5.5in or 6in rear rim, Mark went for 5.5in to keep original handling characteristics, and they come with a rear sprocket in your choice of tooth count.

The main issue is that as there is less mass and material on the wheel, the original long disc bolts from Triumph won't fit (there is literally less 'body' for the bolt to screw into), so Mark had to use Suzuki disc bolts, which are shorter and have a shallower shoulder (29mm total length as opposed to 33mm

Rear of a Dymag forged alloy wheel, showing the shorter Suzuki disc bolts.

originals). Everything else is plug and play; you lose the original cush drive and rear wheel spacers as these are all supplied with the new wheel, but the front wheel spacers are reused.

Original Triumph three-spoke Brembo wheels with all the wheel hardware and tyres on come in 14.7kg (32.5lb) at the front and 19kg (42lb) at the rear. In comparison, the front Dymag comes in at 11.1kg (24.5lb), a saving of 3.6kg (7.5lb). Mark was too eager to fit the rear wheel to do a weight comparison, so that will have to happen later, but Dymag quotes anywhere between 5 and 6.5kg (11–14.5lb) difference here, making about 10kg (22lb) in total.

From the off, the front end was transformed. Steering input is so minimal that you have to continually recalibrate your head and the way you grip the bars – the more lightly you hold the bars the better it feels, as if you weight them up at all you unconsciously put input into the steering and it feels a little weird. Suspension, acceleration and braking all benefit, but the first and biggest result is the quicker steering!

The cost was around £2,000 – not cheap, but then this is a significant upgrade for the bike.

It is possible to fit the later three-spoke wheels to a Tiger, but some work will be required on the spacers and connecting the speedometer drive.

One of the issues with the wheels is that getting an air line onto the front wheels is a real pain. I would suggest fitting some 90-degree valves to the wheels the next time you change the tyres. The size of the hole in the wheels is different between the six- and three-spoke wheels , the six-spoke one being 11.3mm and the three-spoke 8.3mm. These can be bought in silver or black.

Triumph part number T2000248, 'valve assembly alum', is a perfect fit on a three-spoke wheel. Clean the hole before fitting the valves to ensure a good seal.

Ninety-degree tyre valves.

Rear brake reservoir from a later Triumph.

Rear brake reservoir The standard Triumph rear brake reservoir is plastic but is hidden away under the standard side panel. If you are building a CRK or carrying out other modifications then the reservoir can be replaced with one from a 2010 Triumph Speed Triple, which is in blackened aluminium and looks much better.

Stainless pins for the rear brake caliper The standard sliding pins tend to go rusty and prevent the brake pads from sliding. Sprint Manufacturing does a replacement set in stainless steel, which are not cheap but are good quality. If you ride all year round and in all weathers, this is an essential modification.

Stainless steel pins fitted to rear brake slave cylinder.

Removing the oil cooler All the models with fairing panels also had

Oil cooler connections.

Oil cooler bypass pipe; this is required if the oil cooler is removed.

Tokico six-piston front brakes. Note the TTS manifold fitted to the bike.

oil coolers fitted. If you are going to build a CRK or a Speed Quattro – or just remove the fairing – you no longer need the oil cooler. However, the cooler is part of the oil system, so if it's removed a bridging pipe is required, and this can be either a Triumph part or one supplied by CRK.

Alcon six-piston calipers When Triumph launched the Daytona Super 3 they were fitted as standard with American-made Alcon six-piston aluminium calipers branded 'Triumph'.

These calipers were also used on the Daytona SE special edition, and were also listed in the Triumph accessory catalogue, but were expensive, at around £300 pounds each. They were available in two colours, black and gold (from late 1995 onwards). These calipers can give a brake upgrade but they are difficult to find as well as pricey – expect to pay in excess of £500 for a set, and they then may need overhauling so the real cost could be nearer £600. If you buy a set, check the threaded parts on the caliper body as the alloy for the casting of the body is very soft and the steel threads on the bolts can pick up the soft alloy casting. Most castings require a helicoil insert inserted to rectify.

On my Super 3, I found they gave greater braking force but seemed less sensitive than the Nissin four-piston calipers with a very sharp initial bite. Clive Wood, who raced in the Speed Triple Challenge, prefers the Nissin four-pots as they gave better feel under extreme braking. A properly serviced Nissin four-piston system is more than adequate for the road. The Alcons do look nice, though!

Alcon six-pot calipers.

Alcon six-piston calipers sold as an accessory. The reflector on the fork leg on this Super 3 shows it was an American-spec bike.

Tokico six-piston calipers Given that the supply of the Alcon Triumph six-piston calipers is very limited and the cost is high, owners have been tempted to fit the six-piston Tokico calipers, as used on many Japanese bikes, instead. These are readily available and cheap, but owners have reported mixed results.

The seal kits to overhaul these calipers are very expensive and there are reports that complete overhauls are required almost on an annual basis. The Nissin four-pots are much cheaper to maintain. The gain in braking performance over the standard four-piston Nissin calipers is also marginal (*see above*). Gordon Smith fitted the Tokico calipers to his 1997 Trophy but reported that they lacked 'feel' and reverted back to the standard Triumph/Nissin four-pots.

Ivan at National Triumph reports that he sells many Nissin-branded four-piston calipers to Japanese bike owners who have been horrified at the cost of overhauling the Tokico calipers

Sprint Executive fitted with a fuel gauge.

and the general state of corrosion, so consider the Triumph four-pots are a better option.

Fitting a fuel gauge The only bike in the T300 range fitted with a fuel gauge as standard is the revised Trophy from 1996, but many of the other bikes in the range (Sprint, Sprint Executive and Tiger) have a clock included in the dashboard. Gordon Smith has fitted a fuel gauge (from a Mk 2 Trophy) to his Sprint Executive by removing the clock and enlarging the hole by 3mm. To avoid having to use a Trophy tank (which has a float sender unit inside the tank), he performed a bit of wiring trickery to use the Mk1 Trophy low fuel (thermistor-type) sensor, which would normally drive the low fuel warning light.

The other option is to use a Mk 2 Trophy tank and float sender unit.

Replacing the fuel tap with a Pingel-style tap Given that many of the original fuel taps are now over twenty years old, some owners have decided to replace the standard tap with a Pingel-style one. This requires some modification, as the vacuum pipe needs to be blanked off – just remove the vacuum hose and fit a blanking plug to the carburettor top. A high-flow tap with a 34mm adapter plate will cost around £150 and the carburettor float valves need to be in good shape to prevent flooding. Also remember that the fuel inlet pipes into the carburettors are 8mm so the outlet of any Pingel-style tap must be 8mm; anything smaller risks fuel starvation at high speed.

Personally, having got used to a vacuum tap on all my T300s and having fitted a Pingel-style tap to my CRK conversion, I don't always remember to turn the tap off when parking up. I then have to rely on the float levels being correct to stop fuel overflowing into the airbox and sump.

Radiator fan switch As an alternative to the Triumph part, a car part (used on the Mini Metro) can be used. The part number is Lucas SNB748. The fan switch normally initiates at 99°C, but using an alternative means you can set it to come on at a lower temperature. If touring in hot countries, consider putting in a manual override to enable you to turn the fan on at any time.

Gordon Smith suggests wiring in a cooling fan bypass switch is fairly simple to do and he found it very useful for slow traffic on hot days on a bike with a fairing. Below are his instructions.

When you test the cooling fan, the easiest method is to short the two terminals on the fan switch (halfway down the rear left-hand side of the radiator) with a flat-bladed screwdriver or similar. There may be a few sparks but if the fan or fan fuse are OK then the fan will run up (this does not test the fan switch itself). Remove the screwdriver blade and the fan stops. This can be done with the ignition off, meaning the fan switch is always live – if the fan is running when you've been riding the bike and you switch off the ignition, it sometimes runs until the hot coolant has cooled sufficiently to turn the fan switch off.

Pingel-style petrol tap.

Radiator fan switch under the rubber cover.

Manual override switch in the OFF position.

Manual override switch in the ON position.

Connected to the radiator switch.

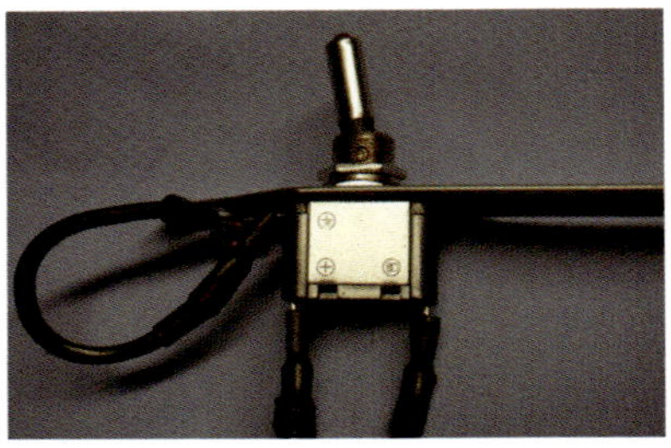

Manual override switch.

Connectors to the radiator switch.

Most motor factors stock a variety of switches – I chose one that costs about £5 and has a red-coloured LED in the toggle. It's 'single pole' – that is, it makes one contact connecting in to out – and 'single throw', so it's either on or off. Motor factors also stock Faston-type crimp terminals in small packs and suitable (15 amp) accessory insulated wire.

A small earth strap is required to ensure the LED works correctly and the ring terminal needs to be attached to the bike frame earth. On the Sprint Executive, that is the fairing mounting frame instrument mounting boss.

Decide where you might want to mount the fan bypass switch. I prefer not to drill through precious original panels but use an existing fixture point. Similarly, I'd rather not cut or splice into the original wiring if I can avoid it.

Make up two suitable lengths of 10-amp accessory wire with a push-fit (Faston) spade terminal at one end and a Faston piggy-back spade terminal at the other. Remove the wiring terminals from the fan switch and push them on to the bare piggy-back blades, then put the piggy-back female spades onto the fan switch.

Test before you decide on a Final Fit.

At the other end of the two wires, push the Faston females onto the switch terminals coming from the main body of the switch, and connect a short strap (ring terminal at one end, Faston female spade at the other) from the switch earth terminal to the switch body for this initial test.

If the fan switches on straight away and the LED illuminates then that is the ON position. Move the switch toggle to the other position and the fan should stop and the LED go out. That is the OFF position.

All you have to do then is wrap the bypass switch wires with electrical insulating tape (I used a plastic spiral wrap made for the purpose of tidying up wiring) and feed them back up under the tank, through the headstock triangle to pass by the steering head, making sure it won't get trapped when the handlebars are turned lock to lock (do not be tempted to tie-wrap it to either the choke or throttle cable – use a wiring harness branch or limb if you have to), and then up to your chosen bypass switch mounting position.

Install the bypass switch. Connect the three wires and test briefly. Bear in mind that overuse of the fan bypass switch when the engine is not running will reduce the charge state of the battery.

Clutch springs If the power of the triple engine has been increased, some clutch slip may be discernible under hard acceleration, so it may be worth fitting the clutch springs from a 1200 Daytona. These are longer than the standard 900 ones so are a bit of a challenge to get started in the clutch gasket, and it is important not to over-tighten the bolts (10Nm). It is reported that some T300 owners prefer the EBC heavy-duty clutch springs (CSK68), available from Sprint Manufacturing. These are 15 per cent stronger than the standard clutch springs and do the same job.

Speed Triple radiator cover reflectors These are still available from Triumph but are very expensive for what is effectively two pieces of orange plastic. These reflectors also have a habit of falling off and they need to be removed from the radiator cover to access the two screws that secure the cover to the radiator. I have used Velcro strips on the reflector and the cover to make removal easier.

KTM offers an identical reflector at a considerably lower price; the part number is 60012080100 and the cost approximately £4. Royal Enfield also uses a similar reflector (581273/A) at a cost of about £2.50.

Speed Triple radiator cover with Velcro to attach the reflector.

Speed Triple radiator reflector with Velcro on the back.

A Speed Triple radiator cover with reflector.

Using 955 parts Internally, the early 955 engines used many components from the 885 engines, and some parts from later engines will fit onto a T300. For example, 955 cams up to 2002 and 955i cams post 2002 will fit, but the sprockets for the cam chain will need changing. Bob Cornforth has used 955 liners and pistons in his Daytona 1200 Sprint bike.

Using T595 cams from the later T500 engines up to the 1050 engines is possible, but you will need to check duration and lift, and then the cam wheels will need to be slotted and dialled in with dial gauges. The piston to valve

Bob Cornforth's sprinting 1200 fitted with 955 liners and pistons.

clearance will also need to be checked. To maximize the benefit of fitting of these cams, the revs need to increase from 10,000 to 10,200. If this is done, then the connecting rods will need to be shot peened and forged pistons. The rest of the engine will then need blueprinting.

You can also fit 955 liners and pistons, but the crankcase will need machining to take the liners.

Aftermarket handlebars on Denis Fitch's 1200 Speed Quattro.

Handlebars The modular quality of the Triumph range means that handlebars from different models can be fitted to most models. The top yokes on some models have the casting such that holes can be drilled to mount those handlebars that are bolted from the top. A popular swap is to fit Sprint Sports bars to Daytonas, as these are a little higher than the standard bars. Very early Trophy handlebars are the same, but neither are easy to find.

There are a number of aftermarket companies, such as LSL, that sell handlebars, and many will also supply twin clamps to place the bars across the top yoke. However, you will need to do a trial fitting as the bars you choose may not clear any fairing panels.

Denis Fitch has fitted a number of different bars to his fleet of bikes, as you can see in the pictures here.

LSL handlebars fitted to a Speed Triple.

Sprint Sports handlebars fitted to Denis Fitch's bike.

Handlebar raising blocks.

Keihin 36/39/40mm FCR flat slide carburettors These carburettors are usually found on race bikes but can be fitted to the T300 for a small increase in performance. They will work best on a tuned engine (hotter cams, ported head, increased compression) – in other words, it allows more airflow through than a standard engine – and a performance exhaust at the cost of dramatically increased fuel consump-

Keihin flat-slide carburettors fitted to the racing Tiger owned by Jonathan Willkie.

tion. For a road bike they are not particularly user-friendly; for instance, if you 'whack' open the throttle, the engine will stumble and hesitate.

If you really want to go down the flat slide carburettor route, then fit 36mm ones, though these still come with a heavy fuel consumption cost.

Paul Humphries has fitted Mikuni 36 flat slides as he prefers the Mikunis to the Keihin ones.

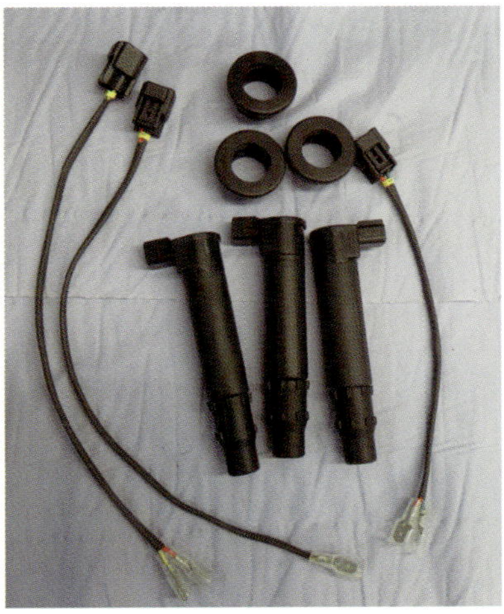

Stick coils from Paul Messenger.

Stick coils (coil on plug conversion) The standard coils sit right above the engine in an extremely hot environment, and over time can fail. The design of these coils is now thirty years old, and both bike and car manufacturers have moved to using stick coils, which are smaller and produce a fatter spark. Until recently there was no source of stick coils for the T300 range, as the coils need to be compatible with the igniter, but Paul Messenger (who has been associated with T300 from the beginning) has spent much time

Stick coil connections with the old coils removed.

Stick coils fitted.

evaluating various stick coils to match the Triumph electronics and igniter.

This is an upgrade that is recommended, particularly if one of the existing coils has decided to fail. Replacing the original coils with like for like will cost around the same as buying a set of stick coils from Paul (around £200). I have these stick coils on both my Speed Triple and my CRK.

Do not attempt to fit stick coils of unknown origin, as they will most likely cause a failure of the igniter. Replacing the igniter is an expensive issue – a PVL will cost upwards of £120 and a Gill closer to £150.

Unfortunately, the stick coil conversion can only be made for the 3-cylinder engines, as the 4-cylinder bikes use a 'wasted' spark system and the igniters are not compatible for use with stick coils.

Standard coils and connections.

Crash bungs On the Speed Triple and Trident, the radiator and radiator covers are the first things that would be damaged in the event of the bike being on its side, so some crash bungs would be useful. The only source of crash bungs that I am aware of is a German company, but they are available in the UK; I bought mine on eBay, following a tip from Mark Gaylard. Look for GSG Mototechnik crash pads and quote the model. I paid £60 for mine on the Speed Triple (also listed for Trident 750 and 900) in 2018 from Square Deals UK. Other companies may also provide crash bungs if you search.

Neutral sender unit As an alternative to the Triumph neutral light switch, a Honda CBR 1000RR Fireblade, 2004–07, gear neutral switch will fit.

Crash bungs fitted to a Speed Triple.

Bottom crankcase showing oil filter cover and oil pressure switch.

Front forks The standard front forks are fine for road use (as long as they have been serviced on a regular basis) but they can be modified. Changing the front springs is a starting point, but beware of using progressive springs as they are not as good as fitting quality linear ones. A number of companies can offer a fork overhaul and upgrade, including Maxton and Nitron, but this is not a cheap option, starting at around £400; if you are a spirited rider or a track day regular, however, this is the way to go.

You can of course fit a set of bottom fork adjusters from companies like Nitron yourself; expect to pay £75 each. Given that the standard fork bottom adjusters are liable to seize up, it is a worthwhile upgrade.

As you will read in Chapter 9, 955 bottoms can be used, or you can change the forks completely. The issue with fitting forks from different brands is ensuring that the fork legs are long

Compression damping: standard at the bottom, replacement at the top.

Tiger front forks with 955 hub and rim fitted to one of Sean Symonds' specials.

enough, otherwise the front of the bike will end up much lower than originally designed, with consequent strange handling. Installing front forks from a different manufacturer will also mean changing the head bearings and possibly the top and bottom yokes.

If you are mixing and matching front fork components, get them checked by a suspension expert, as you don't want the front forks either going solid without warning or collapsing.

Paul Humphreys has fitted a complete set of Tiger 1050 front forks to his modified Trident, but the Tiger 1050 yokes had to be modified to fit the T300 stem. The Tiger forks were the correct length, however, so preserved the stance of the bike and its handling.

YSS rear shock fitted to a Speed Triple.

Rear shock absorbers The original rear shocks are not rebuildable; there are companies who advertise this service, but what they actually do is refurbish the external parts so they look good while leaving the internals untouched. Triumph no longer sells replacement rear shock absorbers but there are plenty of aftermarket suppliers:

Proflex The Speed Triple Challenge race bikes were only allowed one aftermarket rear shock absorber, made by Proflex. This is longer than the standard rear shock, which raises the rear of the bike, and has a remote adjuster. These are no longer available new but Proflex will do a full rebuild; be prepared to pay in the region of £300 for this if you also replace the spring. You will also need to pay close attention to the chain run to ensure that the chain rubbing strip and the swing arm are not being damaged. I myself have found it's not really a road shock absorber (it was fitted to my ex-Speed Triple Challenge bike).

Proflex rear shock after refurbishment.

YSS A recent addition to the UK market, this company originally developed shock absorbers and springs in Thailand for racing, but have now expanded into the road bike market. There are now a number of agents in the UK for these shocks. Expect to pay around £350 for a shock absorber and spring. Paul Messenger can also supply YSS rear shock absorbers. I have a set on the 1994 Speed Triple.

Hagon This UK company has been making aftermarket shock absorbers and springs for many years and has a good reputation for the price. Expect to pay around £350 for a rear shock absorber. I fitted one to my CRK bike and I found their service excellent.

Nitron and Maxton As with front forks, Maxton and Nitron can supply a quality rear shock with a spring customized to the rider's weight. Both are excellent companies to deal with but not cheap.

Hagon rear shock absorber with the revised drop link.

Ignition key I would always recommend having a spare key for your bike. Triumph used to sell keys and blanks but I am not sure if they are still available; you would need to supply the number that is stamped on the original key. Certainly the last time I bought a blank from Triumph they were significantly cheaper than a Triumph fully cut key. The cost of getting the blank cut was very small so this was a significant saving over a full key. If you can't find a Triumph blank then a Kawasaki or Yamaha blank may be the same.

Levers The standard levers are fine in my view, but a host of aftermarket companies sell very flash brake and clutch levers. My only comment would be to beware of buying cheap levers from China: there have been reports of these cheap levers breaking with tragic consequences, and a broken stub for the brake is going to cause major problems as it only breaks when a hard brake application is made. So only buy from reputable brands and companies such as Rizoma, Oberon or ASV, for example, for peace of mind, and make sure that they are not counterfeited copies.

Silicone hoses With the original hoses for the cooling system now over twenty years old, it is prudent to consider changing them. The first thing to do is to carry out a thorough check for any cracks; if in doubt, change them, as a burst hose could cause considerable damage to the engine and having your legs covered in boiling coolant is also not recommended. The choice is then either to replace with Triumph parts or upgrade to some silicone hoses. These are more expensive than the Triumph ones but are well worth the money. I would also change any Jubilee clips to stainless steel, purely for the cosmetic appearance.

Indicators The standard Triumph indicators are big and very noticeable, to say the least. Of course, they are now also getting on in years and are prone to suffer from cracking and breaking stalks. Sprint Manufacturing now sells new stalks.

The indicator stalks are screwed to the back of the lamp unit with two screws, and the indicator lens is held on by a single screw from the rear of the lamp unit.

If you are not obsessive about origi-

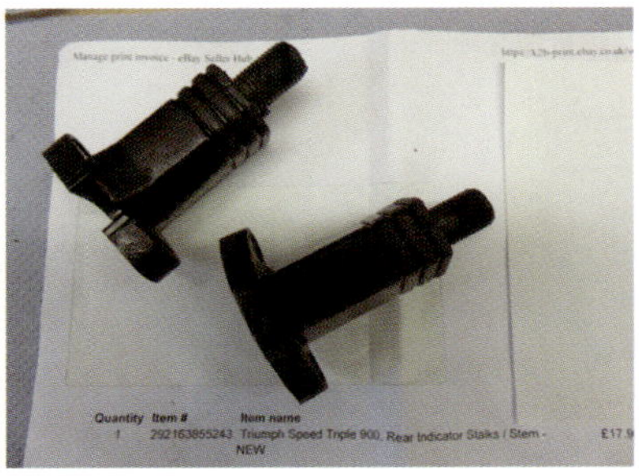

Replacement rear indicator stalks from Sprint Manufacturing.

Silicone hoses fitted to Mark Gaylard's Speed Triple.

Aftermarket indicators on a CRK.

CNC indicators from Norman Hyde.

nality, there are many aftermarket indicators available, as well as indicators from later Hinckley Triumphs. On my CRK, I have used indicators sold by Norman Hyde, which are CNC milled from aluminium.

Speed Triple water hose cover The Speed Triple is fitted with a cover for the water pipe going into the radiator. When building my CRK, I fitted one of these covers, but I had to modify part of it as the CRK tank is a different shape.

Headlight bulbs Most bikes of the 1990s have pretty poor headlights, so if any night riding is on the cards then an upgrade of the headlights is essential. The original headlamp performance is down to the quality of the Triumph lens and accurate alignment (to avoid dazzling oncoming traffic). A number of T300 owners have gone to using LED H4 equivalents. As ever, quality matters; Gordon Smith bought a pair of Phillips Ultinon and they cost £120. LEDs use considerably less of the available electrical energy from the alternator so more can go to keeping the battery charged up, especially important if you ride in daylight with the headlamps on. LED performance does not diminish anywhere near as rapidly as a standard H4 bulb does.

Water pipe cover from a Speed Triple, along with crash bungs.

Non-locking fuel cap If the ignition lock has been changed and you don't want to carry two keys, the

RIGHT: Ducati filler cap mounting rubber; it needed a bit of butchering to fit.

RIGHT: Ducati filler cap mounting rubber with the cap mounted.

LEFT: Ducati filler cap on Mark Gaylard's Speed Triple.

locking fuel cap can be removed and an alternative cap fitted. Oberon do some nice aftermarket ones, and some Ducati caps also fit. Mark Gaylard fitted a Ducati cap but the original Triumph rubber insert did need to be hacked about, as can be seen in the pictures.

Restoring rubber Many rubber components go hard with age, and on the T300 this has happened to many of the rubbers used to fix on the bodywork. Rather than buying new ones, an easy fix is to soak them overnight in a mixture of three parts alcohol and one part wintergreen oil. Overnight the rubber absorbs the oil and the rubber softens. Wintergreen oil is derived from a plant and has many medicinal uses; you can buy it on the internet.

Rear sets The German company LSL makes some lovely parts for Triumph bikes, including rear sets and adjustable handlebars. They currently have an extensive range for the more modern Triumphs and they certainly used to supply rear sets for the Daytona/Speed Triple range, so are worth hunting down. The bike in the photograph is owned by Sean Symonds.

LSL rear sets for a Daytona.

Steering dampers These were fitted to the Speed Triple Challenge bikes and only one brand was available – from Sprint. However, Sprint (not to be confused with Sprint Manufacturing, who supply lots of T300 parts) has now gone out of business and the steering dampers are no longer available. The dampers came with a special bracket that bolted onto the cam cover and allowed the rear of the damper arm to bolt to it, while the front clamped the fork leg. In the earlier versions, the fork tube cover on the Speed Triple would have to be cut back, but a later version did not require the cutting of the cover.

Sprint steering damper, fitted to the author's ex-Speed Triple Challenge bike.

Sprint steering damper bracket.

I had one of these dampers fitted to my ex-Speed Triple Challenge bike and I found it did nothing for the handling unless you were riding at silly speeds. They were only fitted to the Challenge bikes, as the back of the bike was raised and the forks dropped through the yokes, making the bikes a bit 'flighty'. For normal road settings they are not necessary. If you are building a Speed Challenge replica, then it's a must!

Thunderbird clutch cover As mentioned before, the Thunderbird, Legend, Adventurer and Thunderbird Sport had revised engine covers on both sides of the crankcase. During the Speed Triple Challenge race series, to give greater ground clearance when the bike was leaning over, some teams fitted a Thunderbird clutch cover. If you want to follow this path, however, you will not only need the clutch cover but also the two figure-of-eight covers on both sides of the engine and, more importantly, the breathing vane that fits on the end of the crank shaft on the nearside, underneath the cover. When the Thunderbird engine range was produced, Triumph completely revised the engine breathing system hence the revised engine cases and, internally, the breathing vane. Not all bikes have the crankshaft that would allow the fitment of the breathing vane, so check the crankshaft before doing anything. I would presume that only bikes built after 1995 and the introduction of the Thunderbird would have the potential to fit the breathing vane.

Weight saving There is no doubt that the bikes are heavy, particularly when you're moving them around the garage. So any weight saving you can make helps with this as well as improving performance. Mark Gaylard has made the following weight-saving improvements:

Carbon exhaust silencers save around 9kg (20lb). The standard silencers are incredibly heavy!
Lithium-ion battery, 4kg (9lb).
Renthal alloy rear sprocket, 0.5kg (1lb).

This gives a total of 13.5kg (30lb), so is definitely worth doing if you are already upgrading parts anyway.

The next significant weight saving comes from fitting either forged alloy or carbon-fibre wheels. Expect to pay in excess of £2,000 for this, but the benefits go beyond just weight saving, as the reduced mass of the wheels also improves the handling.

Programmable igniter unit Not something that goes wrong very often, the standard igniter (either Gill or PVL) has pre-programmed into it the ignition advance and retard to map the way the bike fires the plugs according to the state of tune, for example what cams are installed, the rev limit and so on. The basic PVL/Gill igniter is fine; the state of tune for the Speed Triple or Daytona, for example, gives pretty good power and torque curve and was also tweaked to help alleviate sprag clutch issues by spinning the engine a few times without any ignition.

If you are tuning the bike or just want a replacement module, the Ignitech TCIP4 igniter for T300s offers a more modern, more compact and cooler-running replacement that will give a sharper, stronger pulse to the plugs; in combination with stick coils, it would update and improve the complete ignition package of a T300.

Furthermore, the TCIP4 is fully programmable to allow you to have two ignition maps of ignition advance, and flip between the two if you wish for different states of tune. It will come with a good functional map already installed that will allow you to plug and play; to take full advantage of its more advanced features, a dynamometer is by far the best and safest way to tweak your ignition map to suit your cams, carburettors and exhaust system and silencers.

The best method is to sort the carburettors to suit your air filter and exhaust first, then try a few runs on the dynamometer to see if plotting the ignition advance up or down improves the power/torque at any given revs.

Clutch and timing cover used on Thunderbirds and Legends.

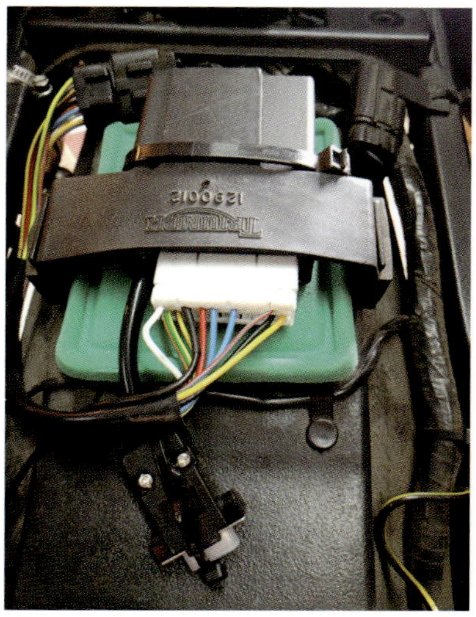

Ignitech programmable igniter unit.

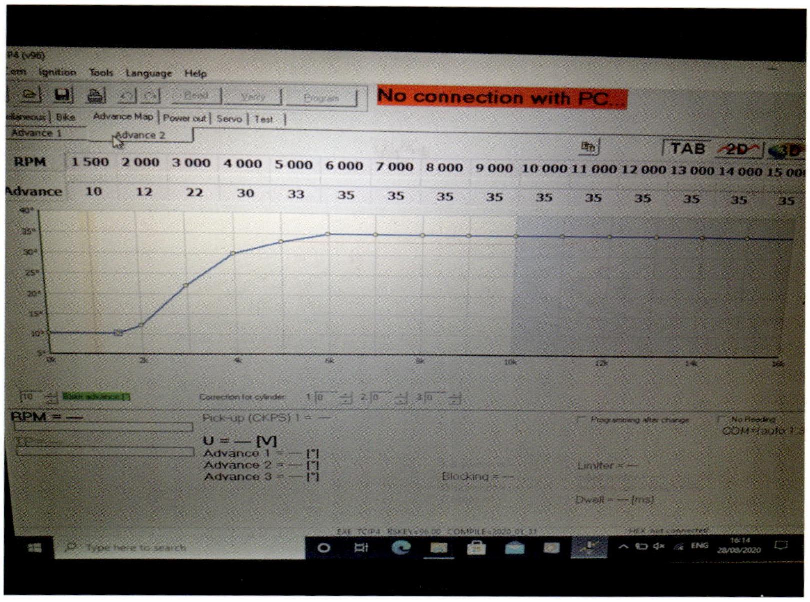

Ignitech graph.

This final map should give you the best possible combination of ignition mapping to maximize any other modifications you may or may not have on the bike.

If your modifying abilities and desires are up to it, you can do a whole host of other modifications with this unit, including the dwell time of the coils, rev limit, the advance at start-up, running a fuel pump, gear shift light, quick shifter, a servo for the exhaust valve, testing tachometer accuracy and adjustment and more.

Caution is needed, though – you can't just rush in and start tweaking, as you risk adjusting things that could potentially make the bike run badly and, worse, damage the engine. The dynamometer is the best place to explore a lot of the options available.

Even to use as just a replacement item, the Ignitech is good value and would cost not much more than a second-hand Gill unit. It comes with a patch lead to plug directly into the loom, and a lead to connect to your laptop. The software has several pages where adjustments can be made, but I say again a dynamometer is the best place to make adjustments unless you really know what you are doing!

Mark Gaylard has fitted this igniter to his Speed Triple along with a digital dashboard.

Electronic dashboard Mark Gaylard yet again is at the forefront of upgrading T300s with modern technology, this time fitting an electronic dashboard to his Speed Triple. Many folk have fitted an alternative dash on a T300 but doing so on a Speed Triple is a whole other ball game. The standard clocks on a Speed Triple help define the bike, and Triumph also made the extra effort by giving them white dials and chrome bezels, making them arguably the best-looking dash set-up in the range – so chopping them out could easily create a mess and be a step backwards in the looks and functionality department.

Mark had the urge for a few years but nothing really made him want to make the jump until he saw a new dash from maker Daytona, the Deva 01. Taking the dimensions from the website, he mocked up a cardboard dummy, painted it black and offered it up; that seemed to work so he ordered one.

Removing the standard clocks leaves a considerable gap between top yoke and the headlight. Until you've done this, you don't realize just how big that clock set-up is and how diminutive digital clocks are! It was clear they

Electronic dash.

Electronic dash 5 showing mounting bracket.

Puig fairing.

needed to sit in that area better so a mounting plate was needed to move them into and a tad down for the right look.

A cardboard template was made up and, once satisfied that all was fine, a metal plate was cut and opinions sought from friends along the way. Once satisfied he was going in the right direction, Mark mounted the plate under the top yoke on the original mounting points but gapped by some tap rubber washers; this moved it down about 5mm and also meant a little vibration damping was built in. This then allowed him to mount the dash with the supplied universal mount to the custom mounting plate. All was painted black and various fixings added, before finishing off with drilled alloy cone washers, helping to improve the look of the finish.

Several features of the new dash include a programmable shift light, where the rev bar flashes at a pre-determined range to change gear. Mark had recently fitted an Ignitech igniter that had a switched earth output for a shift light too, so some nickel-plated LEDS were sourced and attached through some of the decorative drilled holes in the custom mount plate and wired in, allowing him to synchronize the lights with the dash rev shift lights so the whole thing would light up as you hit max revs!

Not wishing to clean bugs out of the back of the new dash all the time, Mark fitted a Puig fly screen, which had the added bonus of Triumph branding on it as was designed for a 2017 Triumph Bonnie Black.

A common question is how you get around the cable drive speedometer to the front wheel. There are a couple of options. You can fit a GPS module, which you would hide away, and take its speed from satellite, or you can use the supplied magnet pickup that you would attach to the wheel/brake disc and then run a pickup sensor to the front fork leg. Both of these options would leave you with a redundant speedometer drive on the front wheel, which you could either plug the input to or replace with a custom-made spacer. Mark, however, found a third option, which was a speed pulse converter that runs the same route (albeit a wire not a cable) to the speedometer drive and has a powered magnetic pickup designed to fit the original speedometer drive. You program the dash with the number of pulses the new pickup receives over ten revolutions to set the speed up.

In order to wire the dash in, Mark used the plug and part of the loom from another set of standard clocks, although replacing the entire lot and crimping in new connecters would be my preferred option, as the original connecter block isn't the most waterproof or best quality! The factory manual wiring diagram is a must here, as Haynes is not 100 per cent accurate from a colour perspective. The basic colours for Speed Triples are as follows:

Left indicator	Green
Right indicator	Grey
Oil warning	Pink
Tachometer pulse	Blue Black
High beam	Red Black
Neutral	Light green/white
Earths	Black/yellow
Power switch	Brown

Some advantages of a digital dash (they all carry slightly different features) are clock, ambient air temperature, programmable shift light, programmable water temperature warning light with real time degrees in centigrade or Fahrenheit, multiple trips, switchable mph or km/h, gear indicator and (soon to be fitted) functioning fuel gauge. You can see the accuracy of the speedo and rev-counter to be bang on, unlike the rather wayward originals with their endearing bouncing needles!

Alternator upgrade This modification has been done by Gordon Smith, whose experience is detailed below.

Most T300s (like Gordon's 1998 Sprint Executive) come fitted with the Nippon Denso 25-amp (single-phase) alternator (T1300014 ND, code 100211-4950).

Some later models, invariably the post-1998 Trophy 1200 with the eleven-hole screen fixing, come with a Nippon Denso 40-amp (three-phase) alternator (T1300350 ND, code 101211-1611). It appears there are similar models of the ND 40-amp alternator from some larger Japanese bikes of the same era, which may also fit the T300s.

Alternator upgrade., the original.

Alternator upgrade completed, with new alternator in place.

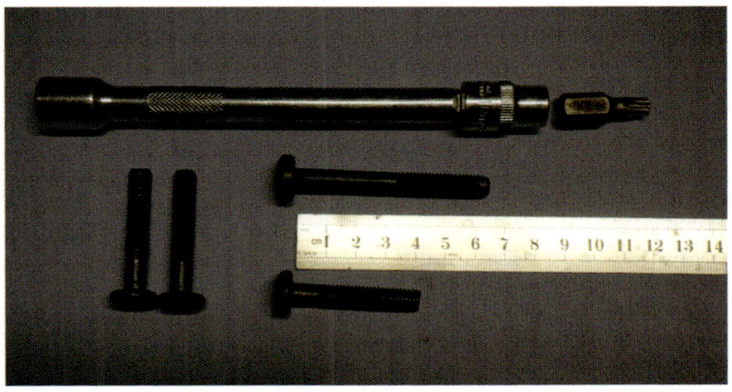

New mounting bolts for the replacement alternator.

The increase in 'capacity' was probably sought to cope with the extra loading from owner-fitted accessories such as sat navs and electrically heated gloves and waistcoats and so on.

The black 4-cylinder engine crankcases are slightly different from the 'normal' T300 range in that the dipstick/oil filler is dispensed with in favour of the sight glass. The oil filler is moved to the clutch cover.

Many owners of the earlier Trophy models wanted to have the advantage of the extra capacity, and reports from Triumph forums showed that it was possible, so Gordon had a go.

A suitable used 40-amp alternator was obtained from an eBay store for

Elongating the mounting hole in the new alternator.

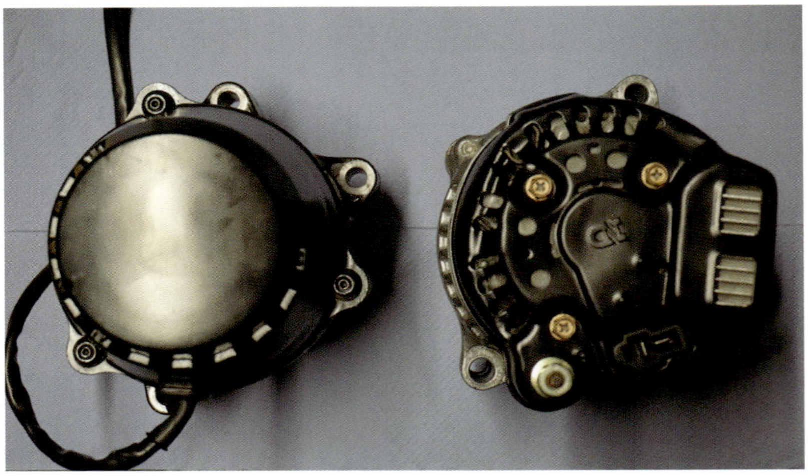

The old versus the new alternator.

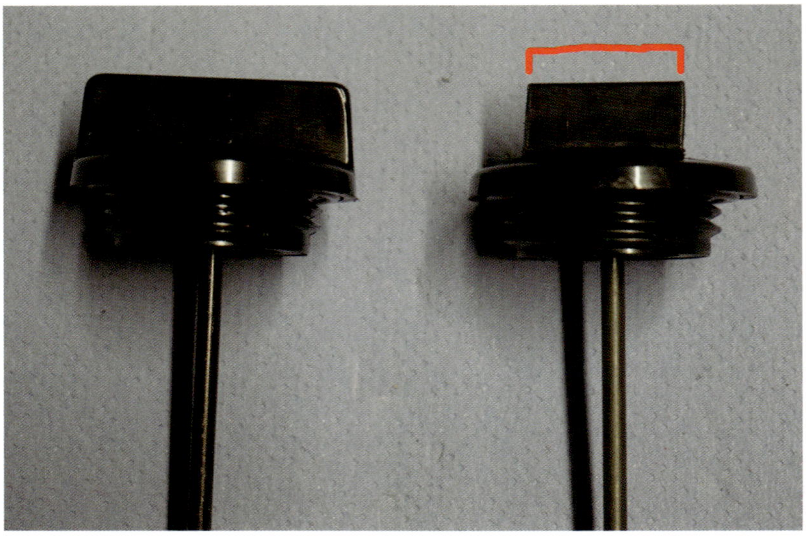

Modifying the dipstick.

about £35. A quick visual examination showed that, other than needing a bit of a clean-up and a new set of brushes, it was a serviceable item.

The first point to note is that any electrical upgrade will not fix an electrical system that is marginal or a bit suspect, so before any extra work is undertaken, underlying faults should be rectified.

Second, the mounting lugs on the 40-amp alternator are quite a bit longer than on the 25-amp alternator so the correct set of mounting bolts will be required – Gordon's came with the correct 65mm mounting bolts.

Third, although the mounting lugs are identically spaced, the normal top-right mounting hole in any replacement/upgrade 40-amp alternator may require opening/elongating inwards by approximately 5mm to match the mounting thread in any earlier version of the crankcase.

This results in the regulator vanes being towards the rear, rather than the top-left position, on the later Trophy 1200.

The fourth point to note is that, if the 40-amp alternator is to be used in conjunction with a lithium polymer (LiPo or $LiFePO_4$) battery, an isolation relay, wired into the smaller (switched by the ignition switch) IG wire, to make the connection to the output wire (10mm hex nut under the rubber boot), will be required to prevent a small parasitic drain current of 0.4mA being seen by the LiPo battery. LiPo batteries do not like small parasitic drains. An alternative solution is to always disconnect the battery positive terminal when the bike is not going to be used for a few days or longer.

Last, note that the dipstick top interferes with the lower-right corner of the 40-amp alternator cover. Either trim the dipstick as shown or remove the alternator cover every time you want to check the oil level.

Fitting the 40-amp Alternator

1. Disconnect the battery.
2. Remove the clutch slave cylinder and tie-wrap it to prevent accidental ejection of the piston.
3. Remove the block to pump coolant hose cover ('Billy the Fish'), if fitted.
4. Undo and remove the three 40mm bolts securing the 25-amp alternator.
5. Insert a suitable tool through the alternator cover holes to aid removal from the crankcase alternator drive cup – a 150mm ¼in extension is ideal. A slight rotational rocking motion on the extension bar with a bit of pulling will separate the alternator from the drive cup.
6. Examine and replace the cush drive rubbers (T1220325) if required, and always replace the alternator O-ring (T3600100).
7. With the original alternator removed, this is a good time to check the security of the alternator driveshaft (splined) through-bolt and nut. Originally two bolts were used, one from either end, but the later sprag clutch upgrade incorporated a different driveshaft that

used a single through-bolt. The hex nut of the through-bolt is visible in the centre of the cush drive cup.

8. Install the cush drive rubbers in the cup, holding them in place with a blob of red rubber grease. Install a new alternator O-ring, suitably lubricated with a smear of fresh engine oil.
9. Apply a smear of red rubber grease to the vanes of the alternator impeller (paddle) and align the vanes with the gaps in the cush drive rubbers, relative to the relevant mounting lugs and holes.
10. Gently ease the 40-amp alternator into position and press home. Slight rotation of the alternator body may be required to correctly align the mounting lugs with the crankcase threaded mounting holes behind. Insert all three of the longer mounting bolts. Check that the top-right mounting hole previously enlarged with a rat-tail file will accept the longer mounting bolt without undue interference or friction. Remove the alternator again and recheck/dress out the elongated mounting hole until a satisfactory fit is achieved. You may need to file away part of the outer edge of the new alternator body where it contacts the crankcase, just to give some latitude to alignment and prevent vibration or wear at that point.

    Refit the alternator, not forgetting the alternator earth strap ring terminal to the top-right mounting bolt. Evenly tighten the three 65mm mounting bolts and torque to 20Nm.
11. Fabricate some suitable leads to connect the 40-amp alternator to the original wiring harness alternator connector. Connect the IG wire (the thinner of the two) to the same thin wire in the harness connector. Connect the output terminal (B) to the thicker wire in the original wiring harness connector; Gordon used half of an old starter motor cable (previously uprated), as it has the correct-size ring terminal, at one end, and a yellow Faston male spade terminal at the other. Fold over the original harness rubber boot and secure

Removing the original alternator.

Alternator upgrade. Check the retaining nut.

Chamfering the casing on the new alternator.

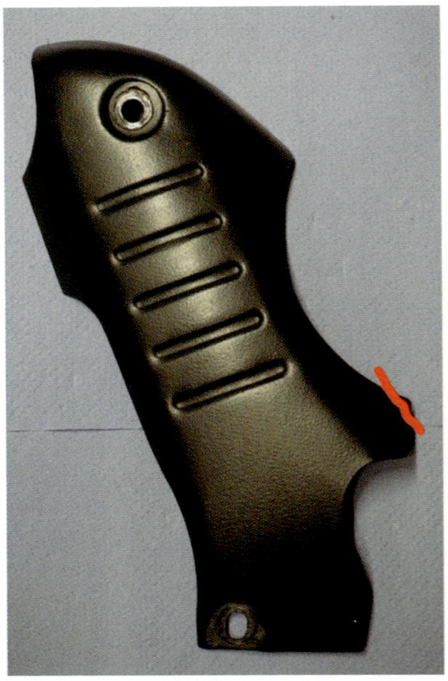

Taking the bottom edge off the cover plate.

Connections into the alternator.

Alternator upgrade completed.

with a tie-wrap or similar. On the alternator, cover terminal B with a rubber boot where possible – there will always be the battery available at terminal B unless an alternator isolation relay has also been installed at the same time.

12. Trim the small corner off the coolant hose cover if you wish to refit it, as shown.
13. Reconnect the battery and start the bike. A check of the alternator charging/battery voltage using a digital multimeter should show something in the order of 14v charging the battery from the 40-amp alternator. The charging output is better regulated with the 40-amp alternator so tends to remain more constant, and variation, depending on the electrical load applied, is minimal. As with the 25-amp alternator, a charging (output) voltage greater than 14.8v at 5,000rpm could well indicate a failure of the voltage regulator. If a LiPo Battery is installed, the upper limit of output (charging) voltage is 14.8v in any event.

Chris Foxley paddock stand and bobbins Having owned three Speed Triples, one Super 3 and a Daytona (now a CRK), I have always found fitting a conventional paddock stand under the swing arm a bit of a struggle, as the underslung rear caliper gets in the way. Some T300 users have suggested that reversing the 'cups' in the paddock stand that go under the swing arm and slide the shaft that holds the 'cups' into the chain adjusters. This will work but I wanted a more elegant solution. Following a discussion with Chris Foxley, he modified the chain adjuster to take a bobbin (also made to fit the chain adjuster) and made up a paddock stand to fit. Subsequently the paddock stand has been modified so that the axle can be taken out to remove the wheel. I have these fitted to both my Speed Triple and CRK.

Modified chain adjusters to take a bobbin.

Replacing engine cover bolts If you buy these bolts new from Triumph they can be very expensive, but there are two alternatives: have the original bolts replated or buy in some stainless cap heads of the various lengths. For my CRK, I replaced all the engine bolts as I already had the stainless sizes in stock (I bought lots of stainless bolts when building a kit car). Remember when inserting to put a little copper slip on the threads to reduce the chances of a reaction with the alloy casings.

Stainless cap head bolts replacing the original bolts, and a polished exhaust.

The Chris Foxley paddock stand, showing the shape to allow the axle to be taken out.

8

building modified bikes

With Triumph's modular approach to bike construction, it is relatively easy to build up a bike using parts from different models in the T300 range, and you can also add aftermarket parts to create a bike that really reflects you.

The X90 by Mecatwin, a French company specializing in Triumph conversions.

MECATWIN OF FRANCE

Mecatwin is a small French company set up in 1986 that originally modified Meriden Triumphs. However, with the introduction of the Hinckley Triumphs, they started to produce models based on different Hinckley models.

The first bike was the x-90, based on a Trident, and a small run of these were made. The bike introduced one of the signature styling features of Mecatwin – the long reverse cone silencers.

The next model was the Ascot TT, which was based on a Thunderbird; this bike featured revised seat, rear bodywork, side panels and indicators. The original Ascot TT had a silver engine, but when Triumph introduced the Legend with a black engine, Mecatwin built another batch using this version. The bike was offered with different exhausts – a 3-into-3 with two silencers one side and one on the other; and two silencers, one each side, using long reverse cone megaphone silencers.

Given the small numbers built and the country of origin, you will not find many in the UK (even though some were sold through Triumph dealer Jack Lilley). I have only seen one and that appeared in the car park for the Triumph Live event in 2010.

The Ascot, a limited edition bike built in France.

SEAN SYMONDS' HYBRIDS

The Bumblebee

Sean has built up a number of hybrids utilizing lots of different parts from the Triumph T300 range and has an extensive parts store – he could probably build at least two more bikes from his stash.

The first example (called 'Bumblebee' because of the yellow tail on a black bike) uses a Legend frame, Super 3 engine, Trident rear swing arm (fitted with Daytona drop links and Daytona shock absorber) and Thunderbird Sport rear sub-frame. The front forks are the adjustable type from a Daytona but with Thunderbird top and bottom yokes.

The original igniter from the Super 3 has been used, connected up with the loom from a Thunderbird Sport. Note that all connectors from the Thunderbird Sport loom matched up perfectly with the connectors from other items of electrical equipment without further modifications.

The speedometer and rev-counter are from a Speed Triple but fitted into a Thunderbird surround. Drop bars from a Speed Triple have been fitted and, to hold the headlamp (from a Thunderbird), the black fork shrouds and ears from a Speed Triple have been used. Because the frame is from a Thunderbird, the radiator, header tank and water pump are also from a Thunderbird.

The carburettors and airbox come from a Thunderbird Sport, although the airbox has been modified to improve airflow.

The wheels are the later three-spoke ones from a Daytona. A Super 3 oil cooler, as well as a Super 3 carbon front mudguard, have been fitted, along with a set of Triumph-branded Alcon six-piston calipers. The seat unit is fitted with the Triumph optional cover for the pillion seat for a Thunderbird Sport, with some LSL Thunderbird rear sets to finish off.

Sean Symonds' Bumblebee, a hybrid of Triumph T300 parts.

The Tiger Bird

The second example by Sean Symonds is a trail bike using both Tiger and Thunderbird parts. This bike started with a 1993 Tiger engine fitted to a Thunderbird Sport frame, sub-frame and a Thunderbird swing arm.

A Thunderbird radiator and header tank have been used and the engine fitted with a Thunderbird water pump, as the hose connections are different.

Sean Symonds' Bumblebee, a hybrid of Legend, Super 3 and Trident parts.

The front forks and wheels are from a Tiger, the wider rear wheel from a later 955 Tiger. The fork spacing on a Thunderbird yoke is slightly wider than the Tiger's so a new spindle and spacers had to be machined to fit the front wheel.

The wiring loom is from a Thunderbird Sport connected to a Tiger igniter (it has a different advance curve from the Daytona and Speed Triple ones), while the rear and the front hub are from the 955 model Tiger, giving two front calipers. The front forks from the Tiger are narrower by 4mm so had to be spaced. A Thunderbird fuel tank has been fitted and a custom seat to be upholstered, based upon a modified Thunderbird seat pan. The exhaust silencers and link pipes were custom made for the bike.

Sean Symonds' Bumblebee loaded up for some touring with a large tank bag.

When he completed the bike in 2020, Sean took it for a shakedown test on a 3,200km (2,000-mile) trip around Northern Ireland, northern Scotland and back to Derbyshire. The trip proved beneficial in identifying some weak points and the bike was subsequently modified.

First, the tyres were 'knobblies', and a low-speed spill proved the need to fit better road tyres, which has now been done. The mudguard's custom-made mounting bracket also broke (as the suspension kept bottoming out), so to give more clearance, a set of Thunderbird Sport drag links were fitted (they are 5mm shorter than the Tiger ones), which raised the rear end of the bike and it looks much better.

Gearing the bike proved to be a challenge; since it had a Tiger engine and wheels, the sprockets were set to Tiger front and back, but the revs at 80km/h (50mph) were too high, so Sean switched to Thunderbird Sport front and rear sprockets (which also meant a change in chain length).

Thunderbird swing arm on Sean Symonds' Tiger Bird.

Tiger Front forks with 955 hub and rim on Sean Symonds' Tiger Bird hybrid.

Sean Symonds' Tiger Bird hybrid.

Since the trip, Sean has sorted out a new seat, tank and side panels. The test run shows that when building hybrid bikes some adjustment is likely to be needed, but that's all part of the fun of creating a unique bike.

JONATHAN WILKIE'S TIGER/ SPEED TRIPLE HYBRID

This started life as a standard Tiger owned by Dave Berry, who used it to tour round Europe. Upon his return, the bike was given to Clive Wood (at that time at Jack Lilley's) to turn into a race bike. Knowing the T300 range backwards, Clive then fitted it with Speed Triple swing arm and wheels and Trident handlebars and brakes. The cylinder head had been ported by George Metz (one of only two T300 heads done by this specialized company).

The ECU was also modified and a lot of lightening and balancing work was done in the engine, which produced over 100bhp. (The engine work carried out was later carried forward to the Saxon Triumph project, where Saxon produced an alloy frame and new front suspension mated to a tuned T300 engine.) The engine in the Tiger was rebuilt by Clive and produced around 108bhp at the rear wheel. The bike was raced at Snetterton in a six-hour relay race, where it won its class, ridden by Clive, Ian Penfold and John Laker.

The bike then disappeared for a few years before the author spotted it for

Sean Symonds' Tiger Bird out for a run.

Sean Symonds' Tiger Bird hybrid, ready for its 3,200km (2,000-mile) shakedown ride.

Racing Tiger being ridden by Clive Wood.

Clive Wood on the racing Tiger.

Clive Wood contemplates what promises to be a long job – restoring the racing Tiger.

FCR carburettors on the racing Tiger.

Racing Tiger.

sale in Derby in 2010, but it was then in very poor condition (and required a huge amount of work, so I declined to buy it). It was then bought by Marcus Hall, who asked Clive Wood to bring it back to life; Clive's comments when he saw the bike again after many years are unprintable (suggesting that it be used as a boat anchor!), but with it now back in his safe hands, it was gradually brought back to life.

After Marcus came across a genuine ex-Speed Triple race bike (ridden by Ron Haslam), he decided to sell the bike and it then passed to Jonathan Wilkie, who not only finished the restoration but did some further modifications, including fitting the upgraded side stand bracket and the longer side stand fitted to the later Trophies, a new clutch slave cylinder, Mikuni FCR carburettors and a new sprag clutch.

Racing Tiger with Sebring manifold, Speed Triple wheels and brakes.

The racing Tiger. Note the exposed front sprocket to allow rapid sprocket changes.

Breather system on the racing Tiger.

The bike now looks much better, but Jonathan would like repaint it in its original race paint scheme, and is looking for a replacement tank, as it is suffering from the dreaded blistering caused by ethanol in the fuel.

MARK GAYLARD'S SPEED TRIPLE

Mark has owned this bike for many years and has been modifying it continuously along the way. The bike started out as a standard Speed Triple but has been upgraded as follows:

- Non-standard paint scheme and Alcon six-pot calipers; these were sold as aftermarket accessories by Triumph and came in black or gold.
- Changed exhausts. There have been various iterations, starting with a set of carbon Scorpions (now on the author's Speed Triple!), then reverse cone silencers from an American company, Cone Engineering, and finally back to a set of carbon exhausts.
- Gaffer brake discs and EBC HH pads front and rear.
- Honda tie rod to the rear brake caliper. This came from a Honda VF1000R, which offered up a treat – even the original bushes popped out and fitted directly in. It was then powder coated.
- Sprint steering damper, K-Tech bottom fork adjusters, Öhlins rear shock absorber.
- Dymag forged alloy wheels (described in Chapter 7).
- Puig cowl fairing (an accessory intended for a 2017 Triumph Bonneville).
- Ignitech programmable igniter.
- Digital dashboard. This replaced the original two-clock set up built by Triumph.

Mark Gaylard's Speed Triple.

Mark Gaylard's Speed Triple fitted with Dymag alloy wheels.

Mark's bike shows what you can do with an older bike to make it your own, improving the original without losing the essence of the bike. The parts may sound expensive, but then how much do you lose constantly changing bikes? Find a 'keeper' and update it, creating a bike that is personal to you and not quite like any other.

Mark has been a trendsetter in the T300 world for adopting new technology to what is a good basic bike and making it better.

Every time I see the bike it looks different, as Mark keeps fettling and applying new technology. To my knowledge it has had at least four different exhaust systems!

Speed Quattro by Denis Fitch.

Instruments on a Speed Quattro, using CRK pods and housing. The bike is fitted with Sprint Sports handlebars.

DENIS FITCH'S CONVERSIONS

The Speed Quattro

With the sales success of the Speed Triple 900, Triumph considered making a 1200 engine version called the Speed Quattro, and two prototypes were built and sent to the USA for evaluation. For whatever reason, Triumph did not go forward with is proposal. However, one of Triumph's dealers, Daytona Motorcycles, built a small number (reportedly two) of these 1200 naked bikes and more have been built by individuals since. Essentially, it's a 1200 Daytona with the fairing panels and lights removed, and replaced with a single headlight, fork shrouds and the instruments and instrument housing from a Speed Triple.

Denis Fitch is a bit of an expert on these conversions and the one in the photos is the second one he has built. The first was sadly sold after he was made an offer he couldn't refuse for it but, when it went, he missed it so much he made another one. Denis has recently taken delivery of another black Daytona 1200, so maybe a third is on the cards.

His second conversion started life as a 1996 (registered in 1997) 1200 Daytona. It was in reasonable mechanical order, although he carried out all the usual jobs like shim check, coolant change, carburettor and fuel tap rebuild and so on as he was working on the project.

The Speed Quattro doesn't actually exist as an official model, so any that you see on the road will have been knocked up in people's sheds, garages and workshops – including the odd ones that were done at a dealer's. Daytona Motorcycles of Ruislip offered them to the buying public, but my research tells me that they only actually built two – one was their own conversion of a new bike and the other was a conversion of a customer's bike. What bothers Denis about their bike is the font on the word 'Quattro' is the wrong size and font! On Denis's bikes, the word has been faithfully matched in size and font to the 'Triple' on original bikes. The Speed Quattro decals were made through Trevor at Sprint Manufacturing, who has a contact who was able to produce an exact match at a cost of around £40 for the pair.

Denis's bike doesn't have the genuine Speed Triple clocks, as it's just impossible to get them (and if you find any, they are very expensive). Instead, he has used the original Daytona clocks in a CRK clock mount, which does the job and looks pretty much right. Others have done this too, although some people on the Speed Quattro Facebook group have used Thunderbird clocks, as these are more readily available.

Another thing that is difficult to find is the Speed Triple top yoke. Denis's bike still has the standard Daytona yokes, but the fork legs are slid through the yoke to give the steeper head angle of the Triple and sharpen up the steering.

The single headlight (replacing the twin headlights of the original) is from a Yamaha RD 250/350LC (readily available as an aftermarket part), as Speed Triple ones are hard to find and expensive.

ABOVE: A second Speed Quattro by Denis Fitch, this time with different handlebars.

LEFT: Speed Quattro fitted with risers on the top yoke.

Speed Quattro.

The long loom from the Daytona was pulled back under the tank to get rid of it, as it won't all go into the headlight shell, as in the Speed Triple.

The bike is fitted with conventional bars (replacing the Daytona bars, which are the same as the Speed Triple ones), as Denis has really bad wrists and needs a more upright riding position – maybe it's not so authentic, but at least he can still ride it! Also, as the model never existed, there's no 'official' specification for it, so all the ones built will have varying specifications to suit the builder/rider. After its conversion, the bike was originally fitted with Sprint Sports handlebars but now has Renthal Ultra Low bars fitted. There are many options available on the internet.

When you think the Speed Triple is essentially a 900 Daytona with the fairing removed, the Speed Quattro is essentially a 1200 Daytona with the fairing removed and a single headlight fitted. As long as the original silhouette and general look is Speed Triple, that's about as authentic as you can get with a Speed Quattro.

Denis has tried different silencers on the bike, but always ended up with the standard ones as they look the best. Also, being a 4-cylinder engine, loud pipes make it sound like any other

4-cylinder motorcycle, unlike the distinctive sound of the triple.

The rest of the bike is standard Daytona. It has a better rear shock on it (a Nitron bought second-hand from a friend who is the suspension guru for the Smiths BSB team) and the foam in the seat is custom. There are lots of detail changes, but nothing the untrained eye would notice. Denis has tried to make it as 'factory' as he can and has preserved the original Speed Triple idea as much as possible.

This bike (like all Denis's bikes) was built on a budget. The second bike Denis built cost £1,400 for the base bike, which was in good condition, and the cost of the conversion was around £1,000. All the original parts have been retained so the bike could in theory be returned to an original specification. The first Quattro Denis built was based on a bit of a wreck, as it had been down the road on its side and then stored under a tarpaulin for two years and therefore cost £600 (after a lot of haggling!). That conversion cost around £300, so the bike was on the road for £1,000, the costs offset by selling all the redundant parts. If you wanted to go the whole hog and fit Speed Triple clocks, clock surround and top and bottom yokes, then expect to add another £1,000.

As far as riding goes, Denis says:

> It's just the same as a Triple, only with another 40bhp or so. It's certainly an entertaining ride. People say it must be heavy, but you hardly notice any difference to a Triple and, once you've ridden it, you never notice. I have a Speed Triple as well and the only thing I notice when I go from one bike to the other is the performance.

We all know the 1200 Daytona never really had 147bhp, but it does have an honest 135bhp, which is plenty in a heavy, old, naked bike.

Yet again it highlights the modularity of the T300 range.

The Sprint 1200 – Sprophy

As with the 1200 Speed Quattro, a model that Triumph never actually produced, you can also create a Sprint 1200. Denis Fitch is a master of putting together bikes using different bits of

A Sprint 1200 hybrid by Denis Fitch.

Another view of Denis Fitch's 1200 Sprint.

The cockpit of the 1200 Sprint.

the T300 range. He has built two Sprint 1200s, one based on the Mk 1 Trophy 1200 (now sold), and the second one based on a 1999 Trophy 1200, originally in Platinum Silver, but, as bought, had a number of bodywork issues. On the later bike, the Sprint fairing is mounted 38mm (1.5in) lower and 25mm (1in) further forward than the factory sub-frame to reduce the buffeting produced by the standard placement. Denis made the fairing bracket himself and built in some adjustability.

The belly pan was made from the lower fairing from a Kawasaki GPX750R, suitably shaped to fit using home brackets. Daytona 1200 SE silencers were fitted and the Sprint fairing came from a Sprint Sports. The handlebars are Sprint Sports, and Denis made use of the Trophy instruments in a Sprint dashboard. Fitting the Trophy instruments proved to be a difficult job.

The 1200 Trophy and Daytonas can be bought for very little money and they make a fast tourer, the only disadvantage being the slightly heavier fuel consumption over the 900. The earlier bikes are fitted with the two-piston sliding calipers, so go for the later bikes with the four-piston calipers or do an upgrade.

GORDON SMITH'S SPROPHY

This is another hybrid created from a 2003 Trophy 1200 bought in April 2018 with only 10,000km (6,200 miles) on the clock! The bike had been stored by its first owner for over ten years (following a bereavement and an Achilles heel injury) and, after some discussions, a satisfactory price was agreed.

Gordon first recommissioned the Trophy (full service, new fork seals, new tyres and a new coil) and ran it on the road, but was unhappy with the nose section and screen. The later Trophies came with an eleven-hole screen fixing and a more upright but shorter screen. This was changed to an earlier nine-hole screen fixing and different screen as Gordon had previously had a 1997 Trophy 900. Gordon then put 20,000km (12,000 miles) on the bike. Things were fine until he bought a Sprint Executive and found that he preferred the riding position and the weather protection, which suited his 1.75m (5ft 9in) stature.

Gordon had helped out with the Denis Fitch Trophy/Sprint conversion (hence the name 'Sprophy'), removing the alarm and sorting out the carburettors, and it was such a good-looking bike that he promised himself he would do something similar if the opportunity arose. Cue Covid 19 and lockdown.

A Sprophy – a Trophy 1200 with a Sprint fairing.

Gordon was determined to do a 'proper' job on the conversion so this meant a change to the wiring harness to relocate the igniter and fuse box from behind the fairing to under the seat. Also modified was the Sprint fairing frame to fit the Trophy frame mounting points (10mm further apart), so that the Sprint fairing wasn't drooping down the front and splayed across the 1200 engine. This involved cutting and splaying the frame, which was then bonded with a two-part adhesive. The Trophy instruments were changed to ones from a Sprint (bought from Ivan at National Triumph).

The original late Trophy wiring harness was removed and an earlier Daytona wiring harness acquired and repaired. The alarm was removed and a side stand relay was added to get everything working. The loom was then threaded through the Trophy frame, and the (extending) crank sensor and neutral/oil pressure wiring limbs modified.

A NOS (new old stock) Sprint fairing was acquired from a Triumph dealer for less than half price (although in the wrong colour, Nightshade). The later Sprint fairings were in three pieces bolted together, which made life easier when offering up the side panels around the 1200 engine. The lower fairing brackets normally mounted on the engine were not required.

Upon completion, Gordon retained the OE silencers, which were handy when he was delivering NHS scrubs and masks as they could go in the panniers. A spare set of 4-cylinder headers was obtained and, after shortening and cleaning a set of Dunstall replica silencers, they were fitted and kept low enough to allow the panniers still to fit; the shortening of the headers enabled the angle of the silencers not to interfere with the panniers. Heatproof tape to the underneath on the panniers keeps the contents cool. The Dunstalls are half the weight of the originals and are not excessively noisy.

The combination of the Nightshade fairing and the Azure blue for the rest of the bike will be sorted when time and fiancés permit.

Gordon Smith's Sprophy waiting for a respray to have one colour.

ABOVE: Instruments on Gordon Smith's Sprophy.

Gordon now has the perfect bike for him, which is what building a 'special' is all about, and this is made easier by the interchangeability of parts in the T300 range.

CAFÉ RACER KITS

Café Racer Kits were created by Ian Saxcoburg and his wife, Tracey. After developing a conversion for smaller Hondas (CX and other models), he then produced a café racer kit for the T300 range and was surprised by the number of kits for the T300 he has sold – at the time of writing, over 270. The conversion is generally aimed at the

RIGHT: The author's CRK donor bike (a Daytona 900) stripped ready for the sub-frame to be removed.

The author's donor Daytona 900 with the seat frame removed for the CRK build.

900 and 750 triples, but some conversions have also been made on 1200 4-cylinder models. They produce two models for the T300, a Café Racer and a Roadster, which is more of a touring bike.

The key issue here is acquiring a donor bike as the base for the conversion. Prices for Tridents, Sprints, Sprint Sports and Daytonas are reasonable and a donor bike can be bought for around £1,500, a lot less if you are lucky. However, don't underestimate the costs of servicing and repairing the donor before any conversion work is even started. The Daytona I bought looked tidy and had some service history but required a new chain and sprocket set – the front sprocket was the original and the bike had 53,000km (33,000 miles) on the clock, so there were virtually no teeth left! – a new swing arm, a new rear shock absorber, a change of oil and filter and a new air filter, as well as replacing the coolant. I replaced the front brake calipers and brake pads with new old stock as well as the brake master cylinder and the rear brake reservoir. The rear brake caliper was also rebuilt, as were the front forks. The clutch had to be changed as there was some water contamination, causing the plates to weld themselves together. A new battery was also required. All this accounted for nearly half of the cost of building the bike, which ended up at around £7,500 in total.

If I was doing a build again, I would take more time selecting a really good donor, even if this meant paying a little more, as this could save more money in the long run as less will be need to be spent on overhauling the base bike.

One issue to consider when making this conversion is that if the base bike is a Daytona (or Trophy) then there will be a considerable weight saving, the CRK weighing in at 218kg (480lb) with fuel, oil and so on, compared to the Speed Triple's 244kg (538lb). I would expect the Daytona to weigh about 10kg (22lb) more than a Speed Triple. Fitting the original shock absorber or buying a direct replacement may give a rear shock and spring that is too stiff for the bike. Certainly in my case, the back of the bike is very stiff even for my 89kg (14 stone) weight, so if replacing the rear shock, get a softer spring.

The conversion kit can be bought in a number of separate modules if you are thinking of only doing a partial conversion.

Instrument module This reuses the speedometer and rev-counter and is helpful if converting a Daytona to a Speed Quattro, or Daytona to a naked bike, as these pods look similar to the ones fitted to a Speed Triple or Thunderbird Sport.

Headlamp and brackets These can be used if converting a Daytona to a naked bike. For my CRK conversion, I used the fork shrouds and headlamp brackets from a Speed Triple and a Speed Triple headlight. Since building the bike, the cost of Speed Triple parts has increased while the availability has declined, so if you want to follow the same path it will require time to find these parts.

CRK instruments using Daytona speedometer and rev-counter in CRK-supplied pods and instrument panel.

Speed Triple headlamp holder and fork tubes fitted to the author's CRK.

The CRK-supplied fuel tank is alloy with a glass-fibre cover. The welding of the tank is a work of art.

The Café Racer Kit sub-frame installed.

Donor Daytona with seat frame removed with an angle grinder!

Fuel tank This fits directly onto the T300 frame at the front and bolts to the new sub-frame at the rear of the tank. The tank is beautifully crafted in aluminium with a glass-fibre tank cover and comes with a Monza-style petrol cap.

Seat and sub-frames The majority of conversions have included all the modules.

The following standard items can then be disposed of: fuel tank, bodywork, exhausts, seat unit and headlights (depending on the model of the donor bike). These can be sold to offset the costs of the CRK parts.

Once the donor bike has been stripped, the original seat sub-frame is removed (take a deep breath and an angle grinder!) and is replaced by one supplied by CRK.

The trick with fitting this sub-frame is to use a substantial ratchet strap to pull down the new sub-frame to line up the holes in the Triumph frame, which makes fitting the bolts significantly easier.

The donor instruments are then housed in two pods provided by CRK, but there is also the option of fitting some more modern dashboard, such as Motogadget – though these excellent German bits of kit are not cheap!

In my view, the bare fork uppers give the bike a strange look, so I fitted the Speed Triple fork shrouds to hold the headlamp, which improved the bike's appearance. However, if spring sports bars are to be fitted, you need the longer fork shrouds from a Trident to fill the space taken up by the Speed Triple handlebars, which sit below the top yoke.

As the rear brake slave reservoir is now on full view (on the original bike it is hidden by the side panel), I used a black CNC reservoir from a 2010 Triumph Speed Triple. I also fitted Speed Triple radiator covers and side reflectors. Again, these are getting harder to find and consequently more expensive. The next upgrade for the bike will be to get some crash protectors similar to those I have fitted to my Speed Triple.

The CRK fuel tank is made of aluminium and sits under a glass-fibre cover, which looks like the fuel tank. There are two sizes of fuel tank; personally, I would go for the larger one, both for

Nearly finished in December 2016, the author's CRK.

Speed Triple headlight holder, fork shrouds and aftermarket indicators on a CRK.

Battery holder installed, along with rear light holder on the CRK.

appearance and the additional capacity, as even the larger tank will struggle to give you more than 90 miles (145km) range. The only issue I have had with the bike has been related to the Pingel fuel tap, as the one supplied has a 6mm outlet whereas the pipework to the carburettor is 8mm. This makes connecting the fuel tap a bit of a challenge; I had an adaptor made to provide the interface. If you buy a replacement tap then you need one with a left-hand outlet (looking from the front of the tap). A right-hand outlet interferes with the air cleaners. It has been suggested that a tap from

A Triumph CNC black reservoir from a 2010 Speed Triple fitted to a CRK Café Racer.

a BMW R80/90 will fit and has an 8mm outlet, but the coupling size is larger than the threaded insert on the tank, so an adaptor will still have to be made.

The beauty of this kit is that you can then add items such as headlight, silencers and so on to suit your tastes. The only regrettable part is that the original silencers offered by CRK (which really look the part and sound fabulous) are no longer available, as the maker, Motad, is no longer in business. Cavan Holden (in the CRK Enthusiasts group on Facebook) has found that the current Triumph Street Cup silencers can be made to fit. He was originally told that the silencers from a Triumph Thruxton 1200 would fit straight on, but he found that they kicked out too much at the rear so they had to be removed. Cavan observed that the Triumph Street Cup silencers did not have the same kink in the pipe at the front of the silencer as the 1200, so he thought he would give it a try, buying a second-hand set of Street Cup silencers and trial fitting them. The only modification needed was to cut the centre stand bump stop off the near-side silencer and reshape the CRK mounting bracket, drilling holes for the silencer bracket to attach to. The sound is louder than a standard Street Cup, presumably because the Street Cup is fitted with a catalytic converter,

The alloy overflow tank supplied by CRK.

Electrics reinstalled in the new sub-frame.

which is not on the CRK, and they have the benefit of being stamped for road use, which makes life easier at the MOT station or if stopped by the police.

Many CRK bikes have been fitted with three separate pod filters, but they can cause fuelling issues (best to get set up on a rolling road), so Cavan also came up with a scheme to modify the standard Triumph airbox. This involves cutting off the intake snorkels and fitting some aluminium or brass mesh to stop large objects being

Battery and earthing installed on a CRK.

Cavan Holden's CRK with Triumph Street Cup silencers; the bike is based on a Trident.

K&N filters installed on a CRK.

A modified Triumph airbox on a CRK.

sucked into the air filter. I have carried out the same modification and, like Cavan, have fitted an aftermarket air filter (Cavan went for K&N, and I have fitted a Pipercross one). I have also modified the airbox cover (by cutting a diagonal across) so that I don't have to take off the carburettors to clean or change the air filter.

CRK now sell a single foam air filter that fits neatly onto the bike once the standard Triumph airbox has been removed.

If the donor bike is a Daytona then it will come fitted with an oil cooler as standard, which is not necessary on a naked bike. If the oil cooler is removed, a different link pipe will need to be fitted under the sump. CRK can supply for around £27, and so can Triumph.

The author's CRK finished in Organic Orange and fitted with the CRK-supplied silencers made by Motad, sadly no longer available.

Roadster Conversion

John Nutting has carried out an excellent conversion to create a Roadster, and this has been fitted with spoked wheels. His donor bike was a Trophy 1200, bought for a bargain £1,000, as Trophies don't seem to command the same sort of money as a Daytona. The engine was then soda blasted (with everything blanked off) and sprayed silver, while the frame and the new CRK sub-frame were painted eggshell black. Having admired the latest Triumph Rocket 3 in maroon, John picked a close match to have the tank, side panels and mudguards painted in a Jaguar colour. The wheels were built on a Thunderbird Sports hub (with two brake discs) and Central Wheel attached some light alloy 17in rims.

John Nutting's CRK 1200 Roadster.

The electronics were simplified by the use of a C-box system that uses thin signal wires for the switches but with a standard ignition switch. The CRK seat and instrument housing was used with the Trophy instruments. The silencers were supplied by CRK, and the Triumph header pipes were polished (the benefit of being made of stainless steel).

As with a number of CRK conversions, the shock and forks proved to be a little hard due to the weight loss, which was resolved by using thinner oil and more preload.

Another view of John Nutting's CRK1200 Roadster.

Again, even though the jetting kit was supplied by CRK, the use of a free-flowing air filter meant that the fuel-

The CRK 1200 Roadster.

The instruments on John Nutting's Roadster.

A CRK built on a Trident 750 base.

A CRK Café Racer based on a Super 3 build by Ivan at National Triumph.

ling was not spot on, but a session on a dynamometer rolling road benefited the bike, and the engine now produces 100bhp at 8,000rpm and a wide torque curve of more than 66lb ft from 2,700rpm onwards. The bike now weighs 234kg (516lb) all in, representing a weight saving of around 30kg (66lb).

LOWERING A STANDARD BIKE

The whole T300 range could never be described as 'petite', and the seat height on some models can be a challenge to some people. However, there are a number of things that can be done to reduce the seat height on these bikes.

First, the chain adjuster eccentrics can be reversed, which will gain approximately 40mm (1.5in). To maintain the handling, the front forks then need to be dropped through the front yokes by about 8mm. This in turn will require the rear hugger to be raised by 20mm at the mounting points to give adequate tyre clearance.

Flipping the adjusters will alter the chain run, and there will be a danger that the chain will cut into the swing arm; to resolve this, the front sprocket will need to be bigger (say, up from a 17in to an 18in or 19in one). But of course this will change the gear ratio, so the rear sprocket will need to be changed as well. The link pipe on the exhaust that goes under the bike (linking the pipes together) may also touch down, but the clamps being rotated towards the rear may give better clearance. Lowering the bike by this method makes using a centre stand a challenge, but rolling the rear tyre onto a 25mm (1in) thick plank or board will lift the rear of the bike enough for the centre stand to be used as normal.

Of course the alternative is to cut down the seat and leave everything else alone!

PAUL MESSENGER'S TRIDENT

Paul started off with a 1991 750 Trident and then started to utilize the modular capabilities of the Triumph range by adding the following:

- Daytona three-spoke wheels (replacing the 18in six-spoked wheels originally fitted) and Daytona front floating brake discs.

- Carbon-fibre front mudguard and rear hugger from a Super 3.
- Speed Triple swing arm with underslung rear brake caliper and torque rod.
- 900 engine fitted with 750 pistons, which give an increased compression ratio and therefore increased power.
- Speed Triple fork tops, later-model Trident side panels, rear light and grab handles, and Thunderbird switchgear.
- Silencers from Dutch company Bros.
- Tokico six-piston calipers (fitted to many Japanese bikes) and a headlight and cowl from a Kawasaki GPZ305, and Maxton rear shock.

Paul Messenger's modified Trident.

This shows how easy it is to upgrade the basic Trident by using standard parts from the rest of the T300 range.

FITTING A SIDECAR

This is not the most common modification in the world, but I have seen a number of T300s that have had a sidecar fitted. I came across a Daytona fitted with a sidecar on my trip to the

A Daytona with a sidecar; this a German bike.

A Daytona sidecar conversion.

Roy Shilling's sidecar conversion with leading link forks.

A four-piston brake caliper on leading link forks on a sidecar conversion.

Not quite a T300 – Roy Shilling's Rocket 3 with sidecar.

Details of the sub-frame required for a sidecar on Roy Shilling's conversion.

More details of the frame required for Roy Shilling's conversion. The cross bar is welded to the seat sub-frame.

More details of the sub-frame.

An even more radical sidecar conversion seen at the Triumph factory, with a single-sided front suspension.

You can also build a trike based on a T300!

Isle of Man Classic TT and Manx TT in 2019. German rider Manfred Gross had a party trick, which was to ride down the street with one of his legs vertical, the foot level with his head; of course he had an artificial leg and that is why he had added a sidecar to the bike.

To do the job properly, the front forks should be replaced with leading link forks, but this is not essential.

The sidecar requires a complex sub-frame to be attached to the bike as shown in the pictures here of Roy Shilling's 1992 Trident 900 with a Squire

RX4 sidecar fitted. Again showing the versatility of the modular build strategy, the bike was fitted with Speed Triple front disc, brake master cylinder and adjustable levers, as well as the full race TTS 3-4-3-2-1 manifold. It had a Wasp swing link front suspension with Falcon shock absorbers.

The wheels are 15in with car tyres fitted. The handlebars have been raised and the foot pegs lowered to give a relaxed riding position, as Roy and his wife have toured all over Europe with the outfit. The bike has now been sold but Roy kept the sidecar (and the new owner of the Trident fitted another sidecar to it) and it is now attached to a Triumph Rocket 3 – just the bike for fast touring! The main reason for keeping the Squire sidecar is that Watsonian wanted over £7,000 for one of their sidecars.

Dual footbrake, one for the sidecar and one for the bike, on Roy Shilling's sidecar conversion.

PAUL HUMPHREYS' THUNDERBIRD SPORT

The bike started out as a standard 1998 Thunderbird Sport but was progressively modified, the most obvious indication of this being the 3-into-3 exhaust made by APH Engineering (at a cost of £1,850).

The front brakes were upgraded by fitting a pair of Pretech six-piston calipers along with a pair of 310mm floating discs. The rear wheel is a 5.5 × 17in Borrani (with stainless spokes), which enables a 180 rear section tyre to be fitted. The engine has been fitted with stick coils and K&N air filter and has been rejetted to suit. There have also been many small fittings and bracket changes, including a Monza-style petrol cap.

The front forks have had K-Tech internals. The headlight has been

Paul Humphreys' Thunderbird Sport with special exhaust system.

changed to a Triumph T120 and the indicators are LED, along with the tail lamp (in Lucas style).

The rear axle has built-in bobbins and the handlebars are by Renthal. Paul designed the paint scheme and it was executed by Hairy Designs. Engineering work was carried out by Andy Rolls.

As you will see in Chapter 9 with Paul's Trident, modifying Triumph triples has become a bit of an obsession, all started by restoring a Meriden T160. When the bike was finished, Paul was so disappointed with the handling and performance of the Meriden triple that he moved onto the Hinckley triples instead.

Details of Paul Humphreys' Thunderbird Sport.

Paul Humphreys' Thunderbird Sport, with six-piston Pretech calipers and larger floating disc.

Paul Humphreys' Thunderbird, showing off the one-off exhaust by APH Engineering.

9

more extensive modifications

CHRISTIAN FORWARD'S BIKES

Christian Forward has taken modifying the T300 to a whole new level and has produced a number of modified bikes that have won prizes in competitions for modified bikes at national shows.

To summarize Christian's experience, his first Hinckley Triumph was a Daytona 900 in Racing Yellow, which he loved even though it was down on power and overweight compared to Japanese sports bikes. That was traded in for a T595 Daytona and he has owned nothing but Hinckley Triumphs since.

Christian did not know how to make fuel tanks or aluminium welding but taught himself how to do these things as and when the skill was required, and was able to turn his visions into reality. The café racer bike was built in stages; he would ride it in the summer and spend the winter modifying it.

The Café Racer

This started out as a Trident, which came into the bike shop as a trade-in where Christian worked. It was mint, with 18,000km (11,000 miles) on the clock, and an excellent bike to start with.

The engine has been severely modified. What started out as an 885 Trident engine has been fitted with T595 Daytona cams, liners and pistons; the cams fitted straight in but the crankcase needed boring out to fit the liners. Con rods and gudgeon pins are the same size. The cylinder head has been ported and gas flowed, and the head skimmed. There is a homemade cylinder head gasket, consisting of the inside of a 955 and the outside of an 885 joined together. The adjustable ignition advancer was also made by Christian, but made no noticeable difference to power on the dynamometer. Stick coils have replaced the standard coils. A spin-on oil filter conversion has been done, initially just to make servicing easier; it required repositioning of the oil pressure relief valve and oil pressure switch. There's a modified gearbox sprocket cover, and Yamaha FZ1000 carburettors, bought from eBay for just £30 (because one of them was broken); he only needed three so removed one and respaced to fit. An aluminium airbox was made to look like bell mouths. The stainless steel silencers are Daytona 900 downpipes with the rest fabricated by Christian. The engine now produces 117bhp and 69lb ft of torque at the rear wheel.

Café racer by Christian Forward.

Another view of the café racer; note the many holes to lighten the bike.

Café racer by Christian Forward, showing the alloy tank and seat unit.

Instrument panel on Christian's café racer.

Christian Forward's Bobber.

The Bobber exhaust.

Bobber details.

The chassis is a Trident 900 with Adventurer rear sub-frame welded on and twin shock conversion. Öhlins fully adjustable rear shocks are fitted on a homemade aluminium swing arm 50mm (2in) shorter than standard, which gives it the same wheelbase as the T595 Daytona. Tiger 900 hubs are laced to 17in rims, 3.5in wide at the front and 5.5in at the rear. The forks are GSX-R1000, with R1 top and bottom yokes and Trident steering stem, as using the standard steering stem makes head race bearing replacement straightforward.

Further modifications include the R6 top-mounted steering damper, Brembo front brake and clutch radial master cylinders. The front calipers are Brembo monobloc, and the front discs Triumph 1050 Speed Triples, on homemade adapter plates. The Daytona 595 seat has been narrowed by 75mm (3in). Seat unit, side panels, front mudguard, chain guard and fuel tank are all hand made in aluminium. The headlight is a Bandit 1200m, and the cockpit has Daytona 900 clocks in Thunderbird cases.

The Bobber swing arm.

The Bobber 955

This bike started out as a 1997 Trident, but the start point for the conversion was the CBR600RR swing arm that Christian came across in his day job of servicing motorcycles. The swing arm is unusual in that it has the top shock absorber mounting not on the frame but on the top of the swing arm. Having acquired a swing arm on eBay, he was cleaning it at work when a customer (Aaron Robinson) came into the workshop and enquired what he was doing; on being told it was going into a special, he then asked if he could buy it when it was finished, and the answer was yes!

Originally the Trident engine was going to remain in the frame, but the Thunderbird engine looked so much nicer that it went in instead. To cope with the extra power, a dual-disc

The Bobber swing arm mounting.

front wheel from a Tiger was fitted to improve the braking. The front fairing went through three iterations before Christian and Aaron were satisfied.

The full specification is as follows:

- Thunderbird engine with 955 liners and pistons.
- Port flowed and skimmed cylinder head, with Daytona 955 cams.
- Six-speed Trophy gearbox; spin-on oil filter conversion; and stick coils.
- 1997 Trident chassis with rear sub-frame removed and replaced with a custom-made one.
- Honda CBR600RR swing arm with custom-made tie rods.
- R1 forks and yokes with Trident steering stem.
- Tiger 955i hubs laced to 17in rims, 3.5 front and 5.5 rear.
- Brembo radial clutch and front brake master cylinders.
- Two-pot Brembo front brake calipers (Honda Deauville 650).
- Brembo rear master cylinder and caliper.
- Custom-made integral rear brake reservoir.
- Custom-made integral coolant expansion tank.
- Thunderbird 900 fuel tank.
- Custom-made aluminium seat pan upholstered by Lucky Foot Trimming.
- Aluminium front and rear mudguards made by Richard Robinson of Causeway Motorcycles.
- Motogadget Mo.unit Blue box and custom-made wiring loom by Aaron Robinson.
- Paintwork by Berkshire Bodyshop.
- Weight 190kg (419lb), power 114bhp, torque 70lb ft.

The X69 Hurricane

This was Christian Forward's first attempt at customizing a bike and is based on the Meriden X75 with its outrageous styling (by American stylist Craig Vetter), especially the use of three exhaust silencers on one side. This styling also inspired Triumph when they produced the Thunderbird Sport with two silencers on one side.

The bike started out as a Triumph 900 Trophy owned by Christian's brother and was built in 2007–08. The engine modifications are minimal, essentially just the exhaust and air filter plus rejetting. The exhaust manifold started out as a Thunderbird Sport, then a friend of Christian's, John Elliot, cut and welded them to create a 3-into-3 system. The fuel tank was also a Thunderbird one and was then covered in carbon fibre and the bodywork created. The three silencers came from Unity Equip and made up to fit the 3-into-3 systems.

The handlebars are from a Suzuki VanVan with a Thunderbird clamp fitted to a Trophy top yoke. The rear mudguard is from a Yamaha XVS1100 with the sides trimmed down and chromed. The rear light was made by Christian to fit the standard tail light lens. The grab rail is from a Triumph Bonneville. Footplates, clock covers, exhaust shield, seat and headlight bracket were all fabricated by Christian. The bike has languished at the back of Christian's workshop for a few years, but he is planning to fetch it out and give it a refresh and possibly a repaint.

Christian Forward's X69.

Two more Christian Forward masterpieces under construction.

The swing arm on another masterpiece by Christian Forward.

Another work in progress based on a T300 by Christian Forward.

THE SPRINT MANUFACTURING SPECIAL

In 1995–6, Trevor Smith of Sprint Manufacturing and his father had an idea to offer a kit to convert a T300 bike so that it was lighter and with more up-to-date styling. The frame was a copy of an Egli but made by Cyril Malem of CTG Racing (who was licensed to make Egli Vincent frames at the time). Cyril made the jig and produced the one-off frame.

The bike was fitted with a Daytona 1200 engine. The bodywork was produced by Trevor's father, originally as a one-piece, but since modified for ease of maintenance into a two-piece.

At the end of 1996, however, Triumph brought out the T595, which was lower, lighter and prettier, so with little chance of selling many kits, the project was abandoned and the bike broken up till only the frame and body remained.

Then, in around 2005, a crashed Sprint Sports with only 1,600km (1,000 miles) on the clock became available and Trevor made the decision to build up the bike as a tribute to his father (who died in 2000), using what parts were available. As the styling was no longer cutting edge, he opted to go down the retro route and use spoked wheels from a Thunderbird Sport (but with wider rims).

Cyril Malem, the maker of the Egli frame for the Sprint Manufacturing bike.

Sprint Sports instruments mounted in a Speed Triple module on the Sprint Manufacturing bike.

Daytona 900/1200 instruments were fitted in a Speed Triple 900 instrument housing.

The front forks were Trophy tubes but with 955 ST sliders with 320mm front discs and Alcon six-pot calipers.

The battery was upgraded to 16 amp hours for better starting, and pod filters were also fitted.

The Egli-style frame on the Sprint Manufacturing special made by CTG Racing.

Details of the Egli frame on the Sprint Manufacturing special.

Apart from the frame and bodywork, all the parts on the bike are Triumph, further illustrating the interchangeability of the T300 range.

Frame builder Cyril Malem visited Trevor in February 2020 and was photographed with the bike.

PHIL OGDEN'S HARRIS TRIUMPH

Harris Performance is well known for making excellent frame kits, particularly in the 1970s and 1980s, when Japanese bikes had great engines but with frames that were less than satisfactory. The majority of the frame kits were built around Kawasaki and Suzuki engines, but Phil's bike has a Triumph T300 1200 4-cylinder engine installed.

The frame was one of twenty-four made by Harris to homologate the chassis for endurance racing and Phil (who bought the frame it in 1985) initially installed a Kawasaki GPZ900 engine in the frame. In 1987, Phil took the bike to the Isle of Man for the TT,

Sprint Manufacturing bike with Egli-style frame.

Phil Ogden's Harris Triumph 1200.

The Harris Triumph 1200.

where he decided to enter Ramsey Sprint, but after the seventh attempt the clutch not only gave up the ghost, it exploded, taking out the rest of the engine.

With the engine completely trashed, the bike was parked for a number of years until Phil saw a photo of a black Kawasaki GPZ900 with a Triumph engine – possibly a test mule by Triumph. This then generated thoughts of putting a Triumph engine into the Harris. Phil approached Triumph, who however refused to sell him an engine as 'they did not want any bastardized bikes on the road', as they were entering the US market. At the time, Triumphs were not common on the road so there were none in breaker's yards, but he eventually found a 1991 wrecked Triumph 1200. The engine and frame were handed over to Dennis Evans, who found that the Triumph engine would be a snug fit and only required an additional upper engine mounting. The Triumph front forks and rear wheel were also utilized.

The 1200 Harris. Note the Trident instruments.

Phil Ogden relaxes while the tyres warm up on the Harris Magnum 1200.

The bike was then taken to Australia in 1995 when Phil emigrated there. After some usage as a road bike, the ignition failed, and with that and Phil's growing family, the bike was parked in the shed in pieces.

Many years later, it was dragged into the workshop again where the ignition problem was quickly resolved. Work now focused on updating other parts, so a Honda 900 front end was grafted onto the frame (after fabricating a new steering head stem). The rear wheel was changed to a Fireblade one (after machining both sides), which enabled a 17in 180 rear tyre to be fitted. The thirty-year-old White Power rear shock was replaced with a Penske one using an Öhlins spring. The Triumph rear caliper was used with a new bracket to mate up with the Honda brake disc. Other parts refreshed included a larger radiator, an undertray and tail unit made out of carbon fibre. A Motogadget Mo.unit Blue box to control the electrics was installed, along with a new wiring harness and some Mikuni RS38 flat-slide carburettors to give more power. Lots of small items, such as grips, tank straps and so on, were 3D printed.

The Harris frame, swing arm and rear wheel.

The finished bike was then run in the Barry Sheene Festival of Speed event and Phil intends to run it at the event in future as well as using it as a road bike.

This is a classic example of a bike being owned by the same person from new and still part of their life forty years later, while being constantly improved and updated with the latest technology.

Bob Cornforth's 1200 without a fairing.

BOB CORNFORTH'S DAYTONA 1200 SPRINT BIKE

The 1200 with a fairing fitted.

Bob Cornforth is a drag/sprint racer who has campaigned Triumphs since 1988 and has raced this 1995 T300 Daytona 1200 since 2000, one of three known to be in regular competition. Bob holds several sprint and UKTA speed records and has written technical articles for *Streetfighters* magazine, *Real Classic* and *Nacelle* (Triumph Owners' Motor Cycle Club magazine).

When the T300 series was launched, and even now, there were very few performance parts available, so racers had to be innovative and come up with their own. The standard 1200 is quite heavy, with most of the weight in the motor, fairing and wheels. Consequently, Bob replaced the fairing on his bike – with a lightweight 955 track fairing – along with the wheels. Removing the balancer shafts also saved considerable weight while not affecting vibration. It required blocking off the oil feeds in the lower crankcase by simply replacing the two banjo bolts with M6 bolts of the same size, leaving the feed to the gearbox intact. Alloy plugs were made to block off the openings where the shafts exited the crankcase to the clamp.

A narrower, lighter, Mk 1 Speed Triple radiator was used, with the temperature monitored by a Koso speedometer and the fan manually switched as required. The lower coolant hose leaves the triple radiator at a different point to the four but, by turning the lower hose upside down, it can be made to fit. The heavy oil cooler and oil cooler sub-frame have also been removed, with the oil circuit reinstated using a CRK link pipe (Triumph also do the same part).

The alternator has been dispensed with and a blanking plate made, the electrics now running total loss off a lightweight lithium battery, its voltage continuously monitored via a handlebar-mounted voltmeter. This gives a reliable two days' racing power, sufficient for instruments, ECU and starter motor. Ancillaries such as side stand, lights, horn and indicators are not needed, so have been taken off. Many of the brackets and fasteners are titanium or alloy, as are some of the engine components, such as the clutch pushrod. Twin Arrow slip-on silencers replace the original heavy OEM pipes, but have had the internals modified to Yoshimura spec, taken from the Yoshimura website some years ago. The exhaust headers are standard, but have had the badly restrictive weld at the head end ground flush.

The motor has been increased in capacity to 1275cc using four first-generation 955i Daytona Nikasil liners and pistons – an increasingly popular upgrade that requires the upper crankcase boring out to fit the 79mm liners.

The pistons have also been machined to take Total Seal gapless top rings, which markedly improve compression pressure. The ported head is fitted with standard 147hp cams with Wilcox vernier adjusters. These allow compensation for cam chain stretch, but also dialling in different cam timings. Standard valves and springs are used, but the buckets have been lightened by having two 10mm holes ground in the walls. Compression is slightly up on standard due to a solid copper head gasket of 1.2mm. Fuel from the tank is

Cylinder head porting, with inlet ports opened up.

The Pingel tap, FCR41 Keihin carburettors and alternator blanking plate.

Nitrous oxide bottle mounting.

fed via a high-flow Pingel tap to four Keihin FCR41 carburettors, mounted on standard carburettor rubbers, which have been opened out slightly to blend to the larger choke.

Although the carburettors ran well with basic settings from the off, considerable time was spent on the dynamometer dialling the mixture in, and some quite large main jets needed making to suit. Bonded into the tops of the rubbers are 'fogger' nozzles for a single shot nitrous oxide system, jetted for a further 12bhp per cylinder.

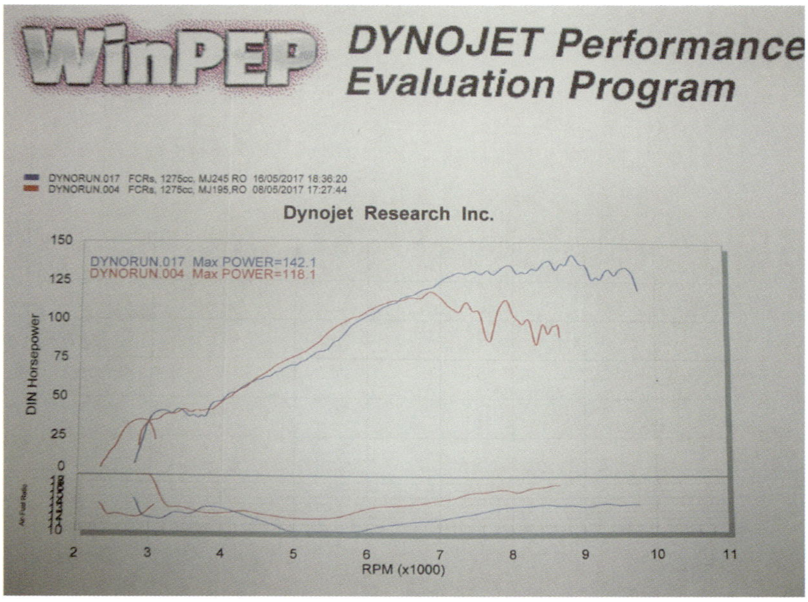

The latest dynamometer printout, showing max power at 142bhp.

Fuel pump and solenoids are mounted under the seat, and fired by a button on the handlebars. The 1kg (2lb) bottle holding the liquid gas is set into the pillion seat behind the rider. The extra power proved slightly too much for the stock clutch, so an overlay MRE-style lock-up plate has been fitted, which has proven light and reliable for both track and street use.

Running gear wise, the bike has been lowered by the construction of a new rear sub-frame that carries the battery and stock ECU under the seat. The ECU fires four JR10B spark plugs through twin DYNA 0.7-ohm coils and Taylor leads, although the standard coils and leads have been used on occasion. A deep-braced JMC Pro Street swinging arm extends the wheelbase by 110mm (4.3in), allowing the bike to be launched hard off the line with no tendency to lift the front end.

The rear wheel is a very much lighter Street Triple R item and fits with minimal effort, only requiring a stop to be made for the caliper carrier.

The forks, yoke and single disc front wheel are Suzuki RGV 250 married to the Triumph headstock with suitable taper roller bearings. In order to facilitate easy engine sprocket changes without the need to drop the oil, the sprocket cover has been cut down, the dipstick replaced by a sight glass and the oil filler cap moved to the clutch cover.

Apart from well-documented issues such as sprag clutch, alternator shaft and cam chain tensioner blades, the T300 motor is robust, with only slight small-end wear over time and a fourth

Rear wheel and swing arm on Bob Cornforth's Daytona. Note the amount of adjustment for the wheel!

Access to the rear sprocket is improved by blanking off the oil filler hole.

ABOVE: *Instrument panel on Bob Cornforth's sprint bike.*

gear that proved fragile if gear changes were overly clumsy. Under good conditions, the bike has run mid-10-second quarters normally aspirated and low 10s with gas. Future plans involve DYNA2000 ignitions and a Cordoba SG quick shifter to try to improve power and lower times.

PAUL HUMPHREYS' TRIDENT 900

Paul has owned this bike, which started out as a standard Trident 900 but has been extensively modified, for nine years.

Even though modifications can be expensive, this is Paul's only motor-

RIGHT: *Paul Humphreys' Trident, extensively modified with one-off swing arm, front forks and many other bits.*

Paul Humphreys' Trident.

cycle and is his main hobby. As with Mark Gaylard's bike, keeping a bike for many years and making it your own avoids the annual depreciation of thousands of pounds incurred buying new bikes every year. The whole bike is a work of art, with many one-off items made to Paul's design, such as the 'banana' swing arm made by Christian Forward. Other changes include mounting Brembo discs and calipers, removing all the original rear suspension linkages, fabricating the airbox for the flat-slide carburettors, fabricating the rear sub-frame, along with a myriad of small parts such as the one-off front axle and spacers. The titanium exhaust manifold and exhaust were made by APH Engineering in Banbury (who also makes F1 exhausts).

One-off titanium exhaust manifold.

The bike has a Motogadget Mo.unit control box and the original wiring has been removed and replaced with a one-off loom. The new loom was made and installed by Aaron Robinson (who does work with Christian Forward), and he wired in the Motogadget box.

The specification is as follows:

Front

- Tiger Sport 1050 forks (because they are long enough to fit a T300), handlebars and modified Tiger Sport 1050 yokes.
- Drilled Tiger Sport 1050 handlebar clamp with a cut-down Tiger 1050 front mudguard, T300 steering stem and Daytona 675R front wheel.
- Thruxton 1200R headlamp with LED running lights, covered by a modified Suzuki SV650X headlamp fairing with a CRK instrument panel fitted with Sprint Sports speedometer and tachometer.

LEFT: Tiger 1050 front forks and Brembo discs and calipers.

BOTTOM: Tiger Sport handlebars.

Suzuki SV650X bikini fairing and Bonneville headlight.

Top-quality Rizoma mirrors and Motogadget bar end indicators.

YSS rear shock fitted to one-off swing arm.

One-off swing arm and silencer.

LEFT: Dished adjusters on the swing arm, Brembo rear caliper and Brembo disc.

BOTTOM: Swing arm and shock absorber mounts.

Engine details; note the Thunderbird figure-of-eight engine cover.

- Mirrors from Rizoma of Italy.
- Motogadget handlebar switches and Motogadget bar end indicators with Domino quick-action throttle cables, Adelin radial brake and clutch master cylinders and black-coated stainless brake lines, and a one-off mini fluid reservoir.
- One-off double-tube banana alloy swing arm made by Christian Forward with a side-mounted YSS shock absorber fitted with dished T300 eccentric chain adjusters (all original suspension linkages have been removed).
- One-off drilled alloy engine mounting plates.
- Daytona 675R rear wheel with one-off rear axle and spacers and a modified Street Triple caliper hanger.
- Brembo rear master cylinder and caliper with a one-off mini rear fluid reservoir with black coated stainless brake line.
- Stainless paddock stand bobbins.
- One-off front and rear sprockets for 520 chain conversion and a one-off alloy chainguard.

Rear lights.

The Trident's unique paint scheme.

The bike is fitted with Mikuni 36 flat-slide carburettors.

Polished rocker cover.

Petrol tank filler.

Middle

- One-off lightweight sub-frame with a one-off battery box with lithium battery.
- T300 tank with lightweight filler cap with a Pingel fuel tap.
- Cut-down and modified Speed Triple side panels.
- Twin LED stop and tail lamps.
- Basketweave recovered seat and pad.
- Modified and drilled frame covers.
- Modified Bonamici GSX-R12000 rear sets.
- Titanium fasteners all round, including one-off engine mount bolts.
- VFR750 front sprocket-driven speedometer drive.
- Trident 900 engine fitted with Mikuni RS36 flat-slide carburettors and Ramair filters in one-off airbox and stick ignition coils.
- One-off alloy radiator shaped to follow frame tubes and radiator grille with a polished Thunderbird rocker, clutch and timing covers with a one-off balancer cover and drilled alternator cover, and one-off titanium rocker cover bolts.

appendices

National Triumph in Wolverhampton have extensive second-hand parts for early Hinckley Triumphs.

appendix I
parts supply

Triumph Triumph have been brilliant in maintaining full supply of parts for about twenty years, but over the last four or five years, parts have been gradually deleted to the point that most of the large parts, such as fuel tanks, body panels, exhausts, carburettors, brake calipers and so on, are no longer available. Check with your local dealer to see what parts they have or, if you don't have a local dealer, try Jack Lilley's or Fowlers of Bristol over the phone.

National Triumph National Triumph was set up by Ivan in Wolverhampton, and is an excellent source of second-hand and refurbished parts for Hinckley Triumphs. Ivan has owned many T300 bikes and has extensive knowledge of the inter-changeability of parts; he can supply anything from a brake caliper to a full set of bodywork.

Obviously what he has in stock will vary depending on what bikes and parts he can buy in, but he should be first port of call for most parts, particularly for tanks, body panels, brake calipers and similar. He can also supply refurbished engine covers in a close approximation of the original 'crackle' finish from Triumph.

With Triumph no longer supplying many items, and the relative scarcity of bikes to break, the cost of some second-hand parts has risen considerably, particularly for models such as Speed Triples and Daytona Super 3s, so don't expect to pay peanuts.

Ivan can be contacted on 01902 421798 or 07768 113636 or emailed at nationaltriumph@aol.co.uk.

He also regularly posts items for sale on eBay – if the item you're looking at has a green background it's probably Ivan's at National Triumph – so it's worth checking regularly.

Trimax-Moto This French company, run by Maxence Sonilhac, has one of the largest stocks of parts of T300/T400 bikes. At any one time, he has sixty bikes being broken for parts and, like Sprint Manufacturing, he also sells generic parts as well as making specific glass-fibre or carbon parts. Only 10 per cent of the available parts are actually listed on the website. Max has been riding T300s since 1995 and has also raced them on track and road racing. Although French, his English, both spoken and written, is excellent.

The website is www.trimax-moto.com and there is also a Facebook page under the name Maxence Trimax-Moto; he can be contacted via Messenger or phone (00 33 09 65 23 55 04). If you fancy a trip, he is located near Clermont Ferrand in the centre of France, a town that is also the home of Michelin and was the home of Voxon Motorcycles.

Sprint Manufacturing Trevor Smith runs Sprint Manufacturing, based in Warminster, and can supply many parts for Hinckley Triumphs. Trevor has been a Hinckley Triumph enthu-

Part of National Triumph's extensive stock.

siast for many years and, where Triumph have stopped supplying spares, Trevor has stepped in; as in the case of Nissin brake parts (seals, pistons and so on), where Sprint have bought supplies direct from Nissin. For some parts, Sprint have upgraded the original part, so, for example, the swing arm chain rubbing strip is made by the original supplier to Triumph but now with a harder grade of material. Other parts, such as the rear brake pins, have been re-manufactured in stainless steel, which is more expensive but a worthwhile upgrade as the standard steel pins are prone to rust.

Sprint are based at 30B Upton Lovell, Warminster BA12 0JW. Contact them on 01985 850821, by email to mail@sprintmanufacturing.co.uk, or go to their website, www.triumphparts.co.uk.

Allens Performance This is a specialized carburettor and parts supplier, and what they don't know about carburettors is not worth knowing. The T300 range is fitted with both Keihin and Mikuni carburettors, and Allens Performance can supply just about everything you may need. Their address is Unit B9, Moorbridge Road, Bingham, Nottingham NG13 8GG; www.allensperformance.co.uk.

Paul Messenger Stick Coils Paul Messenger was for many years part of the Jack Lilley race team with Clive Wood, and has extensive experience of the T300 range (as well as the T595 range), and has used his aerospace engineering background to develop stick coils to replace the standard Triumph coils. These give a much fatter spark and utilize the latest stick coil technology. The price for a set of stick coils is approximately the same as replacing the standard Triumph coils. Paul also sells YSS shock absorbers for Hinckley Triumphs.

Contact Paul through his Facebook profile or email him at pauljlracing@aol.com.

LSL This German company specializes in making aftermarket parts for Triumphs (although it does also make parts for other manufacturers). The range includes handlebars, rear sets, headlamps, headlamp surrounds, to name but a few. Parts are excellent quality, if expensive, and I have many of them on my 2008 Triumph Thruxton. I am not sure if they still supply rear sets for the T300 range, but the handlebar conversions (there are lots of variations) are still available.

Café Racer Kits CRK, as described in Chapter 8, not only supply parts for their kits, but some parts (such as instrument pods) that can be used on other conversions.

CRK can be contacted at enquiries@caferacerkits.co.uk. CRK also have a website, www.caferacerkits.co.uk as well as a Facebook page.

Koos Groenewald Koos lives in Holland and seems to find all sorts of parts (including NOS) and Triumph literature. He can be contacted via Facebook and is a member of all the T300 related groups. He has a day job but nevertheless seems to find bits all the time. If you want any early Triumph brochures or marketing material then he is the person to contact.

CRK stand at Stafford Classic Bike show in October 2017.

appendix II
specialized services

T300 MAINTENANCE SERVICES

Most Triumph dealers do not have many mechanics with first-hand experience of working on the T300 range, so where to find this expertise? There are three people in particular who have established themselves in this field and fortunately cover different parts of the country:

Clive Wood Based in Lincolnshire, Clive's knowledge and experience is second to none, having worked on T300 bikes and raced them over many years. He can offer everything from a straightforward service up to a complete rebuild. Clive lives in Swineshead in Lincolnshire and can be contacted on 07752 477738 or via email at clivejlracing@aol.com.

Chris Foxley Chris has been racing and rebuilding bikes all his life and knows the Triumph ranges extremely well. Before becoming self-employed, he was the service manager at a major Triumph dealership and now works from home in Hatton, Derbyshire. He operates under the name Foxley Starters, so check out his website (www.foxleystarters.com) or contact him on 01283 815064 or 07770 602484.

Paul Barnett Triumph Motorbike Spares. Paul specializes in carburettor refurbishment and rebuilding for all Hinckley Triumph models. This can include stripping, inspecting, diagnosis, ultrasonic cleaning and then rebuilding with replacement jets, needles and sliders. He also has used spares for all Hinckley Triumph carburettors.

Paul's contact details are as follows: tel 07867 785912, email t300spares@gmail.com. He also has a Facebook page, Triumph Motorbike Spares.

Christian Forward's workshop.

Forwardstein Design Christian Forward has now set himself up to offer services not just for servicing and repair but also for custom builds. Based in Tadley (on the Hampshire/Berkshire border), he can be contacted on 07801 250456 or by email to forwardstein@aol.com.

Custom Made Rads Paul Humphries had a one-off radiator made by this company and was very impressed with the quality of the work. They are based near Nottingham at the following address:

Unit 7, Mushroom Farm Court
Meadowbank Way
Eastwood
Nottinghamshire
NG16 3SR

ENGINE BUILDING COURSES WITH CLIVE WOOD

The guru of all things T300 is Clive Wood, who started racing the T300 bikes almost as soon as they came out. He raced in the Speed Triple Challenge series and then built and engineered Jack Lilley's race team bikes (along with Paul Messenger). Clive now works for himself, servicing and repairing anything Hinckley Triumph and, in the winter months, runs a two-day course on T300 maintenance that goes into the rebuilding of engines and carburettors, including how to change the sprag clutch. If you have any interest in getting your hands dirty then I can thoroughly recommend booking a place. Attending this course will give you the knowledge and confidence to rebuild the sprag clutch and overhaul carburettors yourself. You also get to meet other T300 owners, eat the free bacon rolls, and spend two days talking Hinckley Triumphs!

Clive works from home in Swineshead in Lincolnshire, and his contact details are given above.

GROUPS AND CLUBS

There are many Facebook groups catering for T300 bikes including:

- T300
- Mark 1 Speed Triple Owners
- T300 Modifiers
- Triumph Daytona 750/900/1200
- T300 Passion
- CRK Enthusiasts

All are worth joining, although it can be a pain trying to find postings once they are more than a few weeks old, although there is a search function.

Before Facebook, a number of internet forums became established and these are still going for those that don't want to use social media. For example, try:

- TriumphRat at www.triumphrat.net
- The Triumph Forum at www.thetriumphforum.com

Mark Gaylard's website, www.mottleybiker.com, is full of useful information and photographs.

Clive Wood's T300 and engine course.

Clive Wood's T300 and engine course.

appendix III
Triumph T300 paint colours by model

All the colours listed below were sourced from the official Triumph press packs, brochures and paint codes from Triumph documents given in Appendix IV. However, some of the descriptions in the press packs and brochures don't match exactly with the paint codes and descriptions. For example, the brochure listed Quicksilver and Cobalt Blue as a colour combination for the Trident but Quicksilver does not appear on any Triumph internal paint list. It may well have been that Triumph gave a colour in the press packs and brochures, which are printed some months before the bikes are made, and then decided not to proceed with it for whatever reason.

DAYTONA

1991	Assam Black, Lancaster Red, Radiant Red
1992	Assam Black, Lancaster Red
1993	Racing Yellow, Pimento Red, Barracuda Blue (metallic)
1994	Racing Yellow, Pimento Red, Barracuda Blue (metallic)
1995	Racing Yellow, Pimento Red, Barracuda Blue (metallic)
1996	Racing Yellow, Pimento Red, Diablo Black
1997	Not in the brochure
1998	Jet Black, 1200 SE model only, with gold decals

Daytona Super 3

1994	Racing Yellow
1995	Racing Yellow
1996	Racing Yellow

TROPHY

1991	Burgundy, Charcoal Grey Metallic, Oxford Blue Metallic, Caribbean Blue Metallic
1992	Lancaster Red, Caribbean Blue, Charcoal Grey Metallic
1993	Caspian Blue, British Racing Green, Candy Apple Red
1994	Caspian Blue, British Racing Green
1995	British Racing Green, Nightshade Purple
1996	British Racing Green, Merlot Red, Pacific Blue
1997	British Racing Green, Merlot Red, Pacific Blue
1998	Platinum (silver), Pacific Blue, British Racing Green, Turquoise
1999	Platinum (silver), Pacific Blue, British Racing Green
2000	Platinum (silver), Pacific Blue, British Racing Green
2001	Sunset Red, Platinum, Pacific Blue
2002	Sunset Red, Azure Blue, Emerald Green (1200 only, 900 no longer available)
2003	Graphite, Azure Blue, Sunset Red (1200 only, 900 no longer available)

SPRINT

1993	Caspian Blue, Candy Apple Red, British Racing Green
1994	Caspian Blue, Candy Apple Red, British Racing Green
1995	Nightshade Blue, Candy Apple Red, British Racing Green
1996	Nightshade Blue, Candy Apple Red, British Racing Green
1997	Nightshade Blue, Candy Apple Red, British Racing Green

Sprint Sport

1997	Jet Black
1998	Jet Black, Tornado Red

Sprint Executive

1997	Pacific Blue, Volcanic Red, Platinum, British Racing Green
1998	Pacific Blue, Volcanic Red, Platinum, British Racing Green

TIGER

1993	Caspian Blue, Sandstone Gold, Pimento Red
1994	Caspian Blue, Pimento Red
1995	Caspian Blue, Pimento Red, Diablo Black
1996	Caspian Blue, Pimento Red, Diablo Black
1997	Chilli Red, Khaki Green, Jet Black
1998	British Racing Green, Volcanic Red, Jet Black

SPEED TRIPLE

1994	Racing Yellow, Diablo Black
1995	Fireball Orange, Diablo Black
1996	Fireball Orange, Diablo Black

THUNDERBIRD

1995	Cherry Red, Diablo Black, Aegean Blue, Cherry Red and Cream
1996	Aegean Blue, Diablo Black, Cherry Red, Cherry Red and Cream, British Racing Green and Cream
1997	Cardinal Red and Silver, Imperial Green and Silver, Jet Black and Silver
1998	Jet Black and Tornado Red, Imperial Green and Silver, Cardinal Red and Silver
1999	Not listed
2000	Cardinal Red and Chromium Silver, Aston Green and Champagne
2001	Cardinal Red and Chromium Silver, Aston Green and Champagne
2002.	Sunset Red and Opal, Graphite and Jet Black
2003	Cardinal Red and Silver, British Racing Green and Silver

Thunderbird Sport

1998	Racing Yellow and Jet Black, Tornado Red and Jet Black
1999	Racing Yellow and Jet Black, Tornado Red and jet Black
2000	Opal White and Tangerine, Racing Yellow and Jet Black
2001	Bike not listed in the brochure
2002	Bike not listed in the brochure
2003	Tangerine Orange and Jet Black

ADVENTURER

1996	Heritage Gold and Ivory, Violet and Ivory
1997	Amber and Copper, Turquoise and Silver, Aubergine and Silver, Heritage Gold and Ivory, Violet and Ivory
1998	Jet Black and Silver, Turquoise and Silver
1999	Jet Black and Silver
2000	Jet Black and Lucifer Orange
2001	Jet Black and Lucifer Orange, Jet Black and Fireball Orange

LEGEND

1999	Obsidian Black, Cardinal Red and Silver, Imperial Green and Silver
2000	Cardinal Red and Silver, Imperial Green and Silver
2001	Obsidian Black, Cardinal Red and Silver, Imperial Green and Silver

TRIDENT

1991	British Racing Green, Cherry Red (metallic)
1992	Metallic British Racing Green, Cherry Red (Metallic)
1993	British Racing Green, Cinnabar Red, Diablo Black
1994	750 British Racing Green
	900 British Racing Green and Cream, Diablo Black and Pimento Red
1995	750British Racing Green
	900 British Racing Green and Cream, Diablo Black and Pimento Red
1996	750 British Racing Green
	900 British Racing Green and Cream, Diablo Black and Pimento Red
1997	750 Quicksilver
	900 Quicksilver and Cobalt, Cobalt Blue, Jet Black and Red
1998	750 Pacific Blue
	900 Pacific Blue and Silver, Jet Black and Ruby Red

appendix IV Triumph colours and paintcodes

This list of paint codes only applies to the T300 range of bikes. Triumph have listed many more colours over the years after the T300 range was no longer in the brochures, but these are beyond the remit of this book.

There are also references in the brochures to Silver as a colour for Tridents (listed as Aubergine and Silver, Jet Black and Silver, Imperial Green and Silver, Cardinal Red and Silver, Pacific Blue and Silver), but I cannot find a specific paint code as Triumph list six different silvers, each with a different prefix name (Warm Silver, Flamboyant Silver and so on) but nothing as plain Silver!

Be aware that many paint suppliers now no longer use the Dupont or IVC paint schemes and your local paint supplier may be unable to supply what you need. If you have a panel and tank you can take with you; they may be able to get close enough by using a scanner to give them a paint match.

Name	**Manufacturer**	**Code**
Aegean Blue	Dupont/AVC	BEC1717/L3885
Amber	Schoch	673 OME 28
Assam Black	Dupont	BEC089
Aston Green	Dupont	487850101
Aubergine	Schoch	673 OME 24
Azure Blue	PPG	Triumph Azure
Barracuda Blue	Dupont	BEC1393
British Racing Green	Dupont	46120101
Candy Apple Red	Dupont	BEC1396
Cardinal Red	Schoch	673 OME 25
Caribbean Blue	Dupont	462110101
Caspian Blue	Dupont	462110101
Cherry Black	Dupont	BEC650
Chromium Sliver	IVC	L3119
Champagne Gold	IVC	L3126
Chilli Red	Schoch	674 OME 30
Cobalt Blue	IVC	L2263
Cinnabar Red	Dupont	
Copper	IVC	L2398
Charcoal Grey Metallic	IVC	L3725
Cream	Carrs	485970101
Cream/Ivory	Dupont	VAC

Name	Manufacturer	Code
Diablo Black	Dupont	BEC1342
Emerald Green	PPG	Triumph Emerald
Fireball Orange	Dupont	BEC1657
Graphite	IVC	L3725
Heritage Gold	Dupont	BEC1889
Imperial Green	Schoch	673 CAL 28
Ivory	Carrs	BEC1893
Khaki Green	Schoch	674 CAL 28
Jet Black	IVC	L2344
Lancaster Red	Dupont	BEC 858
Lucifer Orange	IVC	L2501
Merlot Red	Dupont	BEC1936
Nightshade	Dupont	BEC1656
Obsidian Black	IVC	L2819T3120300-PP
Opal White	Dupont	486950101
Pacific Blue	Dupont	BEC1954
Pimento Red	Dupont	BEC1479
Quicksilver		
Platinum	IVC	L2367
Racing Yellow	Dupont	BEC1514
Roulette Green	IVC	L2589
Ruby Red	IVC	L2342
Sandstorm Gold	Dupont	3120059-GA
Sunset Red	Dupont	BEC1661T
Tangerine	Dupont	BEC2647/F1875
Tangerine(2K)	Dupont	485940101
Tornado Red	Dupont	BEC2211
Tornado Red	IVC	L2804
Turquoise	Schoch	673 OME 29
Violet	Dupont	BEC1890
Volcanic Red	Schoch	674 OME 39

Some of the colours are listed as combinations of paints, so Aubergine and Cardinal Red are both described as Flamboyant (whatever colour that is!) sprayed over Aluminium Silver.
Opal White was also called Fusion White.

appendix V
carburettor jetting sizes

The table below only relates to the Mikuni BST 36mm flat-slide CV carburettors.

Idle speed	1,000rpm plus/minus 50rpm
Float level (from joint face)	14.5m
Fuel level (above joint face)	1.5mm
Float needle	NVAssy N198008
Choke jet	No. 45

Model	Cylinders	Main jet	Main air jet	Pilot jet	Pilot air jet	Needle jet	Needle	Pilot screw
Trophy 1200	1 and 4 2 and 3	112.5 117.5	1.0	40	1.5	0-8	5E60-3 5E77-3	2 turns out
Trophy 1200 (100hp)	1 and 4 2 and 3	115 120	1.0	40	1.5	0-8	5DH11-3	2 turns out
Trophy/ Trident 900	1 and 3 2	130 127.5	1.5	40	1.5 1.45	0-6	5E56-3	2 turns out 2.25 turns out
Trident/ Daytona 750	1 and 3 2	135 127.5	1.5	40	1.5 1.4	0.6	5E56-3 5E56-3	2 turns out 2.25 turns out
Trident / Daytona 750 (50hp)	1 and 3 2	150 142.5	1.5	40	1.55	0.6	5E60-3 5E56-3	2 turns out 2.25 turns out
Trident/ Daytona (27hp)	1 and 3 2	180 180	1.5	40	1.55 1.5	0.6	5E60-3 5E56-3	2 turns out 2.25 turns out
Daytona 1000	1 and 4 2 and 3	117.5 120	1.0	40	1.45	0-8	5E77-3 5F95-3	1.5 turns out

appendix VI
wheels and tyre sizes

Trophy 900 and 1200

1991–3	Front 17in 120/70; rear 18in 160/60; six-spoke wheel
1994–2003	Front 17in 120/70; rear 17in 170/60; three-spoke wheel

From 2002, 1200 only, as the 900 had been replaced by Sprint ST

Daytona 750 and 1000

1991–2	Front 17in 130/60; rear 18in 170/60; six-spoke wheel

Trident 750 and 900

1991–8	Front 17in 120/70; rear 18in 160/60; six-spoke wheel

Sprint 900

1993–3	Front 17in 120/70; rear 18in 160/60; six-spoke wheel
1995–7	Front 17in 120/70; rear 17in 170/60; three-spoke wheel

Sprint Sports and Sprint Executive

1998	Front 17in 120/70; rear 17in 170/60; three-spoke wheel

Tiger

1993	Front 19in 110/80 radial; rear 17in 140/80 radial
1994	Front 19in 110/80 or 110/90; rear 17in 140/80 radial
1995–8	Front 19in 110/80; rear 17in 140/80 radial

Daytona 900 and 1200

1993	Front 17in 120/70; rear 18in 160/60; six-spoke wheel
1994	Front 17in 120/70; rear 18in 180/55; six-spoke wheel
1995–6	Front 17in 120/70; rear 17in 180/55; three-spoke wheel

Speed Triple

1994–6	Front 17in 120/70; rear 17in 180/55; three-spoke wheel

Daytona Super 3

1994–6	Front 17in 120/70; rear 17in 180/55; three-spoke wheel

Thunderbird

1995	Front 18in 110/80; rear 16in 160/85; spoked wheels on alloy rims
1996–2000	Front 18in 110/80; rear 16in 160/80 or 150/80; spoked wheels
2001–02	Front 18in 110/80; rear 16in 150/80; spoked wheels

Thunderbird Sport

1998–2000	Front 17in 120/70; rear 17in 160/70; spoked wheels
2003–04	Front 17in 110/70; rear 17in 160/70; spoked wheels

Legend TT

1998	Front 17in 120/70; rear 17in 160/70; spoked wheels
1999–2001	Front 17in 120/70; rear 17in 160/60; spoked wheels

Adventurer

1995	Front 18in 110/80; rear 16in 160/80; spoked wheels
1996–8	Front 18in 110/80; rear 16in 160/80 or 150/80; spoked wheels
1999	Front 18in 110/80; rear 16in 150/80; spoked wheels
2000	Front 18in 110/80; rear 16in 160/80 or 150/80; spoked wheels
2001	Front 18in 100/80; rear 16in 150/80; spoked wheels

index

RELATED TITLES FROM CROWOOD

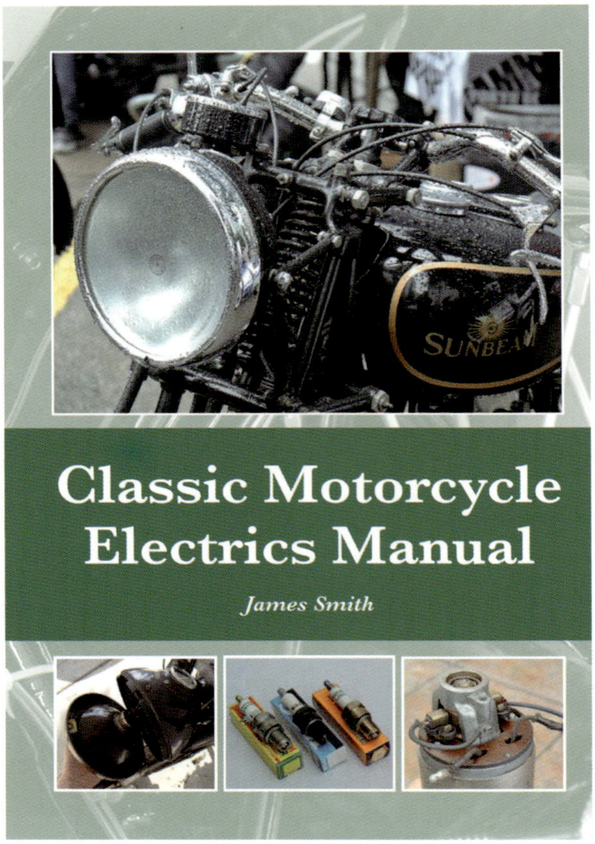

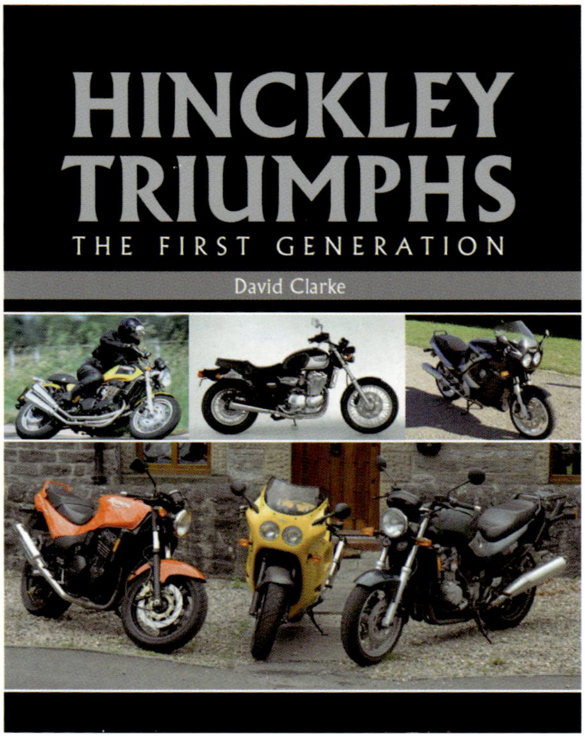